CHEERS

The Cultural History of Television

CHEERS

A Cultural History

Joseph J. Darowski
Kate Darowski

ROWMAN & LITTLEFIELD
Lanham • Boulder • New York • London

Published by Rowman & Littlefield
An imprint of The Rowman & Littlefield Publishing Group, Inc.
4501 Forbes Boulevard, Suite 200, Lanham, Maryland 20706
www.rowman.com

6 Tinworth Street, London SE11 5AL

British Library Cataloguing in Publication Information Available

Library of Congress Cataloging-in-Publication Data

Names: Darowski, Joseph J., author. | Darowski, Kate, 1988– author.
Title: Cheers : a cultural history / by Joseph J. Darowski and Kate Darowski.
Description: Lanham : Rowman & Littlefield, 2019. | Series: The cultural history of television |
    Includes bibliographical references and index.
Identifiers: LCCN 2018056821 (print) | LCCN 2018059817 (ebook) | ISBN 9781538113882 (elec-
    tronic) | ISBN 9781538113875 (cloth : alk. paper)
Subjects: LCSH: Cheers (Television program)
Classification: LCC PN1992.77.C473 (ebook) | LCC PN1992.77.C473 D37 2019 (print) | DDC
    791.45/72—dc23
LC record available at https://lccn.loc.gov/2018056821

Printed in the United States of America

To Shelley Long, Ted Danson, and Kirstie Alley
(and Coke Zero)

CONTENTS

ACKNOWLEDGMENTS

We would like to thank Ken Levine for responding to specific questions we had about his time writing on *Cheers* as well as the wonderful insights about working in the television industry that can be found on his blog, . . . *by Ken Levine* (kenlevine.blogspot.com). Also, we would like to acknowledge Dennis Bjorklund's book, *Toasting Cheers*, which catalogued a huge amount of information from *Cheers*.

"HOW 'BOUT A BEER, CHIEF?"

A now-sober alcoholic who owns a bar. A self-styled intellectual who serves drinks in a sports bar. The least watched show on television becomes a number-one hit. *Cheers* is full of contradictions both in front of and behind the camera, yet at its core the premise is very simple. A former athlete owns a bar and is friends with his staff and patrons. In what is revealed as simple complexity, *Cheers* became one of the most famous and influential series to ever air on television.

Cheers eventually found a devoted fanbase and remains beloved to this day. The respect for the series is particularly strong among creators. In 2013, the Writers Guild of America named *Cheers* the eighth best-written television series of all time.[1] Amy Poehler, alumnus of *Saturday Night Live* and star of *Parks and Recreation*, calls it "the best TV show that's ever been."[2] Michael Schur, a creative force behind *The Office* and creator of *Parks and Recreation*, *Brooklyn 99*, and *The Good Place*, has said that "*Cheers* is the greatest comedy of all time. Sam Malone is the best character of all time. Ted Danson's interpretation of Sam Malone is the best interpretation of any character in television history."[3]

Several aspects of the series that were groundbreaking at the time have become so commonplace in television that it's possible to forget how revolutionary *Cheers* was in 1982. Whether building a show around a will-they-won't-they relationship or planning out a season's worth of evolving stories rather than twenty-two self-contained episodes, *Cheers* set up many of the staples of sitcom television that viewers expect from modern serial storytelling. The idea of a series arc was an innovation, and now, television writer and producer Sam Simon explains, "producers sit down with the network at the beginning of the year and talk about the arc of the show."[4] The creators of *Cheers*, Glen and Les Charles and James Burrows, established a new style of sitcom storytelling that has since become the status quo for network television.

Of course, it's possible to simultaneously acknowledge that *Cheers* earned the praise it received, and that the show has flaws. Not all aspects of the series have aged well. And it's not only Frasier's sweater vests and Rebecca's shoulder pads that belong in a different time period. The absence of characters of color does stand out. It was noted at the time of its airing—a 1984 *Washington Post* article wondered if the producers had "sound artistic reasons for not serving drinks to blacks" before speculating about what the tipping point would be before "the white masses out there feel uncomfortable with all those strangers"[5] if actors of color were cast more frequently. *Cheers* is still well enough known that in 2018, a joke about the absence of people of color in the series was used in the opening monologue of the Emmy Awards—Michael Che quipped, "You're telling me they made a show about an all-white sports bar in 1980s Boston, and not one black dude walked in, saw everybody, and then walked right back out immediately?"[6] Obviously, this was not an issue unique to *Cheers*; many sitcoms of the era (and the next decade too) lacked characters of color. And there are other aspects of *Cheers* that are markers of a different time period.

There are punchlines scattered throughout the series that are homophobic and transphobic and wouldn't be used today. However, it should also be noted that the 1983 episode, "The Boys in the Bar," in which Sam defends an ex-teammate who comes out as gay, was given an award by the Alliance for Gay and Lesbian Artists in the Entertainment Industry; its writers, Ken Levine and David Isaacs, were nominated for an Emmy for this episode and won a Writers Guild Award for it.[7] Though he should be praised for defending his gay friend, Sam Malone would be sweating out the #MeToo movement, not only because of the rampant sexual advances that were core to his personality, but specifically the employer-employee dynamic of several of Sam's conquests. There are also numerous barbs tossed at Carla referring to her as a midget or dwarf that wouldn't be added to a script today. These aspects of the show are time capsules of an earlier era, best relegated to the last century. But, while

The core members of the *Cheers* cast in its first season. Front row: Sam Malone
(Ted Danson) and Diane Chambers (Shelley Long). Back row: Cliff Clavin (John
Ratzenberger), Ernie "Coach" Pantusso (Nicholas Colasanto), Carla Tortelli
(Rhea Perlman), and Norm Peterson (George Wendt)

acknowledging that some issues exist, the show undeniably earned its status as one of the greatest television shows in American history.

Clever one-liners, skilled plotting, comedic performances, layered punchlines—these stand the test of time and age remarkably well. The overall quality is what ensures *Cheers* remains a syndication staple, can be found on streaming services, and is readily available on DVD. Many decades-old series become relics. Even highly rated television shows can become footnotes in popular culture history as tastes evolve and audiences move on. *Cheers* struggled in the ratings its first year, but perusing the television network's prime time schedule for 1982–1983 reveals many shows that must have had higher ratings but are almost entirely forgotten today—shows like *Matt Houston, Bring 'em Back Alive*, and *Tucker's Witch*. But with its well-earned classic status, new fans are still discovering *Cheers*.

Among those new fans are the authors of this book, who came to it years after it went off the air. Joseph was born the year the show premiered and never saw it during its original NBC run. Kate, his younger sister who was born several years later, also was too young to watch its first run. However, their parents had a tradition in the era before DVRs (or even commonplace VCRs) that included a Thursday date night to watch *Cheers* in its 9:00 p.m. time slot on NBC. Joseph and Kate actually came to the show in something of a reverse order, first becoming fans of its spin-off, *Frasier*, and seeing the entirety of that show's eleven seasons before watching a single episode of *Cheers*. What becomes apparent, even thirty-five years after the show started airing, is that smart writing, brilliant directing, and talented acting age very well—even if fashion does not.

I

A JEW AND TWO MORMONS WALK INTO A BAR

Cheers Begins and Nobody Cares

Welcome to Cheers.

It's a tale worthy of Hollywood. Unexpected protagonists, difficult obstacles, the odds stacked against success, a fellowship to help shoulder the burdens, setbacks and failures, and the eventual triumph. While millions are familiar with the plots of *Cheers* episodes, less well known is the behind-the-scenes journey that resulted in what many consider to be *the* classic sitcom. The struggle to create the award-winning show is in many ways as interesting as the story that aired on television.

Glen and Les Charles and James Burrows are deservedly famous as the creators of *Cheers*, their names emblazoned over the still frame of a young man toasting with a beer at the end of the opening credits. However, the trio took an improbable path to television immortality. Like so many success stories, it is possible to view their triumph as inevitable in hindsight, but so many details of their story are implausible—from the Charles brothers finding work in Hollywood by sending production companies unsolicited scripts to *Cheers* surviving its abysmal ratings of its first season—that it's a minor miracle that *Cheers* exists as an eleven-season, 275-episode icon. Add in the fact that it premiered on the least watched network and was one of the least watched shows on all of television, and the unlikelihood of *Cheers* becoming a success increases even more.

CHARLES/BURROWS/CHARLES

In 1982, NBC was desperate to find new talent and infuse their lackluster lineup of shows with something worth talking about. Mired in years of low ratings, NBC sought out Glen and Les Charles and James Burrows and gave them a deal they couldn't refuse. Warren Littlefield, NBC's manager of comedy development at the time, recalls that "we had to wave a series commitment at Les and Glen Charles and Jimmy Burrows. . . . We guaranteed them thirteen episodes on the air just to lure them to pitch us."[1] At this point, the Charles brothers and Burrows had never created a series. NBC's interest was based purely on faith in their talent. How did these three collaborators come together and gain such a strong reputation that they were promised thirteen episodes before even making a pitch to the network?

Glen and Les Charles were raised in Las Vegas, and their parents emphasized the importance of education.[2] They both attended the University of Redlands near Los Angeles where they graduated with liberal arts degrees. After college, Glen became a schoolteacher while Les went on to

The *Cheers* logo

law school and worked as an advertising copywriter.[3] One afternoon, Glen recalls seeing the film *Chinatown* with Les, and afterward they both expressed how unhappy they were with their current jobs.[4] Glen had been a literature major in college and always wanted to write,[5] and Les majored in English and had always wanted to be a novelist.[6] Les noted that television had better writing than what they remembered watching as kids.[7] After that, the brothers would meet on the weekends to start exploring writing for television.[8]

If you're going to be inspired, be inspired by the best. In 1974, CBS had the best comedy. The network aired a block of sitcom programming on Saturday night featuring *All in the Family*, *M*A*S*H*, *The Bob Newhart Show*, and *The Mary Tyler Moore Show*. Those two hours of laughs would be enough for many viewers to schedule time at home on Saturday evenings, and among the devoted viewers were Glen Charles and Les Charles. They weren't only entertained; they studied what they watched and decided that writing for television made more sense than their current jobs.[9]

So they did something that probably wouldn't work today, and certainly wouldn't have worked then if they didn't have a combination of talent and luck. Without any expression of interest from production companies, the brothers started writing scripts for every sitcom on television and mailing them to offices. As Les Charles recalls, "We blanketed the town with spec scripts,"[10] and Glen Charles added, "We even wrote a spec script for 'Gunsmoke'!"[11] Before the Charles brothers even sold a script, they both quit their jobs to try to become professional writers.[12] Whatever alchemical blend of timing, quality, and curiosity from TV producers needed for this scheme to work actually came about, and they found their way into the television business. First, they sold a script to *M*A*S*H*, and then the very first spec script they had sent out was rediscovered in the MTM production offices.[13] Grant Tinker, who was the cofounder of MTM Enterprises with his then wife, Mary Tyler Moore, was impressed with the script for *The Mary Tyler Moore Show* and hired the Charles brothers for the *Phyllis* writing room.[14] *Phyllis* was the second of three spin-off series spawned by *The Mary Tyler Moore Show*. Eventually, the brothers also played a role in several other series produced by MTM, including *The Mary Tyler Moore Show*, *The Betty White Show*, and *The Bob Newhart Show*.

It was while working on these shows that Glen and Les Charles first worked with a director named James Burrows. Of course, odds are good that a sitcom writer working in Hollywood between the 1970s and the present day would have the chance to work with James Burrows. He is an incredibly prolific director in network television. To call Burrows a legend is actually understating his reputation in the industry. In 2016, NBC hosted a tribute show to Burrows after he directed his thousandth television episode. It was hosted on NBC because so much of Burrows's career has been with that network, as a consistent director on *Cheers*, *Frasier*, *Will & Grace*, and *Friends*, among many other shows. Burrows has directed episodes of more than one hundred television series and also directed the pilots for fifty different sitcoms that have gone on to air.[15] But in the 1970s, Burrows's career was just starting.

James Burrows was familiar with show business from a young age. While his father, Abe Burrows, had written for radio sitcoms including *The Milton Berle Show* and *Duffy's Tavern*, he was best known for writing the books for the Broadway musicals *Guys and Dolls*, *Can Can*, and *How to Succeed in Business without Really Trying*, for which he won a

Director James Burrows and Rhea Perlman

Pulitzer Prize with Frank Loesser.[16] James Burrows received his bachelor's degree from Oberlin College and then went on to obtain a master of fine arts (MFA) from Yale University's School of Drama.[17] Eventually, James ended up working as a stagehand for a Broadway musical that Abe Burrows wrote with Edward Albee. *Holly Golightly* (also referred to as *Breakfast at Tiffany's*) was a musical adaptation of Truman Capote's famous novella that inspired the even more famous Audrey Hepburn film. Unfortunately, the musical flopped with critics and audiences and closed soon after opening. However, James Burrows made an important professional connection. The star of the musical was Mary Tyler Moore. Through that meeting, Burrows was put in touch with Grant Tinker, who brought him to MTM Enterprises to observe how television directors worked.

Burrows was mentored by Jay Sandrich, a prolific television director who worked in the industry from the 1950s through the early 2000s. Burrows learned the ropes quickly and before long he was directing episodes of *Phyllis*. Airing on December 29, 1975, the fifteenth episode of the first season, "Paging Dr. Lindstrom," is the first collaboration between Glen and Les Charles and James Burrows. Things clicked quickly between the three, and Burrows directed four more Charles brothers' scripts that season. The fact that they all entered the television business through MTM Enterprises around the same time certainly helped them to bond. Glen Charles recalls, "We'd always gotten along extremely well. I think we felt like contemporaries—like we were in the same college class, and suffered a lot of the same injuries and blows to our egos."[18] Les Charles added jokingly, "We were a Jew and two Mormons, so we kind of banded together. We felt persecuted [*laughs*]."[19]

It was no accident that Glen Charles referred to their entry into television as being part of "the same college class."[20] MTM Enterprises deliberately acted as a training ground for behind-the-scenes talent, and the Charles brothers and Burrows were certainly not the only creators to graduate out of the system. Four other employees—James L. Brooks, David Davis, Stan Daniels, and Ed Weinberger—left MTM to create their own production company, the John Charles Walters Company. Having all worked together on MTM productions, the founders of the John Charles Walters Company asked the Charles brothers and Burrows to be the producers and showrunners of their new show, *Taxi*. In *Taxi*'s first season, the Charles brothers wrote five of the twenty-two episodes, and

Burrows directed all twenty-two. Similarly, in season 2 the Charles brothers wrote five episodes and Burrows directed all twenty-five, and in season 3 the brothers wrote four of the twenty episodes produced, and Burrows directed all but two. After season 3, though, the Charles brothers and Burrows began to explore creating a show themselves. They had enjoyed showrunning *Taxi*, but wanted to work on their own series and decided to form their own production company. Burrows said that they thought of naming their production company "A Jew and Two Mormons" before settling on Charles/Burrows/Charles.[21] The three friends were well enough known and respected in the industry that networks were immediately interested in what they would produce.

THE PEACOCK NETWORK

NBC in the 1970s was a mess. In an era with only three American broadcast networks—NBC, CBS, and ABC—the National Broadcasting Company was jokingly called the fourth-place network.[22] At the time, the head of programming was Paul Klein,[23] a man whose most significant contribution to NBC was a concept called Least Objectionable Programming (LOP), which basically attempted to air shows that nobody would turn off because they didn't like the content. With only three channels to choose from, Klein hoped people would land on NBC and leave the channel there.

Klein laid out his argument in a 1971 *TV Guide* article, "Why You Watch What You Watch When You Watch," in which he argued, "The fact is you view TV regardless of its content. . . . You are viewing programs which by necessity must appeal to the rich and poor, smart and stupid, tall and short, wild and tame, together. Therefore, you are in the vast majority of cases viewing something that is not to your taste."[24] Klein goes on to explain that even if a show is not to your taste, you will watch anyway simply because it's on. If it's in the home, odds are the TV will be turned on every night, whether or not there is an appealing program being broadcast. Klein argued that in all likelihood there will be nothing on that meets viewers' tastes, but "the medium meets their taste."[25] Thus, most people select television viewing over reading or any other activity they might claim to prefer. Eventually a viewer settles on "one channel whose program is *least objectionable*," not because it is satisfying, but because it's there and it's not antagonizing.[26]

With this ethos, NBC was not in the practice of putting on shows that would be talked about. They aired content that would simply be. However, new NBC executives in the early 1980s—including Fred Silverman, Brandon Tartikoff, and Warren Littlefield—were looking to produce shows that audiences would actively seek out rather than passively not turn off.

Trusting in the new Charles/Burrows/Charles company, NBC was willing to "overcompromise and overpay" to get them to come to the struggling network because "nobody wanted to be on NBC."[27] Bob Broder was the agent for Glen and Les Charles and James Burrows and oversaw the negotiation to secure a series pick-up. After negotiating this deal, Broder's reaction was, "Good news: we had a series commitment. Bad news: it was NBC."[28] Having a network agreeing to air the show, Charles/Burrows/Charles still needed a studio to produce. Broder approached Paramount Television, which eagerly agreed to produce the as-yet-unnamed-and-unpitched show. John Pike, the head of Paramount Television, said, "We made the deal without having any concept of what the idea was. We really didn't know. We went into business with Charles/Burrows/Charles."[29]

CREATING *CHEERS*

With a series order and a studio ready to produce the show, Charles/Burrows/Charles had to decide what they would make. One reason the Charles brothers had wanted to write for television in the first place is that they had seen a transition from the era of *The Munsters* and *The Beverly Hillbillies* to *The Mary Tyler Moore Show* and *M*A*S*H*. "After a mindless decade of witches, genies, and talking horses, television suddenly seemed capable of delivering bright, literate comedy you could laugh at without feeling ashamed."[30] *Cheers* is correctly identified as a watershed series in network television, one that broke the mold of classic network sitcoms. But the series owes a debt to the creative voices of 1970s sitcoms that had already cracked it.

There are clear antecedents that inspired aspects of the show, both in general television history and in the work experience of the creators of

Cheers. As Brian Welk argues, "While 'Cheers' remains one of the most successful sitcoms, it wasn't the most groundbreaking or innovative."[31] The workplace as surrogate family had been seen in the writers' room scenes on *The Dick Van Dyke Show* and on the series for which the Charles brothers and James Burrows had first gained some of their television experience: *The Mary Tyler Moore Show* and *Taxi*. While the creators were also looking for something akin to the British show *Fawlty Towers*,[32] they chose a bar setting rather than a country inn. This actually put the show firmly in the tradition of the classic radio comedy, *Duffy's Tavern*, which had been cocreated by Abe Burrows—James Burrows's father—who was also the head writer of *Duffy's Tavern* for the first half of its decade-long run. The Charles brothers and Burrows settled on setting their show in a gathering place rather than strictly a workplace. The show would combine the lives of workers and regular patrons, with the promise that anyone could walk in the door to provide a story.

It should be noted that there exists a "*Cheers* conspiracy," that a local Boston TV show called *Park St. Under* served as an uncredited inspiration for *Cheers*. *Park St. Under* was produced by WCVB Channel 5, which aired all thirty-six episodes of the series from 1979 to 1980. *Park St. Under* was a show set in a Boston bar, with a former Red Sox player who was the bartender, and an assortment of workers and regulars who would make up the recurring characters. The creators of *Park St. Under* insist that their show was ripped off by NBC, with the head writer of *Park St. Under*, Arnie Reisman, calling the pilots of the two series "teethgnashingly similar."[33] A reporter named Dan McCarthy tried to get to the bottom of the conspiracy in 2018, and while everyone involved in *Park St. Under* insists that *Cheers* ripped them off, he was able to locate a few episodes of the difficult-to-find series to watch and concludes that the "similarities between the two make an argument for some kind of influence," but "the things that are so lovable about *Park St. Under*—the local feel, the rough-around-the-edges inside jokes that make it seem familiar—aren't the things that made *Cheers* a hit."[34]

Ken Levine, who was a part of the writers room from the very beginning on *Cheers*, insists that he never heard mention of *Park St. Under* until he became aware of Dan McCarthy's 2018 article. Levine recalls that when breaking stories on *Cheers*, "if we learned an element even approximated something done on another show, we automatically threw it out. That was one of the Charles brothers' strictest rules. In eleven years I never saw them waver from it once."[35] Levine concludes that while there are similarities between the shows, based on his experience working on *Cheers* and knowing Glen and Les Charles and James Burrows, "any similarities are purely coincidental."[36] So, it seems there is something of a stalemate when it comes to voices from these two shows, those from *Park St. Under* insisting it was ripped off, while those who spoke on the record from *Cheers* arguing that they had never heard of the locally produced sitcom. Of course, one only needs to be passingly familiar with popular culture to know that simultaneous creative expressions often overlap in unexpected ways, and similarities do not prove plagiarism.

So, if there were antecedents in *Duffy's Tavern, Fawlty Towers, The Mary Tyler Moore Show*, and possibly *Park St. Under*, what was new about *Cheers*? Most famously, there are two inextricably linked elements that varied from the established norms of sitcom production in the era: the will-they-won't-they Sam and Diane relationship, and the long-running story arc for each season. Certainly there had been shows with characters getting together before, and shows with subplots, but on the whole the television model at the time was for every episode to be self-contained. A viewer could drop in on any episode, watch, and not need to be caught up on any continuity to be able to enjoy it. The order didn't matter. In an era without any kind of on-demand viewing, this is what made the most sense to networks. It was impossible to know if a viewer was committed to watching every episode or just might catch it in a syndicated rerun, so every episode had to be its own story. Or, at least that was the common sense of the day. *Cheers* would upend that.

With Sam and Diane's slow-build relationship, and then the on-again, off-again nature of their romance in seasons 2 through 5, the viewer is best served by watching the episodes in order. Whether Sam and Diane were together, or who was pursuing whom, involved a linear, serial plot. Vikram Murthi recognizes that *Cheers* helped "introduce TV audiences to the viability of will-they, won't-they relationships, multi-episode arcs, and disconnected cold opens."[37] Bill Carter noted in the *New York Times* that "unlike most situation comedies, 'Cheers' has always followed at least one linear storyline all season."[38] Before a season begins, the writers meet to map out the direction for the next year's overarching storyline. For the first year, the storyline would be the slow-building romance of Sam and Diane.

With the premise in place, a cast needed to be found. Because there was a writers strike, Glen and Les Charles had more time than usual to look at potential cast members, and they asked to see everyone. They heard the lines given to actors who auditioned so often that they had to be cut from the actual script for the pilot because they got so sick of them.[39] The work paid off in the end; the actors and actresses they found became "arguably the deepest and most talented class in the history of the American sitcom."[40]

Anticipating that the Sam-Diane dynamic would be key to the success of the show, the creators took the unusual step of screen-testing pairs of actors and actresses for chemistry, rather than casting the roles individually. More than three hundred actors were considered, but eventually three actors and actresses were set to audition as Sam and Diane pairs. They wouldn't be reading for one role, they would be auditioning for the lead couple on *Cheers*.

The three pairs of actors who auditioned were Ted Danson and Shelley Long, Fred Dryer and Julia Duffy, and Billy Devane and Lisa Eichhorn. Burrows remembers that they borrowed the *Bosom Buddies* set because it had a bar in it, and then had all three couples read for the producers and network executives who sat where the studio audience would normally be.[41] The network executives wanted Fred Dryer, who had played in the NFL and seemed a natural fit for Sam Malone. At that point, the script called for Malone to be a former New England Patriot rather than a former Boston Red Sox pitcher. However, for Burrows "it was obvious it was Ted and Shelley."[42] The "Danson-Long chemistry was undeniable,"[43] but Burrows did see why the network was interested in Dryer. He told Ted Danson, "You watch Fred. Watch how he moves. Watch how he preens. He's a peacock. That's who Sam Malone is."[44]

At the insistence of Burrows and the Charles brothers, Ted Danson and Shelley Long were cast as the leads in the show. Fred Dryer did appear in two episodes of *Cheers* as a former athlete who was friends with Sam Malone. The rest of the early core characters in the pilot were Carla Tortelli, Ernie "Coach" Pantusso, and Norm Peterson.

Working at Cheers, Carla Tortelli would be a constant presence, and the producers looked for someone they had already worked with on *Taxi*, Rhea Perlman. Perlman was the first to be officially cast in the show.[45] The role of Coach was originally offered to Robert Prosky, but when he turned it down at the last minute, producers were left scrambling. Fortunately, it was recommended that they read Nick Colasanto for the role. Colasanto brings the perfect blend of naive innocence and accidental sage wisdom to the role. Glen Charles has said that Prosky would have been "great in the role," but Colasanto was "special" as Coach.[46]

In the pilot, the only bar regular to be featured prominently was going to be a beer-guzzling patron named George. For inspiration in creating a bar regular, Les Charles turned back to his own experience as a bartender to create one regular who was constantly there, even when promising to only have one drink that night.[47] In casting George, Burrows and the Charles brothers recalled a guest star from *Taxi*, George Wendt, and invited him to read for the role. George Wendt was always the favorite for the role and eventually landed it. Producers changed the character's name from George to Norm to avoid confusion with the actor and the role he portrayed.

Naturally, though they had been interested in George Wendt, they did also audition other actors for the role, including John Ratzenberger.

Diane Chambers (Shelley Long), Sam Malone (Ted Danson), and Ernie "Coach" Pantusso (Nick Colasanto)

When Ratzenberger sensed that "his reading did not enthrall the producers," he suggested that the bar needed a blowhard know-it-all.[48] Ratzenberger talked his way into a role that didn't exist yet and was offered a seven-episode contract as a recurring character. He quickly became a regular at the bar, and by season 2 he was included in the credits as a full cast member.

While Burrows would direct every episode of the first season, there was no way that the Charles brothers could write every episode. An incredibly talented writers room was assembled. Included in the room were the iconic writing partners David Isaacs and Ken Levine (who have written for shows ranging from *M*A*S*H* to *Frasier*), David Lloyd (who wrote the famous "Chuckles Bites the Dust" for *The Mary Tyler Moore Show*), David Angell (who, along with David Lee and Peter Casey who began writing for *Cheers* in season 3, would go on to create *Wings* and *Frasier*), Sam Simon (who would later codevelop *The Simpsons* with Matt Groening and James L. Brooks), and Heide Perlman (an award-winning writer and producer and the sister of Rhea Perlman). The Charles brothers deserve credit for creating the characters, planning out the overarching storyline of the season, and writing several individual episodes, but also for assembling a brilliant writing room to ensure quality on the show. While Josh Kurp argues that the writing room from season 3 of *Cheers* was one of the greatest in all of television history,[49] the room was obviously talented from year one.

CREDITS AND SONG

One of the most recognizable elements of *Cheers* is its title sequence, showing tinted vintage photographs while "Where Everybody Knows Your Name" is played. Both aspects work in tandem to evoke a nostalgic pathos meant to make even new viewers feel comfortable and want to settle in for a familiar experience.

"Where Everybody Knows Your Name" was penned by Gary Portnoy and Judy Hart Angelo, a writing team who were working on a Broadway musical called *Preppies*.[50] One of the planned songs for *Preppies*, "People Like Us," made its way to Glen and Les Charles, who were interested in using it for their new show. As to how their show tune got to a television producer, Portnoy says, "About ten people have taken credit for that. I think that my co-writer had a friend at a television production company, and he was married to one of the producers. It was one of those weird Hollywood connections."[51] However, when the producer of *Preppies* heard about one of his songs possibly being used elsewhere, he "legally stopped" any chance of that.[52] But Glen and Les Charles liked something they had heard in Portnoy and Hart Angelo's style, and they invited them to submit a new song.

In the end, they submitted two songs that were promptly rejected, and then a third that the creators of *Cheers* liked but needed revisions. The original opening lyrics of the song included "Singing the blues when the Red Sox lose/It's a crisis in your life/On the run 'cause all your girlfriends/Want to be your wife,"[53] but the producers insisted that the song was too local. They wanted it to strike a "more universal chord."[54] In revisions, they landed on the iconic, melancholy opening lines of the song that swell into the more optimistic chorus, "Sometimes you wanna go/ where everybody knows your name."[55] One of the most famous parts of the song is the seven-note introduction, which Portnoy recalls he and Angelo wrote to "get someone back from the refrigerator. . . . If someone went to get a beer or a sandwich, we want something that says, 'We're here!'"[56] In an era when viewers often left the television at commercial breaks and had no means of pausing what was airing, an unmistakable audio cue was an important signal.

For the network, having a song written is not the same as having the finished product that will go on the air. There was debate as to whether to allow Portnoy, who sang on the demo tape, to record the finished version, or bring in a more famous singer. Because the show had unknown actors, the network felt that bringing in a "name" artist for the theme song would boost the awareness of the show.[57] In the end, at Glen and Les Charles's insistence, Gary Portnoy sang the song and also layered five backup vocal tracks to harmonize with himself.[58] The song was popular enough that a full-length version with three verses made both the U.S. and UK pop charts.

The iconic tune is only one-half of the *Cheers* opening credit sequence, the other being the old-style photographs with credits laid over them. The opening titles, which won an Emmy award for "Outstanding Achievement in Graphic Design and Title Sequence," were designed by Jim Castle, Bruce Bryant, and Carol Johnsen.[59] Initially, the Charles brothers pitched the idea that the opening credits would track the history of bars, from cavemen sitting around a fire drinking to the present day. Castle, Bryant, and Johnsen came back saying they were struggling to find the right images for that concept but suggested focusing on just the history of the bar the show was set in.[60] They hand-tinted "archival illustrations and photographs of bar life, culled from books, private collections, and historical societies."[61] They also suggested matching the cast members' names with analogs from the archival images. This wasn't always possible with old photos of bars; for example, they ended up using a photo from a butcher's shop to find a match for Woody in season 3.

Castle, Bryant, and Johnsen also employed a clever bit of text placement to dodge the issue of top billing on the show. Ted Danson and Shelley Long had read for the parts of Sam and Diane as a pair, and both were considered stars of the show. And, neither had the sort of resume that demanded top billing. So, their names appear simultaneously on screen, with Ted Danson's name in the lower left-hand side of the screen and Shelley Long's on the upper right-hand side. If a viewer first scans the screen from left to right, Ted Danson has top billing. But, if they first scan the screen from top to bottom, Shelley Long has top billing. Thus, both Ted Danson and Shelley Long share equal billing in *Cheers*.[62]

The easily recognized font used for the *Cheers* logo and show title is actually a combination of the capital "C" from a font called Candice and the lowercase letters from a font called Flamenco. Castle, Bryant, and Johnsen added a fanciful underline to the show title that was meant to evoke old-style baseball team logos, and the *Cheers* logo was ready for showtime[63] (and eventually all the merchandise NBC could imagine).

CHEERS ON THE AIR

For some sitcoms, it takes several episodes or even a season or two for the series to find its voice. Creatively, *Cheers* hit the ground running. The first review for the show in *Variety* opened by saying, "If quality counts for anything, then 'Cheers' appears bound for success," and closed with, "In short, it looks like NBC's got a hit on its hands and 'Cheers' may well turn out to be the best of the new season sitcoms."[64] That praise for the pilot continues to the present day. As Harry Castleman and Walter J. Podrazik note in their exhaustively researched *Watching TV: Six Decades of American Television*, 2nd ed. "*Cheers* had all its key elements in place starting with the first episode, and never looked back."[65] It quickly became apparent that *Cheers* was "one of the best written and best executed situation comedies ever, with parallel subplots and throwaway background comments that were as funny as the main punch lines."[66] In *TV (The Book)*, the pilot of *Cheers* is ranked as the second best pilot ever, behind only *Twin Peaks*.[67] *Time* magazine included it in their list of "ten most watchable pilots in TV history."[68] Todd VanDerWerff argues that "*Cheers* boasts the best comedy pilot I've ever seen."[69]

Getting a perfect pilot takes a blend where the sum becomes greater than the parts. The writing, acting, directing, and set design have to come together to make something that works together seamlessly to entertain the audience and capture their interest. The *Cheers* pilot, "Give Me a Ring Sometime," confidently and assuredly introduces all of the characters and the narrative stakes for the first season. Because so much of sitcom comedy relies on character interactions, navigating a pilot episode that manages to introduce all the core characters, tells a complete story, and is actually funny is difficult. Television frequently launches shows that get better as they go along, and it's not just actors getting more familiar with each other and writers writing to their strengths; it's also the audience getting to know the characters better. That familiarity makes some of the jokes much easier to land, but "Give Me a Ring Sometime" balances these competing needs perfectly.

There is a patience to introducing characters and building the world of *Cheers* that helps the quality to shine. Appropriate for a show that will not leave the bar at any point during its first season, the series begins with Sam Malone walking down the bar's hallway only nine seconds into the pilot. After an underage patron unsuccessfully attempts to order a beverage in the cold open, the story really begins with the appearance of Diane and her romantic partner, Sumner Sloane. This happens two minutes and forty seconds into the episode. Sumner Sloane is an excellent foil to Sam Malone, with Diane pulled between them. Their names are similar, but Sam Malone sounds appropriately working class while Sumner Sloane smacks of upper-class elitism. And as Diane works as Sumner Sloane's teaching assistant and as Sam Malone's waitress, Sloane and Malone will both be Diane's work superiors who pursue a romantic relationship with her.

Slowly, the bar fills with other patrons and workers. Coach, the dimwitted bartender, appears seven minutes and twenty seconds into the pilot. When his opinion is easily swayed by whomever has last spoken, his lack of mental sharpness is quickly and comically established. Next, Carla appears a little less than a minute later, at eight minutes and eighteen seconds. Entering with a loud and angry rant, her bitterness and lack of tact is known seconds into her appearance. The most regular of Cheers regulars, Norm enters and receives the first of many, many cries of "Norm" as he calls for a beer and settles into his obviously familiar barstool. The last regular from the first season, Cliff Clavin, doesn't have an entrance. After a commercial break he is sitting at the bar near Diane, twelve minutes and forty seconds into the episode. After engaging in a debate about the sweatiest movie ever made, Cliff delivers his first "little-known fact," this one about women's sweat glands.[70]

Halfway through the episode, every character has been introduced and allowed to reveal key characteristics. For viewers, their types are familiar enough (jock, pretentious intellectual, dimwit, etc.) that the laughs come easily even if we haven't yet come to know these characters as individuals.

Mike Schur, who worked on *The Office* before creating *Parks and Recreation*, *Brooklyn 99*, and *The Good Place*, believes *Cheers* created something special right from its first episode, and the casting was key. Schur argues that if you had an actor who was ten percent worse than Ted Danson playing Sam, or an actress who was ten percent worse playing Diane, then you'd have a show that people like and watch, but "certainly doesn't hold the legendary place in time like it does currently."[71] The casting was important for audiences to immediately understand each of these characters. Especially when so many of them are defined by unlikable traits, the charisma of the actors and actresses is essential.

The season would continue with creative strength, tracing the through line of Sam and Diane's flirtations and building to their famous fight that ends in a passionate kiss. Along the way, there would be serious moments—Coach's perfectly written and acted exchange with his daughter or Sam's raw openness with Diane about his drinking problem—as well as detours into broad comedy—Diane's unbelievable hair after a motorcycle ride with a murderer whom Sam accidentally set her up with, for example. But the writing, acting, and directing was consistently a step above the expectations for television productions in 1982, a fact that would be rewarded with multiple Emmy nominations and wins.

ONE SEASON, TOO FEW VIEWERS

Cheers premiered at 9:00 p.m. on September 30, 1982. While NBC would dominate Thursday night television ratings in the late 1980s and throughout the 1990s, that was not the case in 1982. Most viewers' eyes were on CBS, which aired a block of two Top 10 shows on Thursday from 8:00 to 10:00 p.m. Eastern, *Magnum P.I.* and *Simon & Simon*, followed by a Top 20 show, *Knots Landing*. *Cheers* struggled the entire season in its time slot, but despite the low ratings, NBC increased the initial thirteen-episode order to twenty-two episodes.

Despite *Cheers'* ratings struggles, one three-minute clip was among the most watched scripted pieces of entertainment that year, though it then was lost for decades. NBC, showing faith in the series and a desire to boost its status, aired a short original scene just before Superbowl XVII on January 30, 1983. The scene was written by Ken Levine and David Isaacs, and Levine says, "They ran it just before game time and it was seen by 80,000,000 people. Nothing we've ever written before or since has been seen by that many eyeballs at one time. But the scene was never repeated."[72] It is not included on any *Cheers* DVD sets and never aired again. A sportswriter named Joe Resnik had recorded every Superbowl broadcast and had the *Cheers* scene included in his recording. Levine was able to have the scene digitized and put up on his blog, . . . *by Ken Levine*, in 2017. The scene is brief, featuring Diane arriving at work and surprised to see Carla, Norm, and Cliff already there. It quickly establishes the characters through jokes (Norm calls Superbowl Sunday the "only reason for living not found in a mug").[73] It does an admirable job in only three minutes of providing a brief peek into the world of *Cheers*, though it didn't make the series a sudden hit.

There's one other odd little-seen production from *Cheers* during this period. In an effort to promote the sale of U.S. Savings Bonds, the government paid for the production of what were essentially commercials featuring casts from television series in the late 1970s and early 1980s. Among the series that produced these were *Taxi*, *WKRP in Cincinnati*, *Benson*, and *Cheers*.[74] The one for *Cheers* was written by Ralph Phillips and is a twelve-minute scene involving everyone discussing Cliff cashing in Savings Bonds to take a vacation. Like the *Cheers* Superbowl spot, it has never been included in any DVD sets.

A useful time capsule of how *Cheers* was perceived after its first season comes from television historian Rick Mitz. In 1983, Mitz, a self-professed "child of the tube,"[75] published *The Great TV Sitcom Book*, an exhaustive catalogue and commentary on television sitcoms that aired from 1949 to 1983. In the layout of his book, Mitz addresses each season's best and most popular new shows as "Front Runners" and every other new series as "Also Rans." In writing up the 1982–1983 season, Mitz noted, "It's too early to tell the fate of this season," because "no true hits have emerged—except for a few critical faves."[76] And, in a mark of how the new shows had been received, Mitz includes no "Front Runners"—only "Also Rans." This is hardly the only year that Mitz employs this tactic; in fact, the previous three years had also consisted solely of "Also Rans"; *Mork and Mindy* and *Taxi* from the 1978–1979 season were the last "Front Runners" in Mitz's hierarchy of series. When Mitz does write about *Cheers*, it is acknowledged to have been "the most highly touted show of the season" but "did awfully in the ratings," and it was only "an act of faith on the part of NBC" that the show was renewed for a second season.[77]

Other critics clearly loved the series and were disappointed to see it struggling. David Bianculli, who wrote a column for the *Akron Beacon Journal* that was also syndicated nationally, printed an improbable offer to his readers. He offered to host any homeowner with a Nielsen box attached to their television set at his own house for dinner on Thursday nights, so long as they left their televisions on NBC.[78] Of course, his bid did not work—though it did get him a phone call from both the Nielsen company threatening a lawsuit and a call from Grant Tinker to thank him.[79] At the end of its first season, *Cheers* finished as the seventy-fourth most watched show on television, out of ninety-nine shows.[80]

Clearly, even though critics had enjoyed *Cheers*, following the conclusion of its first season there was little expectation that the show would become a hit. Even less likely would have been the assumption that it would become a ratings juggernaut and also forever change audience expectations for sitcoms. Of course, there was some hope that the show could find an audience. In 1983, Fred Rothenberg noted that "the history of commercial TV suggests repeatedly that programs with heart and intellect take time to build an audience. 'The Dick Van Dyke Show' was about to be canceled until viewers found it in summer reruns. 'All in the Family' was an initial disaster. And 'The Mary Tyler Moore Show' didn't soar right away. Last season 'The A-Team' was NBC's only immediate hit."[81] *Cheers* was saved from cancellation because the network didn't have anything better to put on. Quality counted for the executives in charge of programming. And, eventually, viewers discovered the quality of *Cheers*.

2

WHEN EVERYBODY KNOWS YOUR NAME

How *Cheers* Became a Phenomenon

A lot of people may not know this, but I happen to be quite famous.

Working in television, there are any number of ways you can gauge success. When you consider how many would-be writers and actors are out there attempting to make a TV show, even getting a television show on the air is one level of success. Getting picked up for additional seasons is another. Becoming a hit is another. Transforming into a cultural touchstone is a level that a very small number of television shows are able to achieve.

Some shows, like ABC's *Lost* or NBC's *Friends*, achieve all the levels at once (and in the opinion of some, may wane as their seasons run along). *Cheers* had to scrape and struggle to achieve each new tier of success. Remarkably, *Cheers* transitioned from a ratings flop in its first season to a hit that redefined the American television landscape. The unlikely path from failure to shining success paralleled and was key to the rise of NBC from the last-place American television network to the dominant home of "Must See TV."

After its first season, *Cheers* was extremely popular, but most people probably didn't know it. The show was particularly beloved by critics and network executives but not the general viewing public. Looking at the Nielsen ratings, the casual television watcher was more likely to be unaware of *Cheers* than a fan. *Cheers* was one of the least watched shows on television, even rating dead last some weeks.[1] But, it turns out, it must be nice to have network executives on your side.

Glen Charles knew things were not looking good for renewal, but he also knew that the most important *Cheers* fans were the decision makers at NBC.[2] It was not only the showrunners who were nervous; the cast had their livelihood hanging in the balance. Ted Danson recalls that his spirits were lifted by the positive things he heard about the show, even as cast members were very aware of its low ratings. "Everyone said that, you're doing great work, the show is wonderful, keep it up. Don't worry, you're doing great stuff. The media found us. The critics loved us. It was one of those things where we as actors were buoyed up."[3] George Wendt knew that it was a corporate philosophy that saved *Cheers* and not its ratings: "Grant Tinker . . . had this mandate to put on the air what he perceived to be quality programming and leave it there until the audience found it. We were beneficiaries of that philosophy."[4]

Grant Tinker, who had replaced Fred Silverman as the president of NBC, and Brandon Tartikoff, the head of programming, were determined to revive NBC's reputation by airing quality television. Fortunately for *Cheers*, they had patience. Their own personal tastes also played a role. "Both executives *watched* the show. They both *liked* the show. So, despite barely measurable ratings, there was no way they could *cancel* the show."[5] Tartikoff in particular appreciated the caliber of comedy he saw on his network[6] and trusted that eventually *Cheers* would find its audience. Warren Littlefield recounts that when the issue of renewing *Cheers* came up, Tartikoff—an evangelist for quality over anything else—asked, "Do you have anything better?"[7] When the answer was "No," *Cheers* got a second season. As Burrows recounts, "Brandon [Tartikoff] used to tell us that: 'I've got nothing to replace you with, so I might as well leave you there.'"[8] If the person who decides what gets renewed thinks a show is the best thing on the network, odds of a second season go up considerably. Les Charles acknowledged that if the network had any other promising shows, a second season would have been unlikely. "We happened to be at NBC, which at that time was a network which didn't have a lot of successful shows. So they had to ride with us. They didn't have a lot of options."[9] While being on NBC contributed to *Cheers* struggling to find an audience, it also helped to ensure a second season.

In its first run, *Cheers* had been airing against one of the most popular shows on television. In summer reruns, many people who had already watched the other shows that aired on Thursday nights were more willing to sample the offerings on other channels. *Cheers* slowly started to pick up an audience across the summer. Because "everybody had seen *Simon & Simon* and *Magnum [P.I.]*," the reruns of *Cheers* climbed above their low rank during their first run.[10] Shortly before season 2 premiered, a large publicity boost came in the form of awards season.

In January 1984, halfway through its first season, *Cheers* won a Golden Globe for Best Television Series, Comedy or Musical. In September, just four days before the second season premiere of *Cheers*, the Emmy Awards aired. *Cheers* won the award for Outstanding Comedy Series, James Burrows won for Outstanding Directing, Shelley Long won for Outstanding Lead Actress in a Comedy, and Glen and Les Charles won for Outstanding Writing in a Comedy Series. Additionally, the show had five other nominations, including Ted Danson for Lead Actor, Nicholas Colasanto for Supporting Actor, Rhea Perlman for Supporting Actress, and David Lloyd as well as Ken Levine and David Isaacs for writing. In an era when the same show could be nominated for more than one writing award, *Cheers* had three of the five nominations for Outstanding Writing (a feat the show and its writers room would repeat the next two years).

With viewers discovering the show via reruns, critics continuing to praise its excellence, and bevy of awards establishing its quality, *Cheers* climbed into the middle of the pack in terms of Nielsen ratings. In its second season, it finished as the thirty-fourth most watched show. *Cheers* was again recognized at that year's Emmy Awards, winning the award for Outstanding Comedy Series; Rhea Perlman won for Outstanding Supporting Actress, and David Angell won for Outstanding Writing for the episode "Old Flames." Additionally, James Burrows was nominated for Outstanding Directing; Ted Danson, Shelley Long, Nick Colasanto, and George Wendt had all been nominated for acting awards; and Glen and Les Charles and David Lloyd were nominated for writing.

In season 3, *Cheers* finished in twelfth place in the overall Nielsen ratings for the year. In its next season, it would climb into the Top 10 of the Nielsen ratings, a position it would never lose during the rest of its time on the air. From seasons 4 through 11, *Cheers* was ranked fifth, third, third, fourth, third, first, fourth, and eighth, respectively.[11]

Along with its success in the ratings, *Cheers* continued to dominate at awards shows. In total, *Cheers* would be nominated for 178 Emmy Awards and win 28 Emmys. It was nominated for Outstanding Comedy series every year it was on the air, winning the award in 1983, 1984, 1989, and 1991. Every single regular cast member was nominated for an acting award, with those that won including Shelley Long, Rhea Perlman (four times), Woody Harrelson, Ted Danson (twice), Bebe Neuwirth (twice), and Kirstie Alley.

It is remarkable that *Cheers* not only jumped from the least watched show on television to the most watched show in its ninth year on the air, but that it did so with so many changes—"frequent cast shifts, which destroyed other sitcoms throughout the years, could not make a dent in the quality of *Cheers*."[12] There are many examples of sitcoms that retained the same core cast for an entire run—*Friends*, *Seinfeld*, and *Frasier*, for example—but just as obviously, there are many sitcoms that have seen cast additions and departures, such as *The Office* or *Spin City*. But in the case of *Cheers*, more than normal changes marked the show's run, yet the show seemed to continue to flourish. The series began with five main cast members, four employees of the bar—Sam Malone, Diane Chambers, Carla Tortelli, and Ernie "Coach" Pantusso—and one regular bar patron, Norm Peterson, and another recurring cast member, Cliff Clavin, who quickly became a regular. It would end its run without Diane or Coach, and with the additions of patrons Frasier Crane and Lilith Sternin, and employees Woody Boyd and Rebecca Howe.

LONG-RUNNING PLOTS AND CAST CHANGES

The Charles brothers insisted that each season have its own long-form storytelling. While every episode would present a self-contained narrative with a beginning, middle, and end (with the exception of the occasional multipart storyline), each season would also progress from its opening to a new status quo at its conclusion. For modern viewers, this may seem to be standard fare, but for early 1980s sitcoms, this was revolutionary. The brothers expressed that, though they loved *The Mary Tyler Moore Show*, they were frustrated that the characters and relationships were basically the same at the beginning of the series as at the end. On their show, Les Charles notes, "Our key concern was not to get stuck in a rut. We didn't want to set up a situation and just ride it out however long the show was on."[13] *Cheers*, more so than any sitcom of its era, is marked by changes in

Carla Tortelli (Rhea Perlman), Ernie "Coach" Pantusso (Nick Colasanto), and Sam Malone (Ted Danson)

the cast, the character's personal lives, and their relationships with each other.

The first season's story begins when Diane enters Cheers. While there is some flirtation between Sam and Diane, it is also important to note that Sam is kindly and a bit protective toward Diane when he sees that she is being used and abandoned by Sumner Sloane.[14] When at the end of the episode Diane casually repeats a long and complex drink order Carla had given Sam, it's mutually recognized that working at Cheers may be a good idea for Diane.

Naturally, in a first season, there are some moments where it's clear that characterizations are still being worked out. For example, right after establishing Diane as having an astounding memory at the end of the pilot, the second episode opens with her screwing up an order.[15] Also in the second episode, Norm runs around crazily when he sees a pair of attractive legs,[16] which doesn't match the lethargically asexual characterization of Norm that viewers would come to know. These sort of continuity hiccups are found in most early episodes of television series and are very minor nits to pick.

There is one odd repetition in the first season when the exact same scene appears in two different episodes. In "Coach's Daughter," there is a scene in the middle of the episode that is disconnected from the major plot of the episode. A patron at the bar reveals that he works in a biology lab where weird experiments take place, and as soon as he leaves, the staff and patrons react like a comedically well-oiled machine as they toss disinfectant and rags to each other to scrub down the bar.[17] The scene is funny, and one of the best bits of physical comedy in the first season, but feels out of place coming in the middle of an episode as it seems much more like a pre-credits cold open. And that is exactly how it is used seventeen episodes later in "Showdown, Part 2."[18] The scene absolutely functions better in its second usage, but it's very irregular to see a scene re-created so completely.

The through line of season one is a slow build of mutual flirtation and frustration between Sam and Diane. One of the best episodes of the season, "Endless Slumper," deepens their relationship as Diane helps Sam when he fears he may fall off the wagon. Vikram Murthi argues that this episode is the one that first lifts *Cheers* from "'very good' to 'all-timer' by surpassing its fixed potential and entering a new plane of quality."[19] The final act of the episode, in which Sam and Diane are alone in the bar and have an emotionally raw heart-to-heart, highlights the quality of writing and acting that *Cheers* was capable of achieving when at its best. Episode writer Sam Simon's tight scripting of the dialogue between Sam and Diane is a highlight of emotion for the freshman sitcom.[20] The fifth episode of the season, "Coach's Daughter"[21] written by Ken Estin, also had an excellent scene between Coach and his daughter, Lisa, which attained depths of emotion that many sitcoms don't even strive for, much less reach twice in their first ten episodes. The romantic tension that is played out between Sam and Diane explodes in the season finale. In one of the most famous scenes, because it is so well acted and so fraught with heightened emotion, Sam and Diane fight before finally embracing and kissing for the first time.[22]

Having moved the core duo of the series from semi-resistant flirts into a full-blown couple, season 2 explores this new dynamic. Of course, because tension is often the source of comedy, it is not smooth sailing for Sam and Diane through these twenty-two episodes. Trouble begins in the season premiere when, in an attempt to consummate their new relationship, Sam goes to Diane's apartment (the first location *Cheers* has ever shown outside of the bar) and makes fun of her stuffed animal collection. Sam leaves, but the patrons at the bar convince him to act macho and perform a more masculine role with Diane, so he returns to her apartment and breaks her door down, which prompts her to call the police. After Sam has an emotional breakdown, Diane reveals she never actually called the police, and Sam then throws her stuffed animals out the window.[23]

Sam and Diane's relationship continues to ebb and flow, and other characters are given spotlight episodes in the season as well. Carla has another baby, Coach takes over a little league team, Cliff gets into a fight with another patron in an uneven episode that does have one of the best finales of the season. Norm is hired as Sam's new accountant in one of those television stories that is a core plot of one episode but is never fully resolved or significantly addressed ever again. Highlights of the second year include "Homicidal Ham,"[24] in which Andy Andy returns to stage a scene from Shakespeare with Diane, and "Sumner's Return,"[25] when the man who first dropped off Diane at Cheers comes back to see her and causes Sam and Diane to consider their relationship.

At the end of the season, all of the roiling stress of Sam and Diane's different lifestyles and interests being forced together boil over in an explosive two-part finale titled "I'll Be Seeing You." In one of the most famous scenes, for good and ill, Sam and Diane have a fight and slap one another. The acting is strong, but the physical hitting is undeniably un-comfortable to watch, even after it comedically devolves into a nose-pulling struggle.[26] Writing about this episode, Meredith Blake identified the difficulty of this scene: "The slapstick is sublimely well-executed, but it also has a troubling subtext, one that the show is brave to acknowledge. When Diane expresses her shock over the violence, Sam fires back that he hadn't hit her as hard as he wanted to. It sounds less like a defense of his behavior than a confession to even darker emotions."[27] Vince Wal-dron identified a "slapstick sadomasochism that plagued their relation-ship," and it is never more unpleasantly present than in this scene.[28]

In a newspaper article published the day the first half of "I'll Be Seeing You" aired, a spoiler-filled interview with the writers of the epi-sode has Les Charles explain, "The audience will have all summer to wonder whether Sam will ever see Diane again." Guarding against com-plaints that they shouldn't break up Sam and Diane, Les adds, "It was always part of the plan. . . . The ironic thing is that at the end of last season when it became obvious they would get together, the letters said

The Cheers staff in its first few seasons; clockwise from top left: Ernie "Coach" Pantusso (Nicholas Colasanto), Sam Malone (Ted Danson), Diane Chambers (Shelley Long), and Carla Tortelli (Rhea Perlman)

'don't let them do it.' Now that people are hearing they will break up, we're getting letters saying 'keep them together.'"[29]

Sam and Diane's fight at the end of season 2 had been highly charged and emotional, so that alone would have been enough to keep Sam and Diane apart in season 3. But, to add to the tension, the producers introduced Diane's new love interest—thus, the creation of Frasier Crane, who would become the first new regular character to join the ensemble. Because so much of the conflict between Sam and Diane had stemmed from their different tastes, in Frasier Crane they created someone more in line with Diane's professed interests. "They envisioned the opposite of Sam Malone. So rather than a jock, they created an intellectual. Rather than a lover of sports, a lover of museums. Rather than a self-assured, egotistic lothario, a pompous but needy romantic."[30] Fans of the series know that Frasier Crane was destined to become a bar regular, but originally Kelsey Grammer was only signed to a three-episode contract. He became a semi-recurring character in seasons 3 and 4 and then a series regular by season 5.

Season 3 is also notable because of Coach's diminished role. Nick Colasanto was struggling with his health, as is apparent in his more gaunt physical appearance. Coach is entirely absent from six episodes and only appears briefly in some scenes in other episodes—such as only appearing in the cold open in the season finale, "Rescue Me."[31]

The primary storyline for season 3 is Diane's new relationship with Dr. Frasier Crane, coupled with her slowly dawning recognition that she still has feelings for Sam. Standout episodes include "The Heart Is a Lonely Snipe Hunter," in which the gang plays a prank on Frasier, but he turns the tables on them and feels that he's become accepted by the guys at the bar. Near the end of the season, Frasier invites Diane to accompany him to Europe where he'll be a visiting professor, Diane accepts and leaves Boston, but frequently calls the bar (and Sam) to touch base. When Frasier proposes to Diane, she accepts, setting the stage for the series finale, in which Sam will fly to Europe to try to stop the wedding.

Diane's departure to Europe was also a clever way to hide Shelley Long's pregnancy. Earlier in the season, Diane sat behind the bar more frequently and also spent an episode trapped inside the floor of Cheers with only her face showing. But, for the final portion of the season, the shorter scenes in Europe were filmed early on, and Shelley Long was on break while the rest of the episodes were filmed. Diane would be present in every episode, but Shelley Long's pregnancy was never apparent. Ken Levine even notes that sometimes those scenes in Europe were shuffled around and ended up in different episodes than was originally planned.

> Since those Europe scenes were independent of the main stories they could sometimes be shuffled around. I remember watching an episode at home one night, written I believe by Sam Simon. I was laughing and enjoying the story and then they cut to one of these vacation scenes. It was odd. I felt a weird déjà vu. I knew this was a first run episode I hadn't seen yet this scene was vaguely familiar. And then it hit me— David and I wrote this scene. It was taken out of our show and inserted into this one.[32]

Rhea Perlman was also pregnant during this season (and several other times throughout the production of *Cheers*), but, as Levine recalls, "since it was established that her character, Carla, popped out kids like a Pez dispenser, it actually made things easier for us,"[33] and the writers simply wrote Perlman's pregnancy into Carla's character.

After fans were left questioning the result of Sam's desperate flight to Europe, the season 4 premiere reveals that he failed to stop the wedding, but Diane left Frasier at the altar anyway. Diane returns to Cheers, as does Frasier. Diane returns for work, Frasier to drown his sorrows. Also, Coach is now absent, because Nicholas Colasanto passed away from heart disease in between seasons.

Colasanto had clearly been a good friend to the cast and crew and that personal loss hit them hard. But for the series, Coach had served a vital purpose that writers needed to replace even as they all missed the actor. Coach was not just dumb, which could cause comedy in and of itself, he was also absentminded and missed a lot of what was going on around him. That meant anytime writers needed to reset the action or make sure that the audience was up-to-date on where any relationships were at, Coach was a character that could ask the questions that kept the audience up to speed. In order to replace Coach, producers introduced a character who was similarly dim-witted, but rather than Coach's nearly seventy years of age, they would look for an actor who could barely legally drink at the bar.

Cheers, which largely avoided heavy messages and sentimentality, did not have a funeral episode for the beloved character. Instead, in the fourth season premiere, Sam Malone acknowledges that Coach recently passed away and that they need a new bartender. The new bartender is Woody Boyd, played by Woody Harrelson. Woody Boyd, a naive young man from a rural town, provides some of the same comedic opportunities Coach had brought to the bar. For both characters there is no subtext, only text. They take everything they hear at face value and respond accordingly. Another new character is introduced, though she only appears in one episode this season. Frasier has a disastrous date with Lilith Sternin, played by the inimitable Bebe Neuwirth. She also is a guest in season 5 before becoming a recurring character in seasons 6 through 9 and a regular cast member in seasons 10 and 11.

One of the strongest episodes of season 4 is "Don Juan Is Hell," in which Diane writes a college paper psychoanalyzing Sam, allowing the audience to see the writers dig into what makes Sam tick.[34] In another episode signaling that Sam Malone is going to (slowly) mature, Sam suffers a hernia while trying to prove he's still as athletic as he was when he played baseball.[35] On a happier note, the gang tries to include Diane and all make a trip to the opera in "Diane Chambers Day."[36]

Near the end of the season, Sam Malone begins dating a Boston councilwoman, Janet Eldridge. While Sam and Diane had flirted on-and-off during this season, they had never gotten back together. Diane, seeing Sam and Janet together, becomes protective (and possessive) of Sam. Janet recognizes this and gives Sam an ultimatum. He must fire Diane if he wants to carry on seeing Janet. The series finale ends with Sam making a phone call and proposing marriage, though viewers don't know whom he has called.[37]

Season 5 reveals immediately that it was Diane who had received Sam's phone call. The creators were well aware that Shelley Long planned to leave the series at the conclusion of this year, so the plan naturally would be to prepare for Diane's exit in the season finale. To add to the drama of Diane's imminent departure, the season sees Sam and Diane become engaged, with the wedding to take place during the season finale.

This season has a strong opening and a strong finale, but there is a muddle in the middle that is one of the weaker points in the series. In talking about their writing for *Cheers*, Glen Charles says that after season 1, they began to chart Sam and Diane's season-long relationship each year. Glen Charles says that "we sit down and figure out where we want Sam and Diane to be at the beginning, middle, and the end of the season."[38] In this instance, it feels like they had a beginning and an end, but the middle was never fully planned beyond them getting back together in order to serve the end.

Seeing Diane pursue Sam so relentlessly is a fun inversion of earlier seasons when Sam was pursuing Diane, but the conceit runs out of steam before it reaches a natural conclusion. In the middle of the season, the thirteenth of twenty-six episodes, a judge orders Sam to propose to Diane again. It feels like the entirely wrong kind of sitcom, something more akin to a 1960s plot development than the sophisticated comedy *Cheers* had demonstrated for more than one hundred episodes. The plot was dictated by the end goals rather than coming about through character-driven action. In terms of getting Sam and Diane on the path to the season finale's wedding scene, the episode works. In terms of plot and character motivation, it's among the biggest misfires of the series. It strains credulity to accept that a judge would have a couple in the courtroom with the woman accusing the man of physical abuse, and end the proceedings by ordering them to become engaged.[39] This is certainly not an indictment on the writer of the episode, David Angell, who wrote many of the most iconic *Cheers* episodes and would go on to cocreate *Frasier*. The task was awkward, and this was the route chosen to complete it.

Despite the court-ordered nature of their engagement, Sam and Diane do proceed with plans for a wedding. A highlight of their path to marriage is in the episode "Dinner at Eight-ish,"[40] written by Phoef Sutton. Frasier and Lilith host Sam and Diane for dinner at their place and a delightful farce ensues.

On the day of their nuptials, Sumner Sloane returns to inform Diane that a publisher is interested in a novel she wrote, but the manuscript needs significant work. Sam recognizes that Diane needs to pursue her dream, and he and Diane cancel the wedding so that she can revise her work. Diane promises to return in six months, and Sam tells Diane, "Have a good life." Diane is surprised, saying, "That's something you say when something's over. Sam, I'm going away for six months, that's all." After a few more words Diane exits the bar and Sam repeats, "Have a good life" to the now empty room.[41] Diane will be mentioned periodically, but not seen again for six years.

Entering season 6, viewers knew big changes were coming. It is undoubtedly the most significant transition for the series. The creators had dealt with Nicholas Colasanto's untimely passing by inserting Woody into the main cast and had introduced a new regular in Frasier, but the finale of season 5 was the end of an era. Shelley Long's departure from the show was well publicized, and as a Top 10 show *Cheers* had millions of fans interested in what the new dynamic would be. Rebecca Howe would be the replacement for Diane. When replacing Coach, producers had created a much younger but similar character in Woody Boyd. In replacing Diane, they decided to change the course of the show entirely. Coming into season 6, viewers learn that Sam has sold the bar and it's now owned by a large corporation. Rebecca Howe is the (for now) serious, corporate-climbing manager who also aspires to marry her boss, Evan Drake.

To establish the changes that have taken place, Frasier sums up what is different while sitting at the bar talking to Woody:

> What happened to the good old days. Everything was better. Sam still owned the bar, he wasn't out circumnavigating the globe. Yonder sat Diane with a book. Norm and Cliff were permanent fixtures in this place. God how I miss those hail-fellows well met. Where has it gone, Woody?[42]

In what must have been a deliberate setup to highlight the changes at the bar in this new era, the cold open of the season 6 premiere omits any of the original cast members. Woody and Frasier are the only two regulars to appear, the two most recent additions to the cast. There are several possible interpretations for this choice. At the moment of its most public cast change, this highlights the show's successful changes since its first season. It also recognizes the significance of the coming change, as the new decor and showing none of the original cast is a break from the comfortable norm that had been established over the previous five years.

While it never reaches the fever pitch of Sam and Diane, Sam does absolutely romantically pursue Rebecca in this season. One reason it never became as definitive to the series' identity is the fact that Diane flirted with Sam, just as Sam flirted with her. They both questioned their own feelings for the other, and the other's feelings for themselves. In season 6, Rebecca does nothing but shut down Sam's innuendos and advances, even as she is attempting to pursue Evan Drake. Sam's constant advances become wearying for the audience as well as for Rebecca, in a way the coy interactions with Diane never did.

While the new romantic setup between Sam and Rebecca doesn't work as well as what came before, the season premiere remains a strong entry for the series and a clear transition from what came before. The ensemble that viewers have come to love rises in prominence just as the attention of the series shifts to a wider focus than in seasons 1 through 5. Excellent episodes from this season include "The Crane Mutiny," in which the new presence of Rebecca throws a wrench into Frasier's relationship with Lilith.[43] "Yacht of Fools" utilizes the entangled romantic interests of Sam, Drake, and Rebecca to introduce a door-slamming French farce[44] similar to what the *Cheers* spin-off *Frasier* would execute to great success and acclaim.

The season 6 finale, "Backseat Becky, Up Front," sees a resolution to Rebecca's misbegotten pursuit of Evan Drake as he leaves the country to take a corporate position in Japan. It also establishes a strong bond between Sam and Rebecca. After one season of mutual flirtation, Sam and Diane had finally gotten together. After one season of one-way flirtation, Sam chooses friendship over sex. When Sam and Rebecca are having a heart-to-heart after she feels dumped by Drake, Sam begins by attempting to seduce Rebecca. But when he recognizes that she needs a friend and Sam is her best friend, he leaves. He doesn't know if he will be able to resist taking advantage of her and leaves her apartment, explaining, "I can't be trusted. Trust me."[45] But he does call her from a payphone so they can talk and he can better resist his sexual urges.

Season 6 had ended with a sign of maturity in Sam and Rebecca's relationship, which disappeared at the beginning of season 7. Sam waltzes into the bar announcing that he has waited long enough for Rebecca to get over Evan Drake, and that his time of conquest has come. Rebecca, establishing a pattern, sees the new vice president of the company that owns the bar and is immediately attracted to him. Sadly, he's there to fire Rebecca and put Sam back in charge. Sam struggles with the corporation's computer systems and hires Rebecca back to help out. But, unlike the previous seasons, there isn't an obvious overarching narrative in season 7. Seasons 1 through 6 have an obvious starting point and ending point so that viewers can see a shift in the relationships between the characters. Season 7 opens with Sam hitting on Rebecca and a reversion to Sam being more in charge of the bar and ends with Rebecca fending off the unwanted advances of marriage specialist Dr. Lawrence

Crandell (though none of her friends believe her when she says Dr. Crandell is hitting on her).[46]

There are two sub-arcs throughout the season. A new, diminutive vice president in the company wants to marry Rebecca, and she refuses. Sam has the chance to help Rebecca by pretending to be her boyfriend, but runs off to tend bar in Mexico the second that option presents itself. The other plot sees the wealthy Walter Gaines ask Rebecca to organize a party at his house where Woody meets Kelly Gaines, played by Jackie Swanson. Woody's long and slow courtship with Kelly Gaines will become the character's primary storyline from this point to the series finale.

There are several very excellent individual episodes. "Norm, Is That You?" sees Norm acknowledging his hidden talent for interior decorating,[47] and in "Jumping Jerks," Sam, Woody, Norm, and Cliff attempt to go skydiving as the tug-of-war between their machismo and cowardice makes them question their decision.[48] And, Bebe Neuwirth provides an excellent turn as a pregnant Lilith who overzealously enjoys her pregnancy in "The Cranemakers."[49]

Season 8 sees a return to a season-long storyline as Rebecca Howe has a romance with the uber-wealthy Robin Colcord, played by Roger Rees. Robin Colcord appears in the season premiere, just as Rebecca is prepared to give in to Sam's constant advances. His relationship with Rebecca continues until the end of the season when it is revealed that he was using Rebecca to gain access to the Lillian Corporation computers using her password.

Season 8 also sees the birth of Frederick Crane,[50] a character who would become the second most common crossover guest from *Cheers* to appear on *Frasier*. Season 8 features the famous episode, "What Is . . . Cliff Clavin?" when Cliff appears on *Jeopardy* and completely dominates the game, which has categories including "Civil Servants," "Stamps around the World," "Mothers and Sons," "Beer," "Bar Trivia," and "Celibacy." However, in final jeopardy, the category is "Movies," with the clue "Archibald Leach, Bernard Schwartz, and Lucille LeSeur." The correct response would be "What were the real names of Cary Grant, Tony Curtis, and Joan Crawford?" Unfortunately, Cliff wagers everything and answers, "Who are three people who have never been in my kitchen?"[51] In the finale, Sam turns in Robin Colcord, causing him to go on the run from federal authorities. As a thanks for saving the corporation from a

business takeover, the corporation sells Cheers back to Sam for one dol-
lar. [52]

Season 9 is more akin to season 7, with several smaller subplots.
Despite Robin Colcord being on the run, and then in jail, Robin and
Rebecca continue their courtship. Kelly travels abroad and returns with a
clingy French ladies' man named Henri who makes Woody jealous. And
Sam begins to question the emptiness of his one-night-stand lifestyle and
considers becoming a father. [53]

In season 10, the primary plot is Sam and Rebecca trying to have a
child together, but not a romantic relationship. This is strictly a procrea-
tive relationship. Halfway through the season, they decide to call off this
venture, and attention shifts to Woody and Kelly's wedding. The two-part
season finale is an exercise in everything-that-can-go-wrong-does plotting, but with the audience kept on the edge of their seats because what
can go wrong is so unexpectedly absurd. [54]

Season 11 gets a burst of energy from the faltering marriage of Frasier
and Lilith. When it's discovered that Lilith has had an affair and also
plans to leave Frasier to go live in an underground eco-pod with the man
she's slept with, Frasier's emotional foundation cracks, with hilarious
results. [55] Of course, the series finale brings back Diane Chambers to
disrupt the status quo at Cheers before allowing things to settle back into
the comfortable routine viewers have embraced. [56] Eleven years, 275 episodes, and an enduring legacy came to a close when Sam told a would-be
patron, "Sorry, we're closed," and turned off the lights at Cheers.

THE NEW CAST MEMBER THAT ALMOST WAS

Notably, one character was introduced and almost upped to a main character, but it seems the actions of the actor prevented that from happening.
During the course of *Cheers*, Carla Tortelli has an ex-husband who shows
up periodically, as well as a string of romantic relationships, but she
marries a hockey goalie named Eddie LeBec. LeBec eventually ends up
skating in a penguin costume for a traveling show called the Wonderful
World of Ice after his NHL contract runs out. [57] LeBec was played by Jay
Thomas, who made some comments that likely resulted in being written
off *Cheers* at a time when he was being considered for promotion to a full
cast member. There are several versions of this, coming from Rhea Perl-

man, Jay Thomas, and Ken Levine, who cowrote the episode of *Cheers* that introduced Eddie LeBec into the series[58] as well as the episode in which LeBec was written off the show.[59]

While working on *Cheers*, Thomas also had a radio show, and a caller asked him about his work on *Cheers*. Thomas told a joke that had a punchline about deserving combat pay for kissing Carla.[60] Thomas insists the joke was about the character Carla, who was abrasive and mean, and not the actress Rhea Perlman, who played Carla. But the joke could have easily been interpreted as a derisive comment about Rhea Perlman's attractiveness. Ken Levine asserts that Perlman heard the joke[61] and then "came up to my office and she was furious—I'd never seen her like this. She said, 'I want him off the show.'"[62] For her part, Perlman insists that she liked Jay Thomas as Eddie LeBec, but "didn't like the idea of Carla being with somebody because that would make you feel like [you're] not part of the people in the bar."[63] We may never know whether it was concern about Carla being tied down domestically or Perlman being upset about Thomas's jokes on his radio show that led to the character being written off, but Levine adds that after the joke on the radio, Eddie was never seen again on *Cheers*.[64] And, when Levine and David Isaacs wrote LeBec off the show, they didn't just write the character off due to a divorce or because he was constantly traveling; they torched the ground and salted the earth of his memory so that audiences would never lament his departure.

Levine notes that writing off a well-received character is a delicate procedure—in this case, they needed "(a) some comic spin for the story, and (b) something to discredit Eddie so the audience would ultimately be glad he was out of Carla's life."[65] The comic spin came in the mode of his death, which was by Zamboni. Carla gets a phone call telling her that Eddie, who had been dancing in a penguin costume, died when there was "a freak accident with the ice show. Happened real sudden. They were cleaning the ice with that big machine after the penguins' salsa number. One of the penguins slipped, fell in front of the machine. Eddie dived just in time, pushed the guy out of the way and . . . he never felt a thing."[66] Certainly without any of the behind-the-scenes drama to inform a viewing of this episode, it seems odd for a sitcom to have a character so comedically and brutally killed off, but in the same episode they make the previously likable character much less sympathetic. At his funeral, when the priest asks Eddie LeBec's wife to stand, Carla and another woman both rise, and each soon learns that her husband had a second, secret family. In how the scene is staged (the head of a penguin mascot costume sits atop the casket) and played (the funeral for an ex-hockey player ends in a hockey brawl) the tragedy becomes comedy, and instead of mourning, Carla is allowed to be angry, a mood that suits the character far more than moroseness.

Allowing Carla's established personality to be retained in spite of the tragedy is an example of how *Cheers* remained successful despite the cast changes. Carla was still Carla. And throughout the show, original characters were clearly defined and the new characters that were added had clear, distinct identities. Some evolution happens (Sam Malone starts to question his womanizing lifestyle as he ages, for example), but audiences wanted to visit a bar with these characters, and the show didn't mess with that formula. *Cheers* is remarkable for its ability to remove beloved characters, whether because of an actor's death, an actress's career decisions, or a disc jockey's ill-planned jokes, and to create and insert new characters that became as beloved as those that came before. It is difficult enough in the television industry to have a successful show—the rate of failure for each pilot season is far greater than that of success—but it is perhaps more difficult to navigate a shifting talent line in front of the camera. The writers, directors, and actors deserve credit for creating a series that was critically acclaimed for all eleven seasons, not just the Sam-and-Diane years or the Rebecca years.

THE FINALE

While the finale is famous, what immediately followed has become a bit infamous. In its efforts to create an event, NBC had focused its entire prime time programming on *Cheers*. The night included a retrospective special hosted by Bob Costas, the three-episode-length finale, and then the entire cast appearing on *The Tonight Show* live from Boston. The latter event is notorious for how poorly it went.

Hoping to piggyback on guaranteed ratings, the entire regular cast appeared live on *The Tonight Show* with Jay Leno immediately after the series finale ended. The special episode of *The Tonight Show* aired directly from the Bull & Finch, the Boston pub that inspired the look and location of Cheers. However, that live broadcast turned out to be a mistake. The cast had arrived hours early, began drinking immediately, and were quite drunk for the interview. Leno had difficulty keeping them focused, a struggle that was awkwardly apparent to viewers. Leno later lamented, "Those people were so drunk I don't know what else we could have done in a live situation," and added that Ted Danson sent him flowers with an apology the next day.[67] *Entertainment Weekly*'s retrospective on popular culture in 1993 wondered "who had the biggest hangover the next day?" after noting that the cast of *Cheers* "sure looked like they were having a good time."[68] Despite this black eye on the night, the ratings clearly made the evening a success for NBC.

It is one of the odd quirks of popular culture that something can receive rave reviews when released and be forgotten only a few years later or receive a mixed reception but gain status as time passes. When it aired, reviews for the *Cheers* finale were mixed, but it is now held in higher esteem. John J. O'Connor, in a *New York Times* review published the day after the finale aired, said the episode was "overly long and uncharacteristically labored."[69] In more recent years, it has routinely appeared on lists of the best finales of all time, with it being noted that "the consummate professionalism that marked *Cheers* during its 11-season run followed through to the end."[70]

Of course, the finale of *Cheers* was not the end of the line for these beloved characters. With Carla, Norm, and Cliff having already appeared on the short-lived spin-off, *The Tortellis*, and Frasier, Lilith, and Norm appearing on *Wings*, as well as most of the cast appearing on *St. Elsewhere*, it wasn't unheard of for *Cheers* regulars to pop up in other series. But, nothing they had appeared on previously had the success that was awaiting the last *Cheers* spin-off, *Frasier*.

After exploring other options, Kelsey Grammer and three writers and producers from *Cheers*—David Angell, Peter Casey, and David Lee— decided to pursue a sitcom centered around the Frasier Crane character. In the pilot, it's revealed that Frasier has divorced Lilith and moved back to his hometown of Seattle, a move that precluded regular drop-ins from *Cheers*. Occasional guest appearances from the Cheers gang would happen (naturally, during ratings weeks for NBC). Lilith, of course, was the most frequent character to visit Seattle from Boston. But Sam, Woody, and Diane each made their way to visit Frasier. And, in the tenth season of *Frasier*, there is the closest thing to a *Cheers* reunion that could be arranged. Frasier is traveling through Boston and accidentally stumbles on Cliff's retirement party, which is being held at an airport reception room rather than Cheers.

John Pike, the Paramount executive who had first agreed to produce an unnamed show with Charles/Burrows/Charles, tried to figure out how much *Cheers* was worth and concluded that in net dollars, one year of *Cheers* was worth about $75 million for NBC,[71] which quickly approaches a billion dollars when a show runs for eleven seasons and remains popular thereafter. Recalling how NBC struggled in ratings when it first began airing *Cheers*, Warren Littlefield insists, "It was worth more. *Cheers* was an absolute game changer for NBC. Successful both artistically and financially, *Cheers* validated our judgment and our taste and marked the beginning of our discovery of who we were as a network."[72]

3

THE POWER OF THE BAR

Location, Location, Location

This is amazing. Hundreds of bottles. Red and white wine glasses. High-grade naugahyde stool covers. And a brass rail. And a big city bartender with a joke at the ready.

THE BAR AS A SET

Wood panels. Brick walls. Tiffany lamps. Stained glass windows. Eclectic staff. Unique regulars. Overall, warm, cozy, and inviting. The Cheers bar is a home, a refuge, and a hangout for the staff, the regulars and, ultimately, for us—the audience.

The unifying element for *Cheers* is the bar, establishing consistency and comfort. The majority of time in almost every episode is spent in the bar, and there is power in that choice. The only episode to never feature the bar is "An Old-Fashioned Wedding, Part 2," which features the chaotic wedding of Woody and Kelly. It originally aired as the second half of an hour-long episode but has been split off to its own episode for syndication and streaming. That split makes it unique in terms of the absence of the bar, as the first half of the original hour-long version featured the bar. Only one exception in eleven seasons proves the rule: The bar is a foundational element of *Cheers*.

The plots were often contained to the main room of the Boston sports bar, which lent a pleasant familiarity to the series. Viewers could tune in with expectations of what storylines they might encounter as opposed to later sitcoms like *Community*, which creatively thrived on throwing curveballs in terms of tone and story. One week of *Community* might feature a mockumentary-style sitcom, the next an episode shot like a 1980s G.I. Joe television commercial, the next a Rankin/Bass Christmas special, and the next a Ken Burns–style documentary. But when you tuned into *Cheers*, you knew you were going to be back at the bar with the gang. These qualities of familiarity and function help solidify the *Cheers* bar as one of the most iconic and revered sets in television history.

While the bar setting catered to character relationships and episode storylines, none of this would have been possible without an aesthetically appealing but narratively functional set design. When first developing the show, the Charles brothers went to Boston in search of the right bar to help bring *Cheers* to life. Glen Charles claims that they "attempted to draw ideas for the set, the characters and the dialogue from reality."[1] Reportedly, they were having a difficult time finding a bar they liked but were told by the concierge at their hotel to "try the Bull & Finch."[2] The rest is *Cheers* history, as the bar is very much inspired by the Bull & Finch, though differing in size and scale and with the location of the bar floating in the center rather than pushed up against the back wall.[3] It seems the perfect location to have based the show on—the Bull & Finch was named Boston's best bar in 1982, the same year *Cheers* began.[4] And, as evidence of how much of the feel of the Bull & Finch bar was reproduced by the writers of *Cheers* in their script, there is this story from when Shelley Long auditioned for the role of Diane: "After reading the script, Long told the producers it reminded her of a bar she knew in Boston Commons. (In 1980, she was in Boston filming *A Small Circle of Friends* and happened upon the Bull & Finch Pub.) In a wake of deafening silence, the creators paused with dumbfounded expressions on their faces because Long had envisioned the exact bar as replicated for the 'Cheers' set."[5] Altogether, it would appear as though it was fate for the Bull & Finch to be the basis for the set.

Worthy of note are some of the ramifications felt, not by the show creators and stars, but rather by the loyal patrons of the real bar, the Bull & Finch. A show's popularity can affect the lives of those who never asked for it. A few years after the show premiered, journalist Georgia Dullea interviewed regulars at the Bull & Finch in Boston, where they complained of the changes and inconveniences due to the bar's new popularity and waxed nostalgic about B.C. (the clever shorthand for "Before *Cheers*"), a time where "you could always get a seat at the bar and a view of the Red Sox game unobstructed by the backs of heads of people from Cincinnati and such."[6] A Bull & Finch regular, financial consultant Dennis Flynn, stated to Dullea, "Before *Cheers* you never saw babies and old people in here. You never saw people in pastel suits and white shoes. They're nice people, some of them, but when it's your watering hole, it kind of gets to you."[7] And Worcester State College professor Virginia Ogozalek complained of the summer season, telling Dullea, "They drop them off in tour buses. The place is filled with tourists taking pictures and stealing ashtrays."[8] However, it's not all frustration and bad news. Naturally, the owners have enjoyed the benefits of such popularity by "opening a replica of the television bar nearby" and "offering 'Lilith's Pan Asian Salad' for $14.95 and 'Carla's Meatball Sub' for $12.95."[9]

The *Cheers* adaptation of the real-life Boston bar was designed by Richard Sylbert with input from director James Burrows and is a truly stunning set. Wooden tables and wainscoting line the bar, enclosed by brick walls and filled with Tiffany-style lamps, complete with the wooden Indian, Tecumseh, in the corner. More personal elements popped up on the set, such as John Ratzenberger carving "Ratz" into the bar next to his seat.[10] The picture of Geronimo featured on the back gallery wall hung in Nick Colasanto's dressing room, and after the actor passed away, they hung it on the wall to be seen in every episode. And more poignantly, toward the end of his life, Colasanto couldn't remember many of his parts from the script and wrote his lines all around the set.[11] Ted Danson tells this simultaneously heartwarming and heartbreaking story of one of those lines:

> When Nick had heart disease, he was getting less and less oxygen. There wasn't a surface on that set that didn't have his lines written down. There was one episode where a friend of Coach dies, and he says, "It's as if he's still with us now." Nick had written the line on the wood slats by the stairs the actors would use to enter the studio. Nicky dies, and the next year, we're all devastated, and the first night we come down the stairs, right there was his line: "It's as if he were with us now." And so every episode, we'd go by it and pat it as we'd come

down to be introduced to the audience. And then, one year, they re-painted the sets and they painted over the line. People almost quit. Seriously. They were so emotionally infuriated that that had been taken away from them. [12]

Through Sylbert's design and all the various personal touches, writer Ken Levine explains why it is such a unique setting:

Although it is modeled after the Bull & Finch in Boston, the Cheers set was much larger with more texture and color. We could get away with doing a whole season in the bar because it was so inviting and visually interesting. As opposed to say *Taxi*, which was a brilliant show, but I don't think the audience wanted to spend much time in a garage. They did however, want to hang out at Cheers. Who wouldn't? [13]

In the end, that is what it's all about—an inviting feeling that makes the audience want to hang out there, even if only for a half hour. Cheers became a place for fans to escape to each week. Regardless of whether a show is watched week by week or via binge watching, excellent series present a world we want to enter. And *Cheers* created just that.

As a set for a sitcom, the Cheers bar is ideal. Multiple points of movement and exits make it easy to move actors in and out of a shot as needed. The main door is perfect for the chance encounter, as anyone, literally anyone, could walk through that door to get a drink. The back room and office are great for getting characters off screen but not out of the bar when needed for a quick return. These also provide a setting for private moments and conversations. And the stairs up to Melville's provides another point of entrance and exit for characters as well as story plots, particularly when the restaurant gets a new owner, John Hill, in the later seasons. Similarly, the physical bar itself created a perfect setup for a sitcom. Mark Lewisohn elaborates, "The bar not only looked real but was extremely practical: the long counter meant that characters at opposite ends could be isolated in shots almost as if in separate sets. Likewise with the customer booths. However, when the plot called for it, a long shot could take in the entire set and once again place all the characters together. Simple but brilliant." [14] With Burrows's input, the set was easy to shoot in, allowing cameras way up into the set and providing new and interesting camera angles. [15] All the elements combine to become a practical and visual masterpiece.

WHERE EVERY EPISODE IS A BOTTLE EPISODE

Bottle episode is a term for a television episode that takes place only on the standard, existing sets. It allows the production to save on costs, as adding locations or sets adds time, cost, and complexity to the filming of a television episode. The first season of *Cheers* takes place entirely in the bar. It's only in season 2 when the audience first leaves Cheers. In the premiere episode of season 2 when Sam and Diane go to Diane's apartment—or Diane's chambers, if you will—it is conclusively revealed that there is, in fact, a world outside the bar. While part of this could likely be attributed to budget constraints, having an entire season take place on one set creates an attachment to the bar itself, not just to the characters that fans would come to know. The significance of this is felt throughout the rest of the series, as it firmly establishes the bar as a home and an escape for the audience, just as it does for the characters.

TV critic Vikram Murthi praises this format, stating, "It established the bar setting as a living, breathing institution, complete with its own recurring faces and unique quirks, which allowed the series to keep the

Bartender Woody Boyd (Woody Harrelson) and barflies Cliff Clavin (John Ratzenberger), Frasier Crane (Kelsey Grammer), and Norm Peterson (George Wendt)

action limited to one location and three sets for its debut year. Taken as a whole, the first season is a minimalist gem that, in its best moments, aspired to the immediacy and tension of live theater."[16] While the following seasons expand to other locations, the majority of each episode is still spent in the bar, and bottle episodes still occur even after other settings have been introduced. Ken Levine, who hosts a "Sitcom Room Seminar," offers this advice to television showrunners regarding budgets: "On *Cheers* one year we thought of a great gag that would require levitating Norm. The cost turned out more than the license fee of three episodes combined. We did a beer joke instead. And think in terms of the whole season not just one episode. If you're using a lot of outside sets or special effects one week, plan on doing little or none the next."[17] Levine was in the *Cheers* writing room from the very beginning and saw this counsel put into practice firsthand. The entire first season of *Cheers* is essentially a bottle episode resulting in the bar itself beginning to feel like a character.

However, this setup also created the challenge that each episode's entire plot must be contained within the bar, resulting in two distinct outcomes: First, the main bar set had to be the stage for many different events—wedding ceremonies, competitions, radio broadcasts, Diane's Shakespearean play, and other various social gatherings.[18] Second, despite so much action being moved into the confines of the bar, significant action inevitably happens off screen and is never shown. The price of this single setting was the violation of the classic writer's maxim: "show don't tell." Levine points outs that "anything that happened outside of the bar had to be explained, and it's always better to show something than hear about it later."[19] This forced stronger writing and acting. Every word uttered and every character's movement and mannerisms matter that much more when they must hold the audience's attention and explain what has happened to the characters before their entrance. This meant the bar had to be comfortable and inviting, yet not distracting. It had to make sense that the characters would want to return there each day, but not overwhelm the viewing audience. Images simply could not carry the scene. The show relied on the writing and acting, and *Cheers* pulled it off spectacularly for eleven years.

A staggering amount of the plot of *Cheers* happens off screen and is recounted as characters enter the bar and share stories with their friends. This required writers who could prepare and actors who could deliver excellent monologues. But it also allows the writers to toy with the story-telling style of limited description, leaving much of the plot up to the audience's imagination. An excellent illustration of this is the season 1 episode in which Sam and Diane set each other up on dates. Much of the comedy lies in what is never shown or told. We don't see what was undoubtedly a disastrous double date. The hints of imminent farcical romance are laid when the group is leaving the bar for dinner, and in reply to Diane's cuisine suggestion, her date, Andy Andy, comments, "Anywhere but Villa Milano. That's bad memories for me. I killed a waitress there." Then, the audience sees nothing of the date, but we do see all four return from dinner for a drink at Cheers. While Sam, Diane, and Sam's date Gretchen have suitably scared looks on their faces, Andy Andy is happily oblivious. When Andy Andy fantastically mutters, "Do you ever dream you had claws?" while staring at his hands, Gretchen abruptly leaves, having had enough. From this we are left with our imaginations running wild over what actually happened at that star-crossed dinner.[20]

This never-seen, only-described aspect of the writing on *Cheers* also extends to unseen characters, particularly the wife of a beloved Cheers regular. We never meet Norm's wife, Vera (we see her on screen one time on the iconic Thanksgiving episode in which she enters the shot briefly, but only after having a pie thrown in her face).[21] On another show it might not work to never see or meet a main character's wife (well, all right, the writers did just that on the spin-off *Frasier*, in which Maris, the wife of Frasier's brother Niles, was also never seen, just hilariously de-scribed), but we get to know Vera very well across the eleven seasons through Norm and his stories. Vera is a familiar presence on the show along with many other family members who rarely, if ever, are shown. These never (or rarely) seen characters are a critical part of *Cheers* in a way Maris never was on *Frasier*—they serve to remind the audience that these characters have lives outside the bar. Lives that matter, yet they choose to spend the majority of their evenings in the bar.

A BAR SETTING AS A PLAY

Featuring a single set of the bar in front of a live studio audience, the show at times becomes more like a staged play. As director James Burrows was known to say, "I stage it like a play and then I film it."[22] Levine confirms how this enhanced the show, as it "made the bar feel more like an oasis from the outside world."[23] However, this style is reminiscent of something somewhat forgotten since the invention of television—the narrative radio play. Burrows recounts, "When I got the first draft of the pilot from Les and Glen, I said to my wife, 'Oh, my God, these guys have brought radio back to television.' They had written this smart, intellectual story. I'd never seen anything like that on TV before—just guys sitting around, talking."[24] *Cheers* writer Cheri Steinkellner confirmed the deliberate likeness to radio, stating, "The brothers said that we were writing radio. It was all about the dialogue, spoken and unspoken. It was the characters, the relationships. They were so interesting, consistent, and mutable, that we rarely had to leave the bar. One set, 11 years."[25]

Alan Sepinwall and Matt Zoller Seitz, in their book *TV (The Book)*, expertly explain how well *Cheers* pulls all this off:

> *Cheers* was always content to be an intimate, even small sitcom— practically a weekly repertory stage production, confined mainly to the bar, Sam's office, and the poolroom, with action on the street indicated by silhouettes, footfalls, and strategically overheard bits of dialogue. But there was nothing minor about *Cheers* artistry. Week in and week out, the show's writers, directors, and cast pulled off tiny miracles of characterization and timing.[26]

There is nothing loud or flashy about Cheers the bar, or *Cheers* the show, but it had an impact in our culture. Perhaps one of the strongest reasons for this is that the show was content to focus on the small, mediocre lives of its main characters, who were equally content with their small, mediocre lives.

Ken Levine believes that the combination of setting and people was key to making the series a long-lasting success:

> *Cheers* was a comedy built around characters you were really invested in. It wasn't enough to make you laugh, our goal was to make you care. Everything about the show was inviting—from the setting to the people to the situations. It's a place you wanted to be with people you liked to spend time with. And that doesn't change with time.[27]

And in his review of a *Cheers* episode, Todd VanDerWerff points out, "But there's something so pure about never leaving the bar that I wish more shows would experiment with it."[28] Single-set shows are not common by any means, but *Cheers* is proof that, when done correctly, great things can come from this style of sitcom.

Notably, this play-like element of the show was even showcased directly on the spin-off show, *Frasier*, when Diane guest-starred for an episode in season 3. After showing up in Seattle, Diane tells Frasier she has written a play that is going to be produced. Eventually she admits that the play lost funding and Frasier, with his compulsive desire to rescue Diane, offers to fund the play. While watching a dress rehearsal, Frasier sees, to his horror, that Diane has written a play about Cheers.[29] There also was a real-life play based on *Cheers* in Chicago in 2016, titled "Cheers, Live on Stage," which re-created the bar setting with the beginning season's characters.[30]

PRIVATE OFFICE AND BACK ROOM

Though a majority of the series takes place in the main room of the bar, there are two other spaces used throughout the series that deserve attention—the back pool room and the office space (Sam's or Rebecca's, depending on the season). Both serve two primary purposes: an exit space for a character who needs to be off camera and a space for private moments. There is no subtlety about this purpose. The office door quite literally says "Private" for all to see, and characters exit to these spaces with the intention of being away from others in the bar. Some of the most powerful conversations happen in these spaces, particularly between Sam and Diane. It is also the location for Coach's famous speech to his daughter, and the most intimate, revealing moment of all—Sam taking off his toupee for Carla.[31] Aside from these, a few other sets are used at various times throughout the series—Diane's apartment, Rebecca's apartment, Cliff's apartment, Frasier and Lilith's home, Carla's home, and Gary's Old Towne Tavern—but none are used frequently or given the same importance as the main bar and side areas.

Interestingly, we never see Sam's apartment. Perhaps this is a means by which the character is kept at arm's length; Sam is guarded and has difficulty committing, so the audience never get to see his private, personal space. But we get that connection through the private space of his office. We get to see all the other main characters' homes and glimpse their lives outside the bar, but never Sam's. Sam's life is the bar. Why, then, would we need to see anything but his space at the bar? In season 6 we're told that Sam has sold the bar and set off to sail around the world. But when this ends disastrously after he sinks his ship on a reef, Sam comes back and tells Rebecca, "This place is the closest thing I have to a home. I want to come back."[32] Sam's identity is linked with the bar, and therefore it is his most personal space we as the audience can see.

When examined closely, the use of Sam's office highlights the two eras of the show—the Sam and Diane era (seasons 1–5), and the ensemble era (seasons 6–11). At the start of the show, the office is a space filled with sports memorabilia, bar supplies, a couch (that folds out into a bed, of course), and, from the looks of it, a lot of junk. Pointedly, in season 6 when the bar is sold and the office is no longer Sam's, the changes were noticeable visually as well as felt. The office, now belonging to Rebecca, is suddenly clean and pristine, with all remnants of sports and junk removed. But suddenly, a piece of Sam is lost—he has nowhere to go at Cheers. George Wendt describes the difference at the beginning of season 6: "The office is not Sam's office anymore, he can't go there and run away. To take away a space like that changes the dynamics of the show."[33] Sam no longer has his safe space. In these latter seasons, Sam is the center of the show, both as the leader of the gang but also physically, as he is suddenly stuck at the bar in the center of Cheers. Whereas in the first half of the series, Sam was the center but alongside Diane, working out their on-again, off-again relationship, with their dynamic mostly taking place inside Sam's office.

At the same time the primary occupancy of the office shifts from Sam to Rebecca, changes in decor were also made to the rest of the bar. In the main barroom there are new green plants in the corners and along the walls. Sam's photo gallery wall is replaced by a giant map of the world. The staff are obligated to wear uniforms of red and white pinstripe button-up shirts, along with soft evergreen pants, vest, and bowtie.

Sam no longer owns the bar—a corporation does. Rebecca Howe is the new manager, and there is a new bartender, the robot-esque Wayne. The real change occurs when Norm walks through the door and only Woody yells, "Norm," instead of the entire bar. Sam finally returns to the bar and notes only one familiar thing: "I can't believe all the changes here. Thank God you're still pregnant,"[34] he says to Carla.

A BAR ON TV (ALCOHOL ON TV)

As powerful and creatively useful a bar can be both in storytelling and as a set, there is a small hiccup that could hinder a show on network TV—the constant flow of alcohol. This was an issue the show's creators were aware of and handled right from the start.

The opening scene of *Cheers* is simple. A clearly underage kid walks into the empty bar and asks, "How 'bout a beer, chief?" Solo bartender Sam Malone sidles over, replying with a smirk, "How 'bout an ID?" The two laugh through their exchange, as the kid tries to fake his age and Sam knows he is trying to get away with it and the kid knows he's not going to get away with it. It's a charming scene that endears you instantly to the bartender and the place he runs. He's friendly and kind to his customer, but firm in the rules of a bar. The simplicity of this scene sets the tone for the show on how the issue of a sitcom taking place in a bar full of alcohol would be handled. Sam Malone's first line is asking for ID, and while it is done with great humor, it also indicates that the implications of serving alcohol would not be taken lightly.

There was immediate concern about the bar setting; NBC development executive Michael Zinberg recounts his experience on hearing about the show:

> When they came in and [pitched the show], you could feel the room shudder. "What kind of show would be in a bar? How do we handle all the alcohol?" But the Charles brothers very clearly said, telling him, "This isn't about the place. This is about a family; it just happens not to be a group of brothers and sisters."[35]

This statement held true throughout the show's eleven-year run. The bar was simply a location that lent itself to plotlines. It was the people that made *Cheers* a show worth watching.

Alcohol and its consumption is a tricky topic to navigate on network TV, but maybe a little easier in the 1980s than it would be today. Glen Charles noted, "I know some people didn't want 'Cheers' initially because it was set in a bar. I think that [attitude] would be even more prevalent now."[36] It is a different world today than in the time of *Cheers*. Issues are different, studies on alcohol are more prevalent, and the potential for backlash is more direct and accessible now compared to the 1980s, thanks to the Internet.

However, at times the setting can be used for good. In 1988, the Harvard School of Public Health's Center for Health Communication launched the U.S. Designated Driver Campaign, which worked with Hollywood studios and television networks in an effort to show the social concept of a "designated driver" could be disseminated throughout society by mass culture, such as prime time television shows. Show writers agreed to include designated driver messages into their scripts. *Cheers* participated in this campaign in a season 8 episode by showcasing a designated driver selection scene. As Norm enters the bar ("Norm!") and Woody prepares his beer, Carla stops everyone: "Wait a minute, not so fast. It's time for us to pick our designated driver for the night," and everyone writes their name on a piece of paper and Carla selects the driver out of a hat. Come to find out, Norm cheats by not putting his name in the hat, and they re-select the designated driver. It's a quick scene, yet subtly acknowledges that the gang does this frequently, if not every night, thereby conveying the social message. In an article on why the designated driver campaign worked, Jay Winston states:

> Entertainment not only mirrors social reality, but also helps shape it by depicting what constitutes popular opinion, by influencing people's perceptions of the roles and behaviors that are appropriate to members of a culture, and by modeling specific behaviors. The strength of this approach is that short messages, embedded within dialogue, are casually presented by characters who serve as role models within a dramatic context, facilitating social learning.[37]

By 1994, annual alcohol-related traffic fatalities had declined by 30 percent due to many factors, such as stricter laws and enforcement and this campaign.[38]

With that said, *Cheers* is still a show that takes place with characters drinking continually throughout every episode, and this had to be balanced with having the bar as the setting. Alcohol is never glorified, and the consequences are shown. Sam is a recovering alcoholic whose baseball career ended because of his alcoholism, and the ramifications of heavy drinking are showcased by Sam telling of his former alcoholic days, of the games he lost, the women he can't remember, the darkness he felt. At the start of season 3, due to his breakup with Diane, Sam begins drinking again. The situation isn't taken lightly, as the Cheers gang becomes increasingly concerned for him, ultimately causing Coach to bring

Diane back to convince Sam to get help through her psychiatrist, Frasier Crane.[39] This scenario more than anything echoes the Charles brothers' claim that the show isn't about a bar but rather about a family who will be there for each other when needed most. Regarding this issue, Ken Levine argues that "Sam of course, was a former alcoholic and the message was delivered many times that you don't solve your problems by drinking. . . . The benefit people got from going to the *Cheers* bar was the camaraderie and support they gained from each other."[40] This, more than the nods to calling cabs or promoting designated driving, is how *Cheers* most successfully dealt with the issue of alcohol. Alcohol isn't the reason anyone goes to Cheers, and it isn't what viewers remember from the show. It's the characters and their relationships that bring the regulars and the viewers back to "Where Everybody Knows Your Name."

A SPORTS BAR IN BOSTON

More than just being a bar, Cheers is a sports bar in Boston where the loyalty to teams runs deep. And with an owner who is a former Red Sox relief pitcher, it is impossible to not have sports matter throughout the series. The bar could have been set nearly anywhere, as bar culture is a commonality among all cities in America. While each one would have come with its own set of quirks and subculture, by setting it in Boston the show gained the passionate sports fans. Among sports towns, Boston has the reputation of being the most parochial. The creators knew Sam Malone was going to be a former athlete, and although the specific sport ended up being determined by Ted Danson's body build, in the end that didn't matter. Boston is passionate about all its teams. And *Cheers* does not shy away from this, but rather embraces it in full force, particularly in establishing connections between the characters. In their book, *The Sociology of Sports*, Tim Delaney and Tim Madigan state that "because of the cultural importance of sports in society, many people have their identities, directly or indirectly, tied to sports."[41] Sam, the former professional athlete, is praised like a god by all in the bar. Coach, a former professional coach, is respected and revered. Carla loves sports just as much as either of them and can go head to head with them when it comes to sports trivia. The show relies heavily on the unity sports brings to people.

Sports are a unifying force across so many other divides. They bring a commonality to those with far-ranging differences. Those of different classes, or in professions with no similarities, can bond deeply over a beloved sports team. There is no greater world unifier than sports. Just look at the Olympics or the World Cup. Every few years, the world pauses to pay attention to these athletes and teams. We place the weight of entire countries on them because it's not just about the sport—it's about life. Delaney and Madigan note in their book:

> Sports are not just physical activities and games; they serve as focal points in the formation of social worlds. Social worlds consist of group members who share a subcultural perspective and are held together through interaction and communication. In order to fit into a social world, group members will adjust their behavior and mindsets to revolve around a particular set of activities. [42]

The TV cast watching TV: Sam Malone (Ted Danson), Norm Peterson (George Wendt), Woody Boyd (Woody Harrelson), and Cliff Clavin (John Ratzenberger)

We see this unfold in the bar, as the majority of the group will be focused on sports; others, wanting to be a part of the group, will participate in any way they can. Frasier will watch games with the gang, and even Diane joins in on weekly football pools by choosing teams—albeit based on their uniform color and which mascot would win in a fight: "Bears. A bear against a dolphin? Come on."[43]

Sports matter culturally; sports provide the stories we share again and again, the ones we relive through our kids. If we don't get to be the sports stars, at least we get to watch them. We place our hopes and dreams on them. And when we can't live those dreams ourselves, we place those same hopes and dreams on the athletes and the team we love—stand-ins for what could not be. Watching a game as if we were them. They are stand-ins for us. This is why Sam is revered so highly among the Cheers regulars. He is their window into a world otherwise forbidden to them and only seen through a screen. In the episode "Sam at Eleven," Sam begins telling a story from one of his glory days. Interrupted, he doesn't finish. But Diane is enthralled and asks what happened in the end. Diane doesn't care what happened at the end of the game, but she cares about how much it means to Sam and what it says about him.

We're constantly bombarded today with new technology to keep us connected yet simultaneously allows us to be more and more disconnected. Back in the 1980s, in the time of *Cheers*, you didn't have complete replays of games, DVRs to record them, Internet to watch them anywhere and anytime. You watched them live, with your friends, as the series depicts. Today, you are never without a game if it is on. You don't need to hunt for a place to watch or listen to it, or to find your crowd to see it with. Arguably, your bar was more important back then. Sports was a more communal experience. Game knowledge was social capital.

A BAR WITH A HISTORY

In the season 8 episode, "The Stork Brings a Crane," Rebecca discovers, much to her delight, that the bar is celebrating its hundred-year anniversary. Quickly, she insists that they celebrate Cheers with a party and invite the mayor. But the years don't add up—as Norm points out, the date on the door outside says, "est. 1895," to which Sam quips, "Don't pay attention to that, I made it up," confessing he did so while Carla was in her "number superstition phase."[44] Having been sent to the library by Rebecca to research the bar, Woody returns with a pile of books and the history of Cheers. Turns out Cheers use to be a brothel for sailors. Rebecca still insists on throwing the party, and true to form for Rebecca, it is a mild disaster.

Although the history of Cheers as a building isn't revealed until season 8, from the start we feel the bar has a long past. This is a place with years' worth of experiences, and we enter for only a chapter of it. The already established relationships among staff and patrons are evident right from the start, and, as TV critic Erik Adams points out, "part of what makes the world of Cheers (the series) so inviting so quickly is that it really seems like Cheers (the bar) existed long before Diane, Sumner, or that kid with the fake ID walked through its door. It's a place with established customs and a little bit of a history, almost as much a character as any of its regulars."[45] Consistently throughout the series, there are the subtle and obvious hints that Cheers is a place where "everybody knows your name." In the second episode we hear mention of a former owner, Gus, when a patron comes looking for him, needing his advice. Coach steps in to help, but we see firsthand how important this bar and the people in it have been to the lives of its patrons.[46] In the opening of episode 7, Sam mentions to a man we've never seen before (and will never see again) that his usual will be right up. These small moments are vital in giving Cheers that home-away-from-home quality. This world doesn't have to be built—it already exists. As viewers, we become envious of the cozy world of *Cheers*.

"IN THIS BAR, EVERYBODY GETS TO BE A HERO"

For many, a local bar can become their home away from home. A means of escape. Their space away from work when they're not yet ready to go home. A safe space to meet up with someone, watch a game, or just pass the time. Notoriously known as a place where the lonely and sad go, or where one can meet a stranger who becomes a friend, or more. *Cheers* cocreator Les Charles claims that "a bar is a place where everything that happens in life can end up. You go to celebrate, drown your sorrows, meet and fall in love, break up. It's an interesting spot for human dynamics."[47] For a sitcom this is ideal because any storyline is fair game. Anyone can walk through those doors, and story possibilities are endless.

It's an overdone joke premise—"*blank blank* walks into a bar, and . . . " You can fill in those blanks with any numbers of the visitors to Cheers over the years: A professional athlete, a veteran, a murderer, a spy (but not really, but could have been. Or was he?), a con man, a reporter, a city councilwoman, a Yankees fan, a man seeking advice, the lonely, the bored, the out-of-towners, and so on. There is a constant flow of people and almost anything can happen (and does happen), and nothing is out of the realm of believability. As writer Ken Levine points out, "The bar had the advantage that anyone could walk in with a story. That's a big advantage over a living room."[48] The writers exploit this in two different directions: (1) Though the show was centered around a standard bar, the writers were more than willing to send the characters down unexpected plotlines and introduce surprisingly zany elements. (2) The writers use random-character episodes to explore deeper themes of human nature. Both provide entertaining television and are necessary for a well-rounded show. It is proof of the bar setting's power that both episode styles are used well and are plausible. The wild outlandish episodes are perhaps more memorable—for example, all the Bar Wars episodes and cons by Harry the Hat. And just to note, in a series with the premise of patrons having conversations while drinking beer, there is a surprisingly large amount of gunplay, with Sam taking the disproportionate number of looks down the barrel.[49] However, in a completely different tone, the deeper, more meaningful episodes explore human nature.

There is something so calming and relatable in the episodes that center around just talking. And Cheers is a bar with plenty of seemingly pointless conversations, whether it be Cliff telling a little-known fact, or Coach sharing an old baseball story, or Woody describing life back in Hanover. The very first episode brings in a bar debate on the sweatiest movie ever made (consensus being, *Cool Hand Luke*);[50] a debate that, interestingly, was based on a real conversation the Charles brothers overheard while visiting random bars in Los Angeles for research for the show.[51] Who among us hasn't been sitting around with friends, or in a setting with near strangers, and the conversation hasn't turned to random, yet interesting topics? It's human nature at its finest—we will always find something to talk about. As the audience, we often enter the bar in mid-conversation, yet this doesn't feel odd or disjointed but rather confirms the continuation of the bar life when we are not viewing. This allows a greater connection between the viewer and the patrons at the bar.

With these random conversations, there is an openness that comes with a bar setting that you can't get from most other environments. In other sitcoms based in a home or office setting, storylines are often driven by the coaxing to get the truth out or to get an individual to open up. This is not the case in a bar setting. Glen Charles explains, "People will talk to a bartender in a way they wouldn't any other stranger. There's an immediate opening up and frankness."[52] Individuals will often just begin speaking and sharing their story right away to Coach, Woody, and Sam as bartenders, and even to Carla, Diane, and Rebecca as waitresses. Frasier even points out to Woody how similar their careers as a psychiatrist and bartender can be, saying, "Our professions are really very much alike. We both have to listen patiently while people unload their grief and suffering." Woody responds with, "I know exactly how you feel, Dr. Crane."[53] It is a skill all bartenders must learn—how to talk to anyone about anything. Because at a bar, you can never predict what the other person might say or the advice they might need.

In the season 1 episode, "The Spy Who Came in for a Cold One," a smartly dressed man arrives at Cheers. Being an attractive man unknown by anyone, Carla immediately takes interest (are you surprised?) and begins conversing with him, soon learning he is a spy. But Diane refuses to believe his story and uses her knowledge of world geography and politics to point out flaws in his story. Called out on the lie, the man then tells them he is actually a poet. Diane believes him as he recites his work, only to embarrassingly discover he is merely reciting other poets' words. The man then tells everyone he is a very wealthy man and offers to buy the bar from Sam for one million dollars. Refusing to believe him at this point, Sam all but laughs in his face. The man's chauffeur walks in the bar, telling him he must leave to catch a flight. The Cheers gang is left wondering who the man really was, what lies and truths he really told. But in the end, the lies don't matter, and neither does the truth. What matters is what the man felt while visiting the bar. Cheers was a safe haven, though Diane's doubt began to erode that. The bar was supposed to be a place you can enter and be anyone you want or be completely yourself and be accepted. Or rather, as Sam tells Diane, "In this bar, everybody gets to be a hero."[54]

Notably, in this episode Diane is found sitting at the bar reading *The Republic* by Plato, a book that presents an idea of the noble lie. The noble lie, at its surface level, is a theory in which people believe something about themselves and are therefore more motivated, or happier, in life. Even though it is not the truth, the lie is justified for the inner harmony it brings to the person and, by association, the people around them. This noble lie is presented in the episode by the man and affirmed to be acceptable by Sam and the rest of the bar. When asked why he lied, the "spy" replies, "Because my life is very unexciting, and it's very dull. I've been a failure at everything I've ever tried to do. But you know, sometimes late at night, in a friendly bar, I sometimes can make someone believe that I'm interesting."[55] Although she is reading about this very concept, Diane struggles to allow the idea as manifested in real life, as she refused to allow the man to go on pretending he is a spy, arguing, "Every lie is eventually destructive." But Sam argues, "Why do you suppose people come to bars in the first place, huh? . . . They come here to shoot their mouths off and get away with it."[56] And arguably, both are correct.

Sam's argument highlights why a bar is the perfect setting for sitcom storytelling. People come to chat and say anything they want there. And the *Cheers* set portrayed an inviting space for the viewers to return to. By returning there every single episode, the bar itself becomes a familiar and beloved character of the show. This constant familiarity is key to the lasting influence of the show, as it explains why the sight of Sam behind the bar can be comforting. Norm at his stool brings someone peace. The first few notes of the opening credits ignites memories. It isn't frivolous to love *Cheers* or any other show; what we see and watch shapes who we are, reflecting what was, and changing us. Just like everything you place in your home says something about you, whether it be an Eames chair that make you feel luxurious or a poster depicting a favorite sports team, the shows we choose to watch have power over us, particularly as we watch them in our homes. They influence our lives in ways we don't realize, whether we are consciously aware of it or not. This is why the design of a set is so important and every detail matters. It is why a color can change your life. A dress can give you confidence. Every experience shapes us. Together with every sight we see and sound we hear, they slowly help mold us into who we are.

For eleven years Cheers and the gang mattered to tens of millions of people, and they still matter today. The bar itself is beautiful and inviting. But the people and the friendships found there are far more beautiful and inviting. The bar is a place where friendships were born and lasted. A place visitors could call home. And in the end, isn't that what it's all about? That it's nice to have a place where everybody knows your name?

4

THE ALCOHOLIC GREEK CHORUS AND THE STAFF THAT SERVES THEM

Loyal Patrons and Steady Workers

Face it: You're a bunch of losers. If it weren't for you guys, how would we know who the winners are?

The setting is ideal. The creators talented. The writing witty and intelligent. Sam and Diane drove the show. But is that be enough to carry a series for eleven years? What really kept people tuning in? *Cheers* writer Ken Levine explains, "Cheers was a comedy built around characters you were really invested in. It wasn't enough to make you laugh, our goal was to make you care. Everything about the show was inviting—from the setting to the people to the situations. It's a place you wanted to be with people you liked to spend time with. And that doesn't change with time."[1] And writer Peter Casey notes, "It was groundbreaking in the sense that it wasn't a family comedy or a joke machine, just character driven."[2] The plots range from unexpectedly mundane—Diane's cat died[3]—to sitcom stereotypes—let's have a bachelor auction to raise emergency funds[4]—to fantastically absurd—Carla's husband is killed in a freak Zamboni accident *and* had a secret second family.[5] But it is undoubtedly the characters that keep viewers coming back to *Cheers*.

While sitcoms are often divided into family or workplace, *Cheers* exists in a liminal place between those. It is not a sitcom about a workplace, it is a sitcom about a hangout place. And *Cheers* is about a family—the staff and bar regulars become one another's family, bonded together by the bar. Popular culture scholar Gary Hoppenstand explains that *Cheers* is a

> reworking and updating of the popular family sitcoms of the 1950s, with the formula twist that features the characters of the cast as a dysfunctional "symbolic" family: the "father" with the wandering eye (Sam), the overbearing "mother" (Diane), the daffy uncle (Coach), the underachieving "children" (Norm and Cliff), and the promiscuous "sister" (Carla). It also is a great working-place comedy (along the lines of BARNEY MILLER), which moves the family sitcom out of the home and into a blue-collar, working-class hangout.[6]

Michael Schur, who knows sitcoms very well as a creator of *Parks and Recreation* and *The Good Place*, confirms this: "That's the theme of [*Cheers*]: You have another family. . . . You want to believe these people really care about each other and that they are a surrogate family."[7] Andy Greenwald adds, "Even though [*Cheers*] was nominally about a sad Boston cabal of barely functioning alcoholics, it was really about a family."[8]

The atmosphere of the bar is inviting, but it ultimately wouldn't be anything without memorable patrons and staff. The bar has patrons streaming through its doors every day (pay attention to how slowly the bar fills up in the pilot to appreciate how carefully James Burrows and the extras created a sense of the ebb and flow of a real bar's business). However, *Cheers* focuses on a few regular barflies that help form the show: Norm Peterson and Cliff Clavin through all eleven years, Frasier Crane appearing in season 3, and later Lilith Sternin once she begins dating (and ultimately marrying) Frasier, first appearing in season 4. The show sticks to these main regulars, while also sprinkling in other faces that become familiar over time such as Paul, Phil, and fan favorite, Harry the Hat. *Cheers* integrates these side characters seamlessly with our regulars as if we should already be familiar with them too. This simple element helps emphasize the simulated reality of a bar with a constant flow of patrons that continues on even when we are not there.

As for the staff, there is the owner and bartender Sam Malone and waitress Carla Tortelli throughout all eleven seasons. Bartending alongside Sam was Ernie "Coach" Pantusso for seasons 1 through 3 before the actor unfortunately passed away. His absence was filled by Woody Boyd for seasons 4 through 11. For the female lead of the show, there is barmaid Diane Chambers for the first five seasons, replaced by bar manager/ waitress/job is unclear/owner Rebecca Howe for the last six seasons. The loyal patrons and steady staff eventually become a Cheers family. These are individuals who are choosing to be around each other every day. Cliff spends every evening after work there. Norm only leaves when forced. Frasier, with his broken heart, returns there even while Diane is still around. Carla waitresses at Cheers for eleven years. Woody bartends for eight years. Diane, with all her visions of grandeur, falls under its spell. Rebecca, despite her grand aspirations, has nowhere else to go. Sam, the magnet for all of them, despite his ups and downs in life, always ends up back at the bar.

What is most interesting about a bar setting is the unique friendships that develop between the staff and regulars. TV critic Brett White points out, "Would Woody and Carla ever hang out were it not for this bar? Or Frasier and Norm, or Cliff and Diane? The characters of *Cheers* are bonded together by a place. They're a subtly disparate bunch, a fact you don't consider until they're off their common ground."[9] Over time, we are shown that they hang out to go fishing, or skydiving, or they discuss a movie they have all just seen together, or show up at Frasier's home to check on Norm when his back is hurt. But in the end, they always return to the bar.

So what is it about these barflies and the staff that serves them that makes them so compelling? The creators deliberately made a show about a different kind of family—a family you choose—but a family that is just as real as any other. They were never overly caring or spoke of their love for one another. Instead, they teased, they made fun, they played pranks, they insulted, and they bluntly told the truth. Writer and producer Bill Steinkellner stated, "Cheers wasn't cynical nor meant to be. It was a warm and inviting place, where everyone insults each other the way friends do. They put down with love."[10] And TV critic Ryan McGee astutely points out, "After all, the people in that bar are family. And since when do we always like everyone in our family?"[11] There are times when lines are crossed and someone—almost always patriarchal Sam—has to call out whomever said the barb that stung too deep, but it never feels wrong to see everyone together and joking again shortly thereafter.

Along with the teasing and pranks, the regulars are fiercely loyal toward one another and unequivocally have one another's backs. Norm loses his job to protect Diane,[12] Cliff stays with Carla when she is afraid her house is haunted,[13] Sam protects Woody from making a bad bet.[14] Even Harry the Hat steps in to help Coach out as he is being scammed by a friend during a weekly card game.[15] TV critic Erik Adams addressed this very episode: "It says a lot about Cheers and the clientele it draws that even its most unsavory customer is willing to step up when one of the bar's own is in need of assistance."[16] And in season 2, when Cliff is upset over a girl and afraid what people at the bar will say about it, Norm tells him, "No one's going to laugh at you. Those people care about you and they know that you're hurting. Anybody that laughs at you has to answer to me."[17] This is a family where everyone takes care of one another when they need it most.

In the iconic (and arguably most famous) episode, "Thanksgiving Orphans,"[18] we are shown the true dynamic of the Cheers bar family. Airing on Thanksgiving day in 1986, Norm, Cliff, Frasier, and Woody join Carla at her house for Thanksgiving dinner (her kids are spending the holiday with her ex-husband). As the day continues, Sam and Diane, both with separate plans, abandon those options and join the rest of the gang at Carla's. In a moment of choice—although most make excuses about not having anywhere else to go—they all come together for the holiday. Woody asks, "Who needs family?" and Frasier responds, "Family is not necessarily limited to blood relations."[19] In a marvelously accurate family moment, the dinner goes horribly awry when Norm's turkey won't cook, they bicker over what to watch on the TV, and Diane is wearing a ridiculous pilgrim outfit. The episode culminates in a massive food fight between all our main characters. Episode writer Cheri Steinkellner describes the scene that ensued:

> It starts with a pea. We wanted it to be the smallest unit of Thanksgiving aggression. Carla flicks a pea at Norm, who brought a giant turkey that wouldn't cook. Next comes a spoonful of mashed potato, then Frasier flings gravy skin, everyone rears back, ready to rumble. Diane enters in her pilgrim suit, scolding them all to behave, then Sam flings cranberry sauce on her crisp white bib and all hell breaks loose.[20]

The fight is hilarious to watch and endearingly ends with the gang gathered around the table to give toasts of thanks to their loved ones who weren't able to join—Carla's kids, Norm's wife Vera, Cliff's mother, and the moment ends with Sam's toast to Coach. It's a touching scene that perfectly doesn't dwell too long on the sentimentality but acknowledges among this family of friends the other important people in their lives.

Though an excellent finale to the episode that plays very well, the food fight was not choreographed. James Burrows confirms, "Once the cranberry sauce hit Shelley, everything was a free-for-all. You can't choreograph that."[21] Speaking of that cranberry, Burrows continues, "I can't believe Teddy [Danson], with that cranberry sauce, hit her right on the Pilgrim outfit. Amazing. It was the perfect shot."[22] When watching the scene play out, you can see how crazily chaotic everything quickly became when Ted Danson performs an unsteady 360-degree spin because the set's floor is covered in slippery food.

THE LOVEABLE LOSERS

There's a melancholy sadness to so many of these characters. Sam is combatting his aging and his shallowness. Carla has too many kids she loves but can't stand. Norm has no drive to accomplish anything. Cliff is a man-child embarrassed about living with his mom. Frasier hates his work and is a borderline alcoholic. Diane believes she wants one thing out of life, but truly wants another. Rebecca steadily falls from business woman to a boy-crazy shell of a woman. The characters deal with issues people face out in the world: marital stress, kids, parents, career, aging. And the show isn't afraid to highlight every character's flaws and negative characteristics—Sam is a sleazy player, Norm is lazy, Cliff is obnoxious, Diane a pompous snob, Carla is harsh and cruel. All these qualities make each character seem real and more relatable.

Adding to the overall inadequacy of the gang at Cheers, the whole gang is constantly being swindled by Harry the Hat and losing in Bar Wars (until these two collide in the last season). Gary from Gary's Old Towne Tavern was first introduced in season 4 with a bowling competition between the two bars,[23] and the rivalry episodes that followed, known as the Bar Wars, showcased pranks and practical jokes between the two bars beginning in season 6 and through the remaining seasons. The rivalry may bring out the worst in the characters, who lie and cheat their way through competitions, but it also highlights the unity between them.

There are seven Bar War episodes,[24] and in all but the very last war, the Cheers gang loses. When asked if this was intentional, Levine confirms, "Yes. Except for the last one. Frustration is much funnier than victory. The trick, however, was to find different ways for them to lose—or screw themselves. Guess I grew up watching too many Road Runner cartoons."[25]

Weirdly, the character Gary was portrayed by two different actors switching off on inconsistent episodes. Levine attempts to explain why this happened, admitting:

> We had two actors who played Gary, in no particular order. The first time the character appeared, Joe Polis played him in a 1985 episode called "From Beer to Eternity." When we wrote the first Bar Wars episode Joe wasn't available. It was the very end of the season. We had no other scripts so we just had to recast. Robert Desiderio became Gary. For Bar Wars II we went back to Joe Polis and used him one other time. Otherwise, it was Robert Desiderio. Confusing? I don't understand why we did it either.[26]

But which actor played Gary when isn't what matters. What matters is what these episodes convey about the gang.

The Bar Wars were some of show's most memorable episodes because rather than sniping at one another, these were the times when the gang fully unites and takes on the common enemy. Together, this is the Cheers gang at its very best. TV critic Alex McLevy perfectly states why this multi-season storyline matters so much:

> And they become the ultimate versions of themselves: Woody gets even Woody-er, Norm is his Norm-iest, and Cliff is accepted by all as one of the fellas. Despite repeated losses, the camaraderie is heartwarming, and gets to the root of the series' appeal. Sending off the show in its final season with a triumphant win against the gang's erstwhile villain doesn't just close the door on a breezily inspired running plot thread: It gives our little group of losers a win. And winning looks awful good on them—because it's a win for the audience, too.[27]

The connection between character and audience becomes so strong that their triumphs are our triumphs, their failures our own. That association is part of the true beauty of *Cheers*.

So where does this strong connection between audience and *Cheers* come from? Why, as viewers, do we love these characters? Perhaps because no one is the hero. And that makes everyone the hero. (Notably, therefore, no one is the villain, either.) They all lead average lives. They are all flawed. They are all lonely. We root for all of them, just as much as we cringe for them. They're all misfits finding a home in the bar. In their book *Watching TV*, Harry Castleman and Walter J. Podrazik state, "These characters were all clearly defined and made true to type even if that meant coming off as selfish, slovenly, or obnoxious. Personal flaws and all, they were all dead-on hilarious."[28] As people, nobody on *Cheers* is particularly likable; as characters, they're lovable.

THE BARFLIES

Norm Peterson

The world needs benchwarmers.

Residing on the most famous barstool in the United States sits Hilary Norman "Norm" Peterson. The frequently unemployed accountant or painter (depending on which half of the series) acts as the steady anchor of Cheers. Even the mise en scene of the wide shots of the bar feel off when Norm isn't holding down his familiar seat in the bar. Ted Danson said, "George [Wendt] was like gravity to the show. There he was sitting at the end of the bar, and if he wasn't there it was almost like, 'What do you do?'"[29] Norm's entrance is one of the most iconic in television history, and it's with good reason that Norm is the last patron to leave the bar in the series finale. Of all the characters, Norm may be the steadiest, and it just felt right for Norm to have one last beer, one-on-one with Sam Malone, before the series closed up shop. He's been at Cheers the longest, knowing multiple previous owners. He is a firm foundation for Sam. He is endlessly likable and endearing, and a fan favorite.

Norm was based on someone real Les Charles met when he worked as a bartender after college. Les recalls,

> I worked at a bar after college, and we had a guy who came in every night. He wasn't named Norm, [but he] was always going to have just

one beer, and then he'd say, "Maybe I'll just have one more." We had to help him out of the bar every night. His wife would call, and he'd always say, "Tell her I'm not here." I think that was the closest we had to a character based on one guy.[30]

The character's influence has continued on in aspects of pop culture and in real life. On *Star Trek: Deep Space Nine*, there was a big alien who sat in the bar and never said a word, never had a storyline, and was rarely acknowledged. He appeared in almost every episode and was named Morn, in honor of Norm.[31]

Norm's legacy even extends to modern app development. Currently in the works is a targeted marketing technique to give the "Norm effect," which in its simplest explanation would allow an individual to be tracked by their cell phone so that when they enter a restaurant, the hostess can greet them by name and know their drink order, in honor of Norm's entrances. Developers of the technology give the simple explanation for the name of their technique: "Norm walks in. Everyone knows Norm. They say, 'Norm!' There is already a drink waiting for him on the bar. Now, we have the technology to do that with our 'Norms.'"[32] More than thirty-five years after George Wendt was first greeted by cries of "Norm," the character's name remains iconic enough to serve as a shorthand explanation for a planned technological innovation.

Clearly, just as iconic as the character of Norm are his entrances, and they became a favorite among fans. These entrances consisted of the other patrons calling out his name as he entered (with Diane fantastically calling out "Norman" after everyone else), a member of the staff tossing Norm a setup, and Norm nailing a punchline. This setup and punchline occurs nearly every episode (particularly in the beginning seasons), and were presented as natural and effortless, but became a burden on the writers. The difficulty, writer David Isaacs claims, was "making a clean joke that didn't come out of the situation. You have a blind setup and write a good Norm response to that. That was always a challenge."[33] After years of writing Norm entrances, finding new setups became a chore that took more and more time. Writer Peter Casey points out, "They became more difficult because the bar kept getting set higher and higher."[34] This high bar culminated in the only episode that featured multiple Norm entrances. While these moments are usually just one-offs in an episode, Norm's entrances became a focus in a season 9 episode. The writer, Ken Levine, recounts:

Norm Peterson (George Wendt)

Norm entrances were difficult and David [Isaacs] and I once pitched an episode where Lilith and Frasier were concerned that their baby, Frederick hadn't spoken a word. "Breaking In Is Hard to Do." When Frasier had the task of watching the baby he brought him to Cheers. We wanted his first word to be "Norm." But to do that we needed lots of Norm entrances to set it up. Great for the story but a bitch for us. We established that new parking meters were installed on the street and every few hours Norm had to leave to feed the meter. We must've done five Norm entrances. Oy. And we did it to ourselves. But the payoff was worth it. When the baby said "Norm!" I think it got a five-minute laugh.[35]

While the setup was difficult, the final punchline more than delivered, resulting in a remarkably funny and memorable moment for the show.

Interestingly, the origin for the bar crowd yelling "Norm" reportedly comes from a real-life experience. Wendt recounts,

Nick Colasanto [Coach] was nearly 60 years old and had a long career as an actor and TV director. One day when we were workshopping with Jim about the characters' possible backstories, Nick [who was sober] said that when he had been drinking, every time one of the regulars walked into his favorite New York spot, everyone would yell out his name. So it stuck for Norm. [36]

There are dozens of these setups throughout the show. Some of the most memorable "Norm-isms" include:

What's shaking, Norm?

All four cheeks and a couple of chins. [37]

Hey Norm, how's the world been treating you?

Like a baby treats a diaper. [38]

Hey Mr. Peterson, there's a cold one waiting for you.

I know, if she calls, I'm not here. [39]

Whatcha up to, Norm?

My ideal weight if I were eleven feet tall. [40]

The audience was so familiar with the rhythm of Norm's entrances that eventually the writers could even get a laugh by implying the joke instead of writing it. In "The Norm Who Came to Dinner," written by Dan O'Shannon and Tom Anderson, Norm calls from Frasier's house and we only see the scene that plays out in the bar. Sam answers the phone, then holds it out the gang and says, "Hey, guys, it's Norm." Everyone at the bar yells "Norm!" and then Sam asks "Hey, what's shaking, man?" After a beat, Sam laughs and holds the phone to his chest and asks, "Where does he come up with these things?"[41] Nobody knows what Norm says, but the audience laughs all the same.

Now, as is the case for most sitcoms, there are some moments early on that feel out of place when revisited after characters have been firmly established. There are two early moments in the series that are notably out of character for Norm. First, in the pilot, he is passed out drunk at the end of the episode, something the network and creators decided should not be shown frequently. Cheers became a show about alcoholics who are never drunk, and portraying the negative effects of drinking too frequently or for comedy became something the show tried to avoid. In the second episode, Norm is a hound dog, jumping up and reacting crazily when he sees a pair of attractive legs coming down the stairs to Cheers. While literally running around the bar he monologues, "Look at those legs! If those legs are attached to anything, even a truck, I'm going to marry it."[42] After this episode, Norm quickly settles into a comfortable asexual malaise for most of the eleven seasons, only expressing interest in hearing about Sam's escapades and disinterested in romantic pursuits of his own.

As any good character should be, Norm is filled with contradictions. His behavior at times is appalling, but then at times endearing. He jabs at his wife among friends, but he truly adores her. He is self-assured and witty at Cheers, but a desperate man out in the real world. Arguably, this is why he loves being at Cheers so much—he is the best version of himself in the bar. As unmotivated as he may be in real life, at Cheers, Norm is a leader alongside Sam. The gang follows what he says, what he likes, and he is respected as much as he can be. Frasier recognizes Norm's social status within the bar when he says, "You get one, you get them all. It's like a hive mentality. Norm must be their queen."[43]

Perhaps these contradictions are manifestations of the idea of you can be anyone you want to be in a bar. Norm frequently talks of how little he likes being around his wife, but through this "dislike" we know he truly loves her, and ultimately he justifies the jokes about Vera to just being bar talk. In the back pool room, he confesses to Sam how much he loves Vera, stating, "People don't go bragging around how they love their wives. When was the last time you saw a bunch of guys sitting around a bar, slamming beers, exchanging great tales of marital bliss, huh?" Sam commends Norm for his attitude and admits he even envies him a little as he speaks lovingly of Diane, and then makes a joke about her. To which Norm replies, "See, there, you're doing it. You're doing it too. And you know why? Because you're a guy."[44] Whatever Norm may be in his life, at the bar he just wants to be one of the guys, and he knows how to do that.

Because *Cheers* ran for eleven seasons, every character had episodes that focused on their adventures. These episodes—for each of the side characters—often feel like a break in the rhythm of the series. In the case of Norm, the episodes that focus on his life inevitably break away from what viewers have become most comfortable with: the caricature of a bar regular who offers commentary on life around him. When we get a Norm episode, he is most likely exploring a new job opportunity or being forced into a romantic relationship (never consummated), both of which feel unlike him. Throughout *Cheers*, Norm lost and gained multiple jobs, tried to get Vera pregnant throughout season 3, had to pretend to be his own boss,[45] almost had an affair, and so on. But the platonic ideal of Norm Peterson is sitting at the lower right corner of the bar, drinking a beer that he had put on his tab, and commenting on the lives of others because nothing was happening in his. The consistent portrayal of Norm is completely apathetic and asexual, so Norm-focused episodes are outliers in viewers' expectations. Ultimately, Norm probably shouldn't be carrying the A-plot too often, but Norm is a perfectly made side character.

Because of Norm's lack of motivation, he is an unexpected character to put on primetime television. Norm is not dynamic and driven; he is a lazy, unmotivated alcoholic. In an episode in season 8, Norm explains to Diane who he really is:

> I'm not a go-getter. I've never been a go-getter. What's more, I don't even want to be a go-getter. I'm very happy right where I am. I'm tired of all these people saying "Yeah Peterson, you gotta push, you gotta get ahead, you gotta make that goal." I don't even want to make the goal, Diane. I want to be a benchwarmer, ok? The world needs benchwarmers. . . . In this great pageantry of life, Norm Peterson may be a motionless lump, but he's a very damn good one.[46]

Norm fully accepts and takes pride in who he is. And while it is commendable to portray a character so comfortable with himself on television, George Wendt sees his character differently. In an interview, Wendt points out the negative qualities of Norm Peterson, stating, "If anything, Norm is an indictment of what hanging out in a bar can do for you. He has a miserable relationship with his wife, he can't hold a job and he's overweight."[47] While Norm is a fan favorite, hopefully he isn't idolized and mimicked too closely by fans, as there is no greater description of Norm Peterson than "apathetic." Norm Peterson is completely and unapologetically uninterested in engaging in his work or home life, and would much prefer to remain steadily perched on the rightmost barstool in *Cheers*. Perhaps Sam summed it up best when he said, "Norm doesn't have much in life except for Cheers."[48]

Cliff Clavin

It's a little-known fact . . .

Maybe it's the voice. John Ratzenberger does have a unique tone and delivery, after all. It's made him a staple voice actor for Pixar films.

Maybe it's the appearance. The mailman uniform and mustache is a unique look inside a sports bar and that dichotomy works well for a sitcom.

Maybe it's the dialogue. The know-it-all trivia that ranges from the believable to the absurd so often, nobody knows what to think.

Maybe it's the name. Cliff Clavin joins the ranks of Clark Kent, Bugs Bunny, and Peter Parker among iconic pop culture characters with alliterative names.

Whatever it was, Cliff Clavin was unforgettable. John Ratzenberger imbued Cliff with a lovable but clearly unearned confidence that made his monologues some of the highlights of the series. Throw in the sadsack romantic failures to play off that braggadocio, and Cliff Clavin is a mold many sitcoms have since used to cast characters. Cliff's ineptitude with women reaches such catastrophic levels that he is unable to speak to potential dates, and he even suffers psychosomatic blindness when the potential for a romantic liaison arises. You can easily trace a sitcom lineage from Cliff Clavin to Raj Patel on *The Big Bang Theory*, a character who can't speak to women unless he's drunk.

And yet, remarkably, Cliff Clavin almost didn't become a regular at Cheers. John Ratzenberger read for the part of Norm and felt he had bombed his audition. Ratzenberger recalls his audition, initially for the role of what would become Norm, but that ultimately led to him helping to create a new character:

> I'd spent ten years in London, writing and performing my own comedy shows. They gave me the *Cheers* [scenes], and I thought it was the springboard for chatting about the show, because in England, that's what you do. So I walk in, and I'm looking around, and Jimmy Burrows said, "What are you looking at? You're not here to have a conversation; you're here to audition." At that second, I felt all the blood rush out of my body. I did a horrible job. As I was leaving, the casting director says, "Thank you, John," and my eight-by-ten was already in a wastebasket. But the writer part of me turned around and said, "Do you

have a bar know-it-all?" Because in the bars in my neighborhood
where my father hung out, there was always a bar know-it-all. Glen
said, "What are you talking about?" I just launched into an improvisa-
tion of what [became Cliff].[49]

That bar know-it-all is a vital component of the Cheers gang. With bi-
zarre, yet hilarious claims regarding facts about the world ("Did you
realize that the tan first gained popularity in what is now known as the
Bronze Age?"[50]), his family ("It's a genetic quirk in the Clavin family
that we all have two extra teeth. You see, that's the only way that we can
prove that we are the rightful heirs to the Russian throne"[51]), and himself
("with a cerebral cortex that's 8 percent larger than the average human's . . ."[52]), Cliff's absence would have been detrimental to the show.

At times Cliff is a sympathetically sad character. He so desperately
wants to be the cool guy, the ladies' man, the successful one. And he
simply is not. He is the mailman know-it-all who, for the majority of the
series, still lives with his mother, Esther, who makes semi-regular appearances on the show. He wants to be liked and seeks approval, yet at times
cannot help himself in a sarcastic quip or attempting to prove someone
wrong. Glen and Les Charles noted that they made Clavin a mailman
because they imagined he would read the headlines of magazines he was
delivering, so that he could know a little bit about everything, but act like
he knew everything about anything.[53]

There is a self-awareness for Cliff that comes in season 7 when he has
to stay in the hospital for surgery. Heartbreakingly, none of the Cheers
gang visits him except for Frasier. Everyone else assumed the others had
visited him, and Carla claims, "Come on, it's just an appendectomy.
They're taking out a useless organ. He's chock-full of those."[54] Cliff
realizes his insensitivity toward others has driven them all away. Using
drastic measures, Cliff attempts to make himself more likable through
shock aversion treatment. He returns to the bar along with a doctor to
eavesdrop in on his conversations and, through a device, shock Cliff
anytime he makes a sarcastic or insensitive comment. It all goes poorly,
as Cliff gets repetitively shocked and begins to fight with the doctor while
the gang all watches, clueless as to what is happening.[55] It is a nice
attempt by Cliff to better himself, but viewers, along with the Cheers
gang, have come to love Cliff just the way he is.

Cliff Clavin (John Ratzenberger) and Norm Peterson (George Wendt)

Although the majority of the time he is known as the obnoxious know-it-all, Ratzenberger elaborates on the truly positive qualities of his character:

> Cliff was totally unpredictable. He was just a silly goose. You didn't know what he was going to say at any given moment. You were always waiting for some outlandish bits of information to roll out of his mouth. He had more freedom than the other characters because his job took him out into the world. He was also a loyal character, even though the other characters didn't like being around him. Cliff was a loyal individual in that if you were in a hospital, he would visit you. If you had a flat tire, he would help you fix it. I admire that quality in anybody.[56]

Despite any annoyance he may bring to the bar, Cliff is never intentionally cruel, and he is fiercely loyal to his friends. John Ratzenberger realized there was a transformation in the character he played over the years: "In the beginning, Cliff was more a font of knowledge. . . . [Coach] was always amazed at how brilliant Cliff was. I enjoyed playing the character because it really comes from the premise that, if you say something with enough authority, people will believe you. So I always got a chuckle out of that. And then later, down the line, Cliff became less of a perceived expert as someone who just interrupted conversations, who was more of an annoyance."[57] Whatever version of Cliff that Ratzenberger was playing, wise sage or bloviating buffoon, with his trademark white socks and too-short pants, Cliff Clavin is a truly unforgettable character.

Frasier Crane

For I am a healer, that is what I do.

First introduced as a foil to the Sam and Diane relationship, Frasier Crane entered Cheers in the premiere of season 3, hoping to counsel Sam on his increased drinking and as the new man in Diane's life. At first a character hated by many, Kelsey Grammer's performance as Frasier became beloved by many in the end—so much so, he was given his own spin-off show, *Frasier*, which ran for another eleven seasons.

Frasier was intended to be merely a solution to a problem the writers had created and appear in only a few episodes. Burrows explains the focus, as always, was Sam and Diane: "We'd get Sam and Diane into some predicament, and then over the summer, when the boys would start writing, we thought, 'How do we get them back together?' That's how Frasier evolved."[58] Glen Charles describes the character as representing "everything Diane always said she wanted: brilliant, erudite, cosmopolitan."[59] He was the anti-Sam. And the writers thought the character would work for one season, tops.[60] Initially offered a limited number of episodes, Grammer kept getting invited back for more episodes. Shelley Long admirably notes, "Kelsey could do anything. He found new things about that character to play in every episode. That's lightning in a bottle. A brilliant performer building a character as much as any writer. You just can't create that."[61] A documentary on Kelsey Grammer observes:

He was so perfectly suited for it, just his face and his manner, it just screamed pompous shrink. He was a great, classically trained actor who could do anything, but he was exceptional in comedy and they could sense that immediately on the Cheers set. . . . He was like this erudite figure and it just mixed so well with the blue-collar atmosphere of the bar. It clashed so perfectly for comedy reasons, they knew they had to do something with him.[62]

Grammer definitely imbued Frasier with a delightful mix of needy self-aggrandizement, and the character was able to neatly slip into the snob role when Shelley Long left the series.

As much as the creators and writers adored Frasier, initially the fan reaction was decidedly the opposite. Les Charles claims they received "horrible fan mail, or anti-fan mail, about Kelsey breaking up Sam and Diane or coming between them."[63] Les continues:

Frasier was the most hated character on TV. No one wanted to see someone come between Sam and Diane. After that season, he took a cross-country car trip by himself. He stopped in a bar filled with rough characters to get a beer. A big guy comes up behind him with long stringy hair and sleeves cut off, showing his tattoos. He taps Kelsey on the shoulder and Kelsey turns around and the guy says, "You're that pencil-necked son of a bitch trying to break up Sam and Diane!"[64]

So when did the shift occur from Frasier being hated to becoming a character that would carry the title role of an equally successful sitcom? At the end of season 3, while in Italy together, Frasier proposes to Diane and plans their wedding for the next day. The season ends with the audience wondering if they were married, or if Sam, who flew to Italy to stop the wedding, achieved his goal. The result was neither—Diane made the decision to not marry Frasier and left him at the altar. Suddenly, Frasier was no longer the character who broke up Sam and Diane, but rather a sympathetic (or pathetic) heartbroken, mildly bitter man. It would have been easy to write Frasier out of the show right then, as there was essentially no reason for him to return for season 4. And yet, Frasier sticks around in the bar, despite Diane being back at work there, and the new dynamic allows for a lighter, more carefree, borderline fun yet still grandiose Frasier. In a plot point best left forgotten, Frasier does threaten Sam with a gun after he returns from Europe. But the gun was never actually loaded; Frasier just wanted to see Sam "quaking in his boots a little,"[65] and they worked it out and became closer friends, bonding over their equal hurt caused by Diane.

As different as he was from the usual regulars at Cheers, Frasier becoming one of the gang can be traced to one defining moment. In the season 3 episode, "The Heart Is a Lonely Snipe Hunter,"[66] the guys at Cheers go fishing. Upset over something at work, Frasier tags along at the encouragement of Diane (they were still dating at the time). However, Sam and the guys play a joke on Frasier by having him go "snipe" hunting. Now commonly known, a "snipe" does not exist, but rather is a popular practical joke in which a naive newcomer is duped into believing a "snipe" is real and is left alone to hunt for one, while the others in the group all gather together to do something else and laugh at the one left alone. Sam and the guys leave Frasier out on his own and return to Cheers. Diane is furious at Sam and the rest for misleading Frasier and insists that they find him and tell the truth. Suddenly, Frasier returns from the "hunt" seemingly angry. However, he begins smiling and laughing with the guys, thanking them for introducing him to such an "intoxicating sport." Rather than tell him the truth, they all continue to play along. Diane protects Frasier by not letting him know what really happened, thinking the truth would hurt him. Frasier gets the guys to take him out "hunting" again, and Diane decides he needs to know to know about the prank. However, Frasier has been aware of what is happening the whole time. Rather than be offended, he decides to play along and plans to prank the guys right back by rushing to the car before them when they get back to the woods; he tells Diane, this is what guys do, and "Boy, it's great to be one of the gang, I'll tell ya."[67]

It would have been easy in this episode to have Frasier be upset and play up the humor and drama through his anger. It's an unexpected and enjoyable turn to have Frasier laugh along with the gang and then attempt to outsmart the guys. And almost as if this prank was the hazing he needed, Frasier is accepted not just as Diane's boyfriend but as one of the gang. Had he remained as the butt of the joke, he would have remained an outsider. Although this episode takes place while he is still with Diane, and when Grammer was still just offered a few episodes for the role, it is a crucial storyline for the character, setting him on a course that will last through the end of the series (and beyond).

The character Frasier Crane as played by Kelsey Grammer was a constant presence on television for twenty years. Such a character could not have lasted so many years (across so many shows) without an incredible actor behind him and dynamic, complicated characteristics. Grammer, in describing his character, recalls:

> The first thing I thought [when I read the script] was that Frasier was an intellectual at some points but also an Everyman—flawed and very insecure. The other thing I thought was that when he decided to love, he was completely—what is it Othello says?—"perplexed in the extreme." What made him endearing in the end was that his love for Diane was without question. [68]

These qualities were explored on *Cheers* as he moved from Diane into new stages of life; he got married to a different woman and had a child, Frederick. None of this would have been possible without the character of Lilith Sternin.

As Frasier grew as a main character, naturally the writers wanted to create a new love interest for him (lest he gaze longingly at Sam and Diane at Cheers). Played by Tony Award–winner Bebe Neuwirth, Lilith Sternin first appeared in season 4 as a memorable bad date for Frasier. [69] Writer Peter Casey confirms the impression she made, stating, "Bebe blew everyone's socks off. We said we have to get this character back because she and Frasier were hysterical together." [70]

However, the new love interest wasn't initially intended to be Lilith. Writer Cheri Steinkellner recounts,

> Bebe started as a day-player, one scene, a terrible date, to set up Frasier meeting his dream date, Candi, played by Jennifer Tilly. That was the romantic arc we planned. But Lilith was the romance we pursued. So much fun. The same antagonism that characterized Sam and Diane showed up—only instead of equal and opposite, they were more like equal and identical. [71]

Candi was a woman Sam set Frasier up with to help ease his loneliness. Candi with "i" because, as she claims, "I used to spell it with a 'Y' but nobody ever took me seriously, so then I switched it to an 'I', you know, like Gandhi." [72] As entertaining as Candi was for the episode, it is impossible to imagine *Cheers* without Lilith.

However, the role of Lilith wasn't intended to be a long-term gig for Neuwirth either as she was a Broadway actress biding her time between roles. She stated,

Frasier Crane (Kelsey Grammer) and Lilith Sternin (Bebe Neuwirth)

In 1985, I was doing a pre-Broadway run of *Sweet Charity* [that] started in LA and had four months off before opening on Broadway. So I stayed and tried to rustle up whatever work I could while I was waiting. The first job was on *Simon & Simon*, and the second was *Cheers*. I don't know that I had seen it. But my parents, who are very smart, very sophisticated, they loved *Cheers*.[73]

Pale, cold, dry wit, no sense of humor, and having hair straight back in a bun became what Lilith was ultimately known for. Neuwirth admits the role of Lilith was tricky to get down at first, noting Lilith was the opposite of the musical roles she usually played, so "when I first auditioned for Lilith, I really struggled. Then her voice occurred to me in my head, and I started reading it out loud to myself, and it made me laugh. That was her."[74] And once she found her, she practically stole the show, and critics agreed as she won back-to-back Emmys in 1990 and 1991. Although often categorized as harsh, Neuwirth points out the softer characteristics of Lilith: "I find Lilith very innocent, very sweet, very naive, she's socially inept. She has no idea how to react with other people. She's shy and uncomfortable with people. She's a scientist, she's very analytical, she's very honest. And she loves her husband very, very much. That's important. And she loves her child, Frederick, too."[75] On their first date, Frasier brings Lilith to Cheers for a drink and it is evident she does not fit the usual clientele, but by the last few seasons it was expected to see Lilith sitting at the bar, reading a book, just hanging out like one of the gang. Lilith found a comfortable home at Cheers, just as Frasier did.

THE STAFF

Diane Chambers

I am not a regular person.

Diane Chambers first enters Cheers only to stop in for a moment with her fiancé (not to mention her professor, boss, and mentor), Sumner Sloane, on the night before their wedding. Sumner leaves Diane at the bar to visit his ex-wife in order to get his "grandmother's antique gold wedding ring"[76] back. Although he returns for a brief moment, he quickly leaves again and never returns, having reunited with his ex-wife. Diane is quite literally abandoned at Cheers and taken in by Sam and the gang by being offered a job as a waitress.

Diane's role is essential for viewers as she is the only newcomer in the already established world of the Cheers bar. This was purposefully done, as Glen Charles states, because "we wanted to introduce the bar and the people in it through Diane's eyes. She was the audience's guide."[77] There are years of friendships and relationships between staff and patrons already established, and notably, there are no introductions. We learn of this world just as Diane does. Diane is a controversial character that many can't identify with, yet whether you love her or hate her, she was the

Diane Chambers (Shelley Long) and Sam Malone (Ted Danson)

audience's proxy, an outsider entering an established world that the audience could follow.

Pompous, arrogant, entitled, snob. These are just a few words that describe Diane Chambers. She was the wide-eyed, annoying, innocent intellectual. Her presence and tastes stand out painfully against the blue-collar environment of Cheers. However, Diane's moral compass is needed, guiding Sam and the gang through various aspects of their lives. Writer Cheri Steinkellner claims that Diane was "the emotional center of the show. She told the ultimate truth."[78] Even when no one wanted to hear it. She changes Sam for the better, igniting a growth in him that is explored throughout all eleven years. But Diane always remains the same, the intellectual barmaid who thinks she is above her station.

In the end, Diane does mean well, and she so desperately wants to be included and become a part of the group. In the season 4 episode, "Suspicion," Diane conducts an experiment for her behavioral sciences colloquium in which she brings a classmate into the bar to play a "harmless" trick on the gang. She has the man sit at a table, watch the bar and look as though he's taking notes, refusing to engage with anyone, leaving the gang to question who he is and what he is doing there. When Sam goes to confront the man, Diane reveals the truth of who he is and why he is there. Annoyed by the trick, Sam walks away saying, "Diane, we don't get mad," with the clear indication of the rest of the sentence being, "we get even." And so Diane paces the rest of the episode, terrified of (yet excited by) the gang's retaliation. When a host and cameraman show up at the bar to film Diane reciting some of her poetry for a poetry show at the recommendation of her professor, Diane assumes this is the gang's elaborate prank. Rather than reading poetry, she bawks like a chicken over and over. Humiliated when her chicken segment really did air on the show, Diane tells the everyone, "I felt kind of good, thinking you guys had gone to all that trouble to get back at me like you would with each other. And I was thinking of myself as one of the gang." Four years at the bar, and she still felt like an outsider. However, as she goes inside Sam's office, a bucket of water is dumped on her, causing her to come back into the bar, exclaiming, "I love you guys!"[79] While Diane may come off as a highbrow elitist at times, deep down she is just like everyone else, hoping to be a part of the place where everybody knows your name.

There are times when life imitates art nearly perfectly. Shelley Long portraying Diane Chambers seems to be one of those times. Les Charles says of Long:

> Shelley knew who her character was and had a much surer idea of herself than the rest of the cast. She was able to carry the show in the beginning while the others were finding their way. That's the way it

worked: The actors got closer and closer to their characters. Or maybe
their characters got closer to the people. [80]

It is high praise to say how quickly she knew her character, yet arguably, Long was perhaps the most similar already to the part she played of
all the cast. In many ways Diane felt she was better than Cheers. She
speaks down to them, particularly Sam, and never is one to shy away
from her opinions on their choice of entertainment, conversations, or
hangout location. She is often secluded away from everyone, sitting off
on her own reading, or not participating in the bar activities. Long admits
to needing time away to prepare for her role, often taking lunch in her
dressing room away from the cast. [81] Of course, Long's reasons for her
seclusion from the rest of the cast are completely justified and under-
standable, but it is interesting that both her process and her character
allowed for the outsider status. In another similarity, Diane always expected more from her life and ultimately leaves Cheers to pursue her
career in writing. Infamously, Long left *Cheers* at the end of season 5 for
a movie career (as well as recognizing that the Sam and Diane saga had
run its course). Just as the rest of the Cheers gang were content in their
life, the rest of the *Cheers* cast were content with their television role.
Even Long states, "Diane was . . . a pain in the butt . . . and I think the
people of Cheers got me confused with that, maybe I did too, which
convinced me it was time to let go of that persona."[82] Whatever challenges may have arisen off screen throughout the first five years of
Cheers, Diane is a powerful and memorable character, consistently mentioned in popular culture, and expertly portrayed by Long. Long's contri-
butions went beyond what was seen in front of the camera. Writer Cheri
Steinkellner states that the writers "used to go to Shelley whenever a
script was in trouble."[83]

While the difficulty of making Diane likable is underrated, so too is
Shelley Long's gift for physical comedy. Perhaps it is overshadowed by
her talent for long-winded dramatic monologues, but Long's facial tics,
her exaggerated reactions, and her overexcited energy when Diane gets
her way all deserve more praise. There's comedic genius to Long's physical performance that gets lost in her character's elitist dialogue. Clearly
others agree about her abilities as Long exited the show with two Golden
Globes and an Emmy for her portrayal of Diane Chambers.

Carla Tortelli

Carla's been in a lousy mood for the last two or three years.

Carla Maria Victoria Angelina Teresa Apollonia Lozupone Tortelli Le-Bec was ultimately written on *Cheers* as representative of "the bittered working class."[84] Carla's life is hard, but she is hardworking. She is mean, sarcastic, and loyal, with strong religious faith and equally strong superstition. Witty, honest, and perpetually pregnant, she can't stand her kids, yet everything she does is for them. In a newspaper ad, she described herself as "divorced female, warm, witty, and Italian in every way except fat. 33, five foot and a quarter inch, dark-brown hair, brown eyes, no visible scars, tattoos or birthmarks."[85]

The small, feisty Italian was played by Rhea Perlman for all eleven seasons. Having previously worked with the Charles brothers and James Burrows on *Taxi*, Perlman was the one actor whose part was specifically written for her, as Les Charles admits, "We always had Rhea in mind because she'd worked with us on *Taxi* and was a friend of ours."[86] The Perlman family had a huge impact on *Cheers*, as Perlman's sister, Heide, was a writer and producer for the show, and her father, Philip, played bar patron Phil, who was often seen but rarely heard.

Despite knowing her previously, casting Rhea was with complete merit, Cheri Steinkellner claims: "Rhea could nail a joke like an Olympic gold medal gymnast sticking the landing."[87] However, she was nothing like the hard, insulting, flailing character she played. Levine states, "Rhea was the complete opposite of Carla—quiet, a little shy, very sweet. I think she really enjoyed playing her. It was an alter ego and she could really let loose."[88] Similarly, Rhea herself echoes these words, pointing out the simultaneous flaws and strengths of Carla: "I can't say I based [Carla] on anybody I knew. She was so foulmouthed and mean, just said what was on her mind. So I guess Carla is somebody I always wished I could be at the right moment, the one who always has the perfect comeback."[89] As mean as she can be, Carla is one to admire. She knows and accepts who she is and is always truthful. In speaking of Carla's character, Cheri Steinkellner said, "She [Rhea] once said, 'Carla's not mean, she's just honest.' That gave us permission to write her the meanest possible things."[90]

At the start of *Cheers*, Carla has four children, all with her ex-husband Nick Tortelli. By the eleventh season, she has eight children—the four additional children are with three different men—one with Nick; one with a man she had a relationship with, Dr. Bennet Ludlow; and twins with her husband Eddie LeBec. Carla first got pregnant in high school at age sixteen and declared herself to be "the most fertile woman alive."[91] Although all three pregnancies were incorporated into the plotlines because Perlman was pregnant in real life, they are pivotal in showing the differences in male/female sexual promiscuity. Both Sam and Carla have multiple sexual partners throughout the series, however, Sam faces no consequences (aside from the occasional hurt female) and Carla has multiple life-altering consequences of having a child for the rest of her life. In her essay, "Sex, Society, and Double Standards in *Cheers*," Heather Hundley states,

> In fact, the dominant ideological message perpetuated in *Cheers* was that casual, unprotected, promiscuous, heterosexual sex was sport for men. Moreover, the juxtaposition of class and gender reveals that *Cheers* advanced double standards, in that upper-middle-class white

Carla Tortelli (Rhea Perlman) and husband Eddie LeBec (Jay Thomas)

men may enjoy the pleasures of sex without guilt, remorse, or health concerns, while working-class women suffer serious consequences for the same actions. Thus, within *Cheers*, Sam represented the male hero figure constructed through his sexual conquests, while bar server and main character Carla Tortelli-LeBec (Rhea Perlman) portrayed a nymphomaniac who reveled in her self-condemnation as a slut and "paid the price" for her loose morals.[92]

In season 6, Carla's son Anthony tells her she is going to be a grandmother. Devastated by the news, Carla declares some of the painful results of her life by having had children so young: "Look at my life. I never had a childhood. I married Nick when I was fifteen. Never got to go to the prom or homecoming, or a slumber party, to Fort Lauderdale on spring break, or on one lousy date with Fabian. Now I don't even get a middle age. Went straight from grade school to granny."[93] This is not to say Carla doesn't love her children. Although she repeatedly jokes about them and admits the difficulties and sacrifices of motherhood, everything she does in her life is for her children.

A bright spot for Carla's character is her relationship with Sam. Their friendship spans years before we ever meet them, and we are introduced early on to how deep their friendship really is. There is a slight unbalance as you sense Sam means a little more to Carla than just a friend, and Perlman deliberately played the role that way. Long explains, "Early on, Rhea came up to me about a line after a run-through and said, 'This feels weird to me because Carla's in love with Sam.' I thought, 'Oh, of course. All this time she's been playing to that because it made sense to her and the character.'"[94] And Les Charles confirms, "We thought that was the subtext of their relationship from the beginning. They both knew it couldn't go anywhere. It's important to establish relationships and how people appeal to one another."[95]

In the third episode of the show, "The Tortelli Tort," Carla assaults a patron after he mocked Sam about his pitching days. The patron tells Sam, "Fire her or I'm gonna take everything you got."[96] Carla immediately quips, "Fire me? Come on. That's crazy." And as an audience you believe her. You already know Sam will do anything he can not to fire her. Throughout the series, they sweetly show how much they know and care about one another: Sam dances with her in a competition she wants to win, she is the only one he will confide in when he thinks he got a woman pregnant, and Sam reveals to her his most-kept secret—wearing a toupee. When arguing over who knows the other better, Sam tells Carla, "Your favorite meal is Chicken McNuggets. Your favorite hobby is drawing underarm hair on all the models in Vogue magazine. And your favorite movie is *Lady and the Tramp* and you always cry when they come to the part about the spaghetti."[97] Sam already knows what the audience comes to learn, that the hard, tough exterior Carla puts on is covering a softer, sentimental, hardworking single mother.

Ernie "Coach" Pantusso

> *Coach: Is there an Ernie Pantusso here?*
> *Sam: That's you, Coach.*

The sweet innocence Coach brought to *Cheers* was a necessary counterpoint to Carla's cruel snark, Sam and Diane's sexual tension, and Norm and Cliff's idle gossip. Played with remarkable comic timing by Nicholas Colasanto, Coach's non-sequitur responses at the end of a conversation could provide the perfect comedic button to a scene. Glen Charles described Coach as "a little bit of Yogi Berra, Sparky Anderson and Casey Stengel,"[98] and Castleman and Podrazik succinctly describe Coach as a "logically illogical bartender."[99] Coach is regarded by many as *Cheers'* most beloved character. Despite only appearing on the show for the first three seasons before Nick Colasanto passed away, Coach left a lasting impression both on the show's audience and the *Cheers* cast and crew.

Nicknamed "Coach" because he used to be a coach for the Boston Red Sox (not because he "never flew first class"[100]), Ernie Pantusso was a kind bartender, whose dim-wittedness was said to have been caused by being hit in the head by too many pitches during his baseball career. Which, incidentally, he may have purposefully caused in order to win over women, as revealed when he explained his dating methods: "I'd spot a cute dame in the stands, and to get their attention, you now, I'd injure myself . . . I'd lean into a pitch, or I'd dive face-first into a bag, I'd take a real hot grounder in the gut. Anything to get their sympathy."[101] Colasanto said of his character, "Coach is not a worldly man. He's not well-read. He comes from the dugouts. He may be intelligent, but he's not worldly wise. He's so positive; that's what makes him funny. He'll say the most absurd thing, but, if someone corrects him, he immediately capitulates because he doesn't want to offend anyone."[102] It was this positive and sweet nature that made both the character and the actor so beloved. Ted Danson believes, "Coach was the heart and soul of the first two or three years of *Cheers*. You know, the sweetness of *Cheers* came out of his character."[103]

That sweetness he projects also leads to more serious moments, and Coach gives some of the most heartfelt moments of true emotion of the entire series. In one of the most memorable scenes of the show, Coach is speaking with his daughter, Lisa, in Sam's office. Lisa wants to marry Roy, a gruff man who treats her terribly. Coach pleads with her not to marry him, but Lisa believes he is her only chance at a marriage and children. Their exchange continues:

Coach: But you're so beautiful, so . . .

Lisa: Beautiful? Daddy, you have been saying that I'm beautiful ever since I was a very little girl. But look at me, not as my father, but like you were looking at me for the first time and please, try to see me as I really am.

Coach: Oh my God, I, I didn't realize how much you look like your mother.

Lisa: I know. I look exactly like her, and mom was not . . . comfortable about her beauty.

Coach: But that's what made her more beautiful. Your mother grew more beautiful every day of her life.

Lisa: She was really beautiful.

Coach: Yes, and so are you. You're the most beautiful kid in the whole world.[104]

Nothing is obvious to Coach and he takes everything quite literally, but it was these qualities that bring out the most truthful, tender moment of the show.

There was a necessary usefulness to Coach's clueless character for the writers—if any information needed to be refreshed to the audience, it was believable to have Coach (and later Woody) be the one receiving the information from another character. But Ken Levine makes sure to clarify

Coach Ernie Pantusso (Nicholas Colasanto)

regarding Coach and Woody stating, "People make the mistake of believing they were 'dumb.' They weren't. They just took everything literally."[105] And Glen Charles continues, in describing the key traits behind these characters: "These were certainly not dumb men, they just had a different perspective on things. We tried to make Coach not so much stupid as indecisive and pursuing his own line of reasoning. Behind the seeming stupidity was a sweetness and innocence and a striving to make sense out of life."[106]

In many ways, Colasanto was the wise father figure to the cast and crew of *Cheers*. Director James Burrows states, "Colasanto was like a father on stage and off. He was the older, more experienced one of all of us. Nick was Coach."[107] His positivity and childlike nature came not just from the character but from the actor himself. Ratzenberger says that when he asked Colasanto, "How do you do what you do?" Colasanto replied, "Ratz, every day, when I pull in the parking lot and I get out of the car, I'm twelve years old." Ratzenberger continues, "If you see Nick's episodes now, think of that: Whatever the line or situation is, he'd react like a twelve-year-old. Perfect, but so simple."[108] And powerfully, Danson admits the influence Colasanto had on himself and Sam Malone, saying, "Nicky is the one who told me . . . you're the leader, you're the owner of the bar, you're the leader, you need to act like one, you need to behave like one, you need to set the tone. It wasn't like I became this amazing leader, he kind of imbued me with 'you stand up a little straighter.' He was important to all of us."[109] Clearly, in his few short years on the show, Colasanto was incredibly impactful and helped shaped *Cheers*.

On February 12, 1985, Nicholas Colasanto died of a heart attack in his home at age sixty-one.[110] Although he was sick when he was cast on the show, the other actors didn't know of the health issues until a few weeks before his death. George Wendt recalls,

> He'd been getting kind of thin. [Earlier in the season], they called us all into Glen and Les' office, and they told us his heart muscle was sort of dying, but they said he had been cleared to come back to work. They said, "Well, it could mean six weeks, could mean six years." So we were all like, "Oh. Well, that's a drag, but it seems like he's ready to come back to work." We were [hoping for] six years. It turned out it was six weeks.[111]

Filming was canceled that night as the cast learned the news. Amid their grief, concern grew among cast and crew as to how the show would survive without Coach and Colasanto. Danson states, "Nick died. Wow, will we maintain the sweetness? Where will we get the sweetness he gave us?"[112] The answer was the youthful Woody Boyd, but Coach was always remembered as he is frequently referenced through the remaining seasons.

Notably, aside from appearing in the cold opening in the final episode of season 3, "Rescue Me," which was filmed far in advance given Colasanto's ailing health, Coach's final full episode is "Cheerio, Cheers," in which Diane leaves for Europe with Frasier, assuming she will never return. Their final exchange is especially poignant, given that Colasanto never returns:

Diane: Oh Coach, I'm going to miss you.

Coach: I'm going to miss you too, honey.

Diane asks him to look after Sam, and in his final moment on screen, Coach says to her, "Bye, sweetheart" as he leaves Cheers. [113]

Woody Boyd

> *Howdy. I'm Woody Boyd from Hanover, Indiana. That's the placemat capital of the world. . . . My favorite color's blue, and I've saved all my baby teeth.*

There was nothing sensationalized in announcing Coach's death on *Cheers*. In the premiere of season 4, when Woody arrives at the bar asking if Coach is around, Sam informs him, "I'm sorry, Woody. I guess you hadn't heard. No, uh, Coach passed away a couple months ago. But yeah, I'd like to think he's still around." [114] It is not dismissive of Coach given that the gang (and cast) has had months to accept his passing, but Danson's delivery portrays the grief that is still felt and continually acknowledged throughout the rest of the series. Coach is gone, but never forgotten.

Replacing the character of Coach with another actor was never seriously considered, but rather the decision was made to create a new but equally genuine character in his place. For Woody Boyd, the show went much younger than Coach, creating a character who could only legally make a purchase at the bar a few years before. In an enjoyable coincidence, twenty-three-year-old Woody Harrelson was cast for the character already named Woody Boyd. Coming off its third season, *Cheers* was climbing in critical praise and rankings, but Harrelson, focused on his

Broadway career, claims he had heard of *Cheers* yet had never seen it. During the audition process he then watched two episodes and realized, "Oh my God. This is really good."[115] Harrelson charmed the producers by both his natural presence and acting ability. As he recalls about one of his auditions, "I didn't know I was going into a room with [all the producers], so I was blowing my nose when I walked in. The room erupted in laughter, and somebody said, "This is Woody."[116] Writer and producer Peter Casey recalls, "Harrelson comes in to read looking like he just came off a basketball court. He had on athletic shorts and unlaced high-tops, and I'm going, 'This is so not the character.' And then he read, and he brought this beautiful innocence to the whole thing, and when [his character] heard the news that Coach had died, he cried a little. No actor had done that."[117]

Because he was filling a narrative void left by Coach, Woody had to adopt some of the storytelling role Coach had in the first three seasons. Coach had been slow on the uptake, often missed nuance or double meaning, and had to have things explained to him. Obviously these character traits are valuable on a sitcom and created great humor, but they also allowed Coach to serve as a reason to catch up the audience on recent events. In explaining Coach's dim-wittedness, writers revealed that he taken too many fastballs to the head during his playing days in baseball. Thus, these characteristics weren't a commentary on where he was raised or his ethnicity or gender; they were a result of life events. Clearly, the writers wanted a character who was similarly dim-witted, but in this case they created a character who was naive and slow on the uptake because he was a country boy. This was a stereotype that *Cheers* certainly did not invent. It had been a staple of American sitcoms in the 1950s and 1960s; Sara K. Eskridge notes that series such as *The Beverly Hillbillies*, *The Real McCoys*, and *The Andy Griffith Show* all embraced and promoted a stereotype of a "naive southern hick."[118]

Some of the humor that the writers gave to Woody definitely leans hard into a stereotype of the country bumpkin, and because of that many of most laugh-out-loud moments break that mold. In the season 5 episode "Tan 'n' Wash," the cast jumps into a business opportunity presented by Norm, which inevitably backfires. However, when egged on by everyone else to also jump into the business arrangement without really looking into the matter, Woody sagely says, "You know, when I left home, my father gave me some very sound advice. Never trust a man who can't

Woody Boyd (Woody Harrelson)

look you in the eye, never talk when you can listen, and never spend venture capital on a limited partnership without a detailed analytical fiduciary prospectus."[119] It is unfortunate the show plays hard into the country boy stereotype, but Woody does have one of the greatest character evolutions of all the Cheers gang.

When Woody enters the bar in season 4, he is new to Boston with a girlfriend waiting for him back home. By the end of season 11, Woody is married to a different girl, the wealthy Kelly Gaines, with a baby on the way, having just been elected to the City Council. These changes are natural, particularly for a character in his twenties during the show. However, his entry marked a shift in the series, as his youthful energy ignited the rest of the cast. Burrows explains,

> I'm telling you, once Woody came, the water-pistol fights, the foosball games . . . the testosterone on the set just went berserk. You know, when you had Woody, he'd jump over the bar. And that was a chance for Teddy to try to jump over the bar. So he brought a youthful enthusiasm, which was infectious. Not to take anything away from Nicky, but it was just a totally different attitude that the cast had.[120]

And Danson recalls of Woody's arrival,

> Most of us were about 37 when Woody joined the cast, and he was 25. And, for a man, 37 is the age when you realise you are no longer 25. So we would do everything to try to beat him, at anything. We tried to beat him on the basketball court, because we all thought we were pretty good—and he killed us. We arm-wrestled, and I still have tendonitis from that. I never had brothers, but I got to have that with Woody.[121]

Woody's presence brought out new dynamics among the characters as well, particularly in Sam. When there was Coach, Sam was in the role of a son taking care of his father. With Woody, Sam was the older brother. As George Wendt explains, "Woody brought this impishness. He brought it out in Ted, especially."[122]

In their book, *Cult TV: The Comedies*, Jon E. Lewis and Penny Stempel describe Woody Boyd as "a farm boy of frightening simpleness from Hanover, Indiana."[123] But Shelley Long points out the overall charm of Woody: "The way Woody played Woody was he thought the best of everyone. He didn't think Carla was mean or Cliff talked too much. That was one of the things that made his performance so luminous."[124] Woody is endearingly courteous and polite. He calls everyone Mr. and Ms. (aside from Sam and Carla), and sends Rebecca flowers when he is running late to work.[125] It is a credit to both the writers and Harrelson that Woody appears on screen and is instantly likable. He oozes an unrehearsed charm and eagerness you can't help but adore. Woody is immediately accepted as part of the group; in his second episode, the gang even flies his girlfriend out in an attempt to make him happy.[126] But more than anything, the immediate welcoming and acceptance of Woody is a testament to the Cheers gang's friendship and openness.

5

THE EVOLUTION OF SAM MALONE

When Age Catches the Magnificent Pagan Beast

I'm Sam Malone. By definition everything I do is cool.

The series premiere of *Cheers* begins with Sam Malone walking down the hallway from the back room to open the bar for business. [1] The series finale ends with Sam Malone closing the bar, turning off the lights, and walking down the hallway to the back room. [2] It's a lovely bit of symmetry and a rather perfect ending for a series set in a sports bar, but it does invite the question, "What's changed?" If the series begins and ends with Sam in the bar, has there been an evolution? Is there progression if it begins with the lights being flipped on and ends with them turned off?

Obviously, for some characters, yes. There are marriages and children and job changes. But what about Sam? He's single at beginning and end. He's the owner, manager, and bartender at beginning and end. Is he the same? Definitely not. Of all the characters, he may have transformed the most in terms of personality. The journey is far from a smooth progression—in fact, it's as herky-jerky as a rickety roller coaster—but Sam Malone does mature away from the impulsive lothario we meet in "Give Me a Ring Sometime."

It's not hidden from viewers that Sam Malone is a broken man. We're told about his greatest demon in the pilot when he confesses that he lost his pitching career due to alcoholism. [3] "Recovering alcoholic" is a part of his identity that he acknowledges it, but hides beneath other aspects of his personality. He projects the identity of a man's man, defined by his attractiveness, his physical prowess, and his success with women. But during *Cheers* we see every part of that projected version of Sam Malone begin to crack.

SAM, THE RECOVERING ALCOHOLIC

There is something appealingly contradictory in the fact that Sam is a recovering alcoholic and owns a bar, choosing to literally surround himself with his greatest vice as he serves his friends drinks every single day of his life. Ted Danson said of Sam Malone, "I don't think the character

Sam Malone (Ted Danson)

would have been worth a hill of beans if he hadn't been an alcoholic. I think that was brilliant. And that brought a little bit of sadness and I like humor that comes out of real human sadness."[4] Sam Malone seems at peace with this inherent conflict; after all, he projects a macho, carefree, lovable attitude at almost all times. But there are moments of genuine vulnerability that break through that performance. Whether it's Sam's insecurities about his brother,[5] or his discomfort when anyone makes fun of his intelligence,[6] or recognition of his loneliness,[7] viewers occasionally see a raw side to the traditionally polished Sam Malone. But never do viewers get a more intimate glimpse of the dark, personal, and somber side of Sam Malone that he keeps hidden than when his alcoholism is addressed head on. Sam's drinking past is often mentioned in passing through a casual reference, but on a few occasions the shows pulls his alcoholism into focus for an episode.

In the first season's most powerful episode, "Endless Slumper," Sam reveals when he stopped drinking. A Red Sox relief pitcher, Rick Walker, currently in a slump, comes to Cheers asking Sam and Coach for advice on how to get back to form. To help Rick, Sam lets him borrow his lucky bottle cap. Turns out that bottle cap is from the last bottle of beer he ever drank before giving up alcohol, and Sam always carries it with him. While Rick has the lucky cap, Sam begins to have horrible luck. He can't slide a beer glass on the bar, he locks his keys in his car, and his TV set explodes. After Diane constantly teases Sam about his reliance on that one little object, Sam confides to her, "You see, that little bottle cap keeps me from drinking. When I was tempted to have a drink, sometimes I'd look at the bottle cap, and it would stop me." After learning Rick has lost the cap late one night, Sam is tempted to drink again. Diane does everything she can to distract him so he does not drink. But Sam points out a very real issue as he tells Diane, "Where am I going to be tomorrow night? And the next? And the day after that, huh? I'm going to be in a bar, right?" revealing a new side to Sam we had yet to see. Sam is the cool, carefree bartender, but in this scene, he is the struggling alcoholic who is just about completely broken. In the end, Sam does pour a beer, but rather than drink it, he slides it along the bar, smiling in his victory to Diane, while flipping a new lucky bottle cap in the air.[8] Diane has more to do with Sam's sobriety in this moment than that bottle cap, but the cap will serve as a memento of this night together—a night when Sam and Diane became more than a boss and employee, or potential romantic interests, but rather humans who lift one another up in their weakness.

The ugliest version of Sam that we see comes at the beginning of season 3. Sam and Diane had been together for a year, but it ended in a fight when Sam tried to control Diane and Diane fought back. The fight was ugly; Diane ended up in a sanitarium to regain her emotional and mental footing while Sam turned back to the bottle. The first appearance of Sam in this season sees him disheveled, unshaved, and unkempt, looking more like a stereotypical street bum than the Boston sports hero and businessman he believes himself to be. Sam tries to play off his problem: "Yeah, I'm drinking again, but it's not the same thing. This time it's good-time controlled drinking. Before it was negative. Now it's fun."[9] The denial is so obvious that even Norm, who spends his life sitting at the bar and drinking, warns Sam that he's drinking too much. With the help of Dr. Frasier Crane, Sam leaves this drinking episode behind him, but for viewers it serves as a stark portrayal of how bad things can get for Sam Malone. But, even as things do turn bad in the coming seasons, it's a sign of Sam's progression that we never see him turn to the bottle again.

It isn't until the ninth season that the origin of Sam's drinking is revealed. Rebecca asks Sam why he started drinking back during his baseball days, and he replies, "I lost my curveball."[10] The only time we see Sam drink on the show is after he loses Diane the first time. Sam lives a charmed life, where things usually go his way—he is the star, and others praise him. When things don't go his way, Sam doesn't always know how to handle it. His growth is shown through the series as he falls on many hard times. Coach passes away, he loses Diane again, he sells the bar but has to come back begging for a job, a fire burns the bar down, but through none of those does he ever consider drinking again. Sam remains on guard—when Woody thinks he's created a new cocktail, he offers it to Sam, who recoils: "Woody, I can't touch that stuff, I'm an alcoholic"[11]—but we never see the simmering addiction bubble up to the surface again.

SAM, THE AGING MAN

Patrice M. Buzzanell and Suzy D'Enbeau, in examining the portrayal of masculinity in popular culture, identified several of the gendered stereo-

types that "indicate men are supposed to be stoic, anti-feminine, competitive, individualistic, successful, and heroic."[12] It doesn't take much familiarity with American television and film to begin listing examples of
iconic characters that match that description: Don Draper from *Mad Men*,
Joey Tribbiani from *Friends*, and Harvey Specter from *Suits*. However, as
Buzzanell and D'Enbeau note, "these stereotypes are premised on a sexy,
successful, attractive *young* man,"[13] and popular culture has historically
presented fewer portrayals of older men or explored the aging of men.
Cheers stands out as an example of presenting the process of aging, as
Sam Malone begins the series as a character that checks every single box
in the man's man stereotype but after more than a decade has matured
into a different character. And while it is possible to identify several
critically successful, hit series that address aging male protagonists
(*Breaking Bad, The Sopranos, Mad Men*), many of these shows are from
the mid-2000s and on. *Cheers* broke new ground for network television in
many ways, but one underrated area is the evolution of Sam Malone.
Alan Sepinwall and Matt Zoller Seitz note:

> Rather than merely put Sam and his castmates through the usual paces
> over and over, the series dared to ask itself, and us, what might actual-
> ly happen to such people were they to experience the situations de-
> vised by the show's writers, taking into account the effects of age and
> disillusionment, the painful recognition (or denial) of failure, and the
> way the inevitability of death makes some people double down on
> their pathologies and makes others work harder to subdue them and
> create something like a contented life.[14]

As Sam Malone ages over a decade, the show explores his need to adjust
to the new normal as his days as a strong professional athlete fall well
behind him.

In "Dark Imaginings," the nineteenth episode of season 4, Sam suffers
a hernia when he attempts to keep up with the younger, stronger Woody
in a game of racquetball.[15] Of course, this being Sam, it was also an
attempt to impress a young woman. The episode front-loads the theme of
aging, making certain the audience is aware that while there is comedy to
be mined from Sam's injury, the episode is also exploring weightier
concerns that will jump-start the evolution of Sam Malone.

Sam enters the bar in this episode with his current date, a younger
woman named Bonnie. The gap between Sam and Bonnie is established

through their taste in music; Sam can't remember the name of John Cougar Mellencamp. Woody, several years younger than Sam, is a fan though. Woody and Bonnie also bond over a shared appreciation of U2, though Sam doesn't recognize the band name. It's natural for musical tastes to lock in on what plays on the radio when you're in high school or college, and Sam is removed enough from the current music scene to be unfamiliar with newer music groups.

Diane notices "a bit of a gap" in Sam and Bonnie's ages and makes a joke about Bonnie losing her baby teeth, which is the first time Sam notes that she might be a bit young. He defensively insists Bonnie is sophisticated and well-traveled because she's been to Hawaii. Sam is further put on the defensive when he realizes that Woody plays racquetball but has never played with him. When Sam asks why, Woody says, "I didn't think the two of us should play." Sam believes Woody is intimidated or overly deferential because Sam played baseball and asks if Woody hasn't played him "just because I'm a professional athlete"[16]—note Sam's use of the present tense, as in his mind this is still how Sam is perceived. Woody says that's not why and then stumbles around pointing out their age difference before clarifying that he doesn't think Sam is old, "just older." In the course of a few lines of dialogue, Sam goes from a position of assumed superiority to realizing he's being pitied by a younger man. Sam immediately overcompensates. When Woody effortlessly hops over the bar, Sam distracts everyone by pointing and saying, "Hey, is that somebody famous?" before he awkwardly scampers over the bar but makes it appear to everyone who looked away that he jumped right over it.

Naturally, Sam and Woody's racquetball game takes place off screen, and we only see them returning to Cheers after it's completed. Sam won, but is limping, his overcompensation clearly having carried over to the court. Diane is worried that Sam has hurt himself, but he laughs her off and grabs some skis from his office. Sam is so concerned about his image that he pretends to be going off on a ski trip rather than reveal to the gang that he's injured. Injury equals frailty. And this particular injury equals aging. Sam is hurt enough to go to a hospital for several days. It's only when Diane overhears two nurses complaining about an aggressively flirtatious patient and tracks him down at the hospital that we learn he has a hernia. He laments to Diane, "I didn't tell you I was in the hospital because I got a hernia and it's an old man's problem." Diane counsels Sam to accept that aging is perfectly natural, but he emotionally retorts,

"That day you start accepting getting old is the day you're old." To prove to Diane—and himself—that he's not getting old, Sam checks himself out of the hospital well before he's fully recovered. When Woody gives Sam a congratulatory slap on the back he instantly freezes. Diane asks if he wants to go back to the hospital, and he admits that he does "very badly" want to go back. [17]

While the episode ends on the unexpectedly somber note, this is key for the remaining plotline of the season. This is a moment of Sam reconciling himself to a different status than the mental image he had held of himself. Sam is moving away from seeing himself as eternally young, and this realization is necessary for the season finale's cliffhanger. Though we'd seen Sam in a serious relationship with Diane, it never really headed toward marriage. At the close of season 4, there's a run of episodes with Sam dating Janet Eldridge. The season ends with Sam on the phone proposing marriage, and the audience left in the dark about whether it's Janet or Diane that Sam is speaking with. Sam reaching the point where it is believable to see him proposing actually begins with "Dark Imaginings," not with the Janet Eldridge storyline.

In season 5, Sam is threatened by Diane's new younger, very attractive love interest and goes around the bar asking everyone who is the handsomest man they know, while always pushing for them to say him. [18] Sam needs constant validation in his life. And typically, Carla is more than happy to provide it, as are Norm and Cliff. In the same episode, Sam again reveals his discomfort with aging when Frasier greets him with, "How you doing, Sam old man?" and he replies, "You know, Frasier, I don't like that phrase 'Old man' anymore." [19]

The final season sees an acceleration of Sam's maturation on several fronts. The most unexpected is a revelation about his aging body that his vanity has forced him to keep hidden. Sam's self-confidence is always a part of the show, but his obsession with his hair gets highlighted more frequently in the latter half of the series. In "It's Lonely on the Top," when Carla is ashamed that she got drunk and slept with Paul, Sam seeks a way to comfort her. In the end, to reveal his own secret he's ashamed of, Sam removes a "hair replacement system" that covers a bald spot on the top of his head. Carla is shocked and delighted to learn that the perfect Sam Malone's hair is fake. Of course, the maturation isn't Sam going bald—it's his willingness to reveal it to Carla in her moment of need. As Carla says, "You are a terrific sweet guy. Anyone who would do what you just did to make someone feel better is just the best friend in the world."[20] For Sam, who is introduced to viewers as "a magnificent pagan beast"[21] who sleeps around, to come to terms with his aging and become "a terrific sweet guy"[22] eleven years later demonstrates one aspect of Sam's evolution.

SAM, THE FADING ATHLETE

When trying to understand the character of Sam Malone, it is important to note his career before owning Cheers. Sam was a relief pitcher for the Boston Red Sox, a position that comes with high fame and accolades when he is performing well, and comes with a lot of scrutiny when he is performing poorly. Danson describes the key characteristic he felt was necessary to play that position: "I had an inkling on how to play Sam Malone, because he was a relief pitcher, which comes with a certain amount of arrogance. You know, you only get called in when you're in trouble and you're there to save the day, and that takes a special kind of arrogance, I think."[23] A relief pitcher swoops in for a moment of glory and is not expected to be committed for a whole game. These are qualities that apply to Sam in his life as well. Sam loves the glory of a single moment, but lacks the ability to commit to a single woman.

Sam Malone's alcoholism cost him his career, but he transitioned, ironically, into bar ownership.[24] Several times in the show we witness Sam attempt to recapture his glory days, whether by trying to cling to his sports fame, parlaying his time pitching into a broadcasting career, striking out his old nemesis, or attempting one final comeback. Each attempt fails spectacularly. Sam Malone is reminded again and again that he has aged beyond his wasted prime.

Sam constantly succumbs to the lure of fame and has endless need for success and validation, but he is proven again and again to be past his prime. In the season 1 episode, "Sam at Eleven," Sam is asked to be interviewed for a sport show. Sam is hesitant, admitting he hasn't done an interview in years. After he agrees to do it and begins his interview, the crew ends up leaving for a more current athlete. Sam is left to lick his wounds in the back pool room, admitting to Diane how much his lack of fame is affecting him.[25] In season 3, Sam attempts again to relive his glory days by participating in a charity softball game, but he just ends up beating a bunch of Playboy playmates who were definitely not there to demonstrate their athletic prowess. Diane points out that Sam has a problem and gets his attention when she says, "You wanted to beat them more than you wanted to bed them."[26] Sam admits to Diane the drive for his competitiveness may come from his father: "When I was about six, I made my dad breakfast in bed on Father's Day. I was really proud of myself. All he could say was the eggs were too dry. And the toast was too light." Diane tells Sam, "Sam, you are an attractive man. You have many friends. You have a lot going for you. But you have one miserable character flaw . . . you and I dated for what seemed like an eternity. And I think I know you pretty well. You get into a contest, and you'd rather die than lose. I'm surmising, but I think your fear of losing drove you to drink and ruined your career."[27]

Not only has Sam aged, but the world has moved well past him, it turns out. When Sam attempts a career as a sports reporter, he can't find a way to present himself to the audience that appeals to a younger demographic. After being told he's boring the audience by using air time to chastise fans for booing the home team or to present an ill-informed take on artificial versus natural turf, Sam decides he needs to be cooler. So, this being a show set in the 1980s, he attempts to appeal to the youth by performing an awkward rap. When that fails, he turns to a ventriloquist act before admitting defeat.[28]

In the most undeniable revelation that Sam is too old for sports, Sam tries to return to professional baseball in season 10's "Take Me out of the Ball Game."[29] Improbably, Sam does make it into the Red Sox minor league system and begins traveling with the team and having success on the field. But when Carla comes to visit him, we see Sam contrasted with his younger, immature teammates, and Sam ends up telling Carla, "That's, that's baseball. That's what it's all about. And God, I hate it so much. Get me out of here, Carla, please!" When Carla asks what Sam is whining about, he explains, "It's just I don't think I like baseball anymore. You know, it's a, it's a kids' game now. And I'm not a kid anymore. You know, I thought it was gonna be like old times. You know, that's the problem. It, it was exactly like old times. I've done all this stuff before. It's just not me."[30] Sam is finally accepting that he's aged past his sports prime.

SAM, THE MATURING LOTHARIO

It might seem that identifying a character arc for Sam Malone would require a retrospective look at the series. Because the popular conception

Carla Tortelli (Rhea Perlman) and Sam Malone (Ted Danson)

of Sam Malone is as an unrepentant womanizer, surely the change to the character came near the end. After all, comparing the early libido-driven Malone from the first episodes of the series with the humbled man who attends a sex addiction group in one of the series' last episodes allows the character's evolution to stand in sharp relief. However, his maturation begins early enough to see the path laid out for Sam from very early on, even if Sam himself didn't realize he was growing up and occasionally reverted to his earlier ways in fits of rebellion against aging. This transformation begins unexpectedly early in show's run.

Viewers learn in the pilot that Sam Malone is something of a ladies' man. When a romantic partner calls and refers to Sam as "a magnificent pagan beast,"[31] the implication is clear. But, in the very next episode, "Sam's Women," Diane has already had an influence on him. A beautiful woman enters the bar and all the men take interest. But they know the drill, and all await for Sam to see her and win her over. Diane refuses to believe that Sam would be taken with a woman of such low intelligence. Sam sees her and heads over to wait on her at the bar. While serving her an "amusing little wine," Sam learns her name is Brandee with two Es, and that she will not go see an Australian film because she hates subtitles. Ultimately, Sam and Brandee with two Es don't work out, but later in the episode Sam brings in a date who pretends to have just gone to a concert with Sam and talks of Mozart. Diane catches them in their lie, and Sam admits to Diane, "You know, this week I have gone out with all the women I know. I mean, all the women I really enjoyed. And all of a sudden all I can think about is how stupid they are. I mean, my life isn't fun anymore. And it's because of you."[32] Sam Malone was a ladies' man, and the personality or intelligence of his sexual partner didn't much matter to him. But after just meeting Diane—not even dating her—he begins to reassess his standards.

Sam's womanizing is not without standards, as he avoids "married, underage, and comatose" women.[33] Despite those standards, Sam does have many low points that just come across as gross to modern viewers. Perhaps the lowest of the low is Sam trying to date a woman, Judy, AND her daughter at the same time—a daughter he used to play with when she was a little girl back when he dated her mother years ago.[34] Another inglorious moment comes in the final season when Sam has the chance to get his beloved Corvette back (he had to sell it when he needed money for the bar) and he pretends to date a recent widow to con her out of the car.[35]

In the first season, we hear Sam tell Diane, "Before you came to work at this bar, I never thought much about morality and integrity. You made me aware of all that stuff for the first time."[36] Though the line certainly earned laughs from the studio audience, modern viewers likely wince when Sam proudly claims that he can't remember how old he was when he lost his virginity, but "I know I couldn't get to her house until the crossing guard showed up." He then follows this admission with the more cringe-inducing (and likely criminal) admission that his second sexual experience was with that crossing guard.[37] While Sam did show growth and maturity throughout the show, many times he reverted to his familiar ways.

Often, Sam's escapades are just for show for the guys at the bar. When Sam asks Norm, "How come you guys remember my love life better than I do?" Norm replies, "I think it meant more to us."[38] And when referring to Sam's dating life, Carla says, "He [Sam] lives to talk about that stuff." Norm follows with, "We live to hear about it." And Cliff sums it all up: "It's a symbiotic relationship."[39] When Sam gets turned down by a woman he had been pursuing because she became engaged to another guy, Sam turns back to the gang and says, "I'm sorry. I've let you all down."[40] And he really does look upset that he didn't pull through for them.

Though the main gang applauds Sam and his womanizing endeavors, it isn't praised by everyone. By episode 2 Diane calls him a "rapidly aging adolescent."[41] In season 4, Carla's son Anthony visits the bar to tell his mother he wants to marry his girlfriend, Annie. Carla has Anthony hang out with Sam for the day, hoping his womanizing ways would rub off on her son and he would no longer want to get married so young. However, the opposite effect occurs, as by the end of the episode Anthony tells Carla he doesn't want to end up "a lonely old skirt chaser, like Sam."[42] Even a sixteen-year-old boy can recognize that it isn't a happy life.

In season 4, Diane takes a human sexuality class in which she uses Sam as a case study. While Sam is thrilled to be studied for such a class, Diane's analysis is less than favorable toward him. She writes:

> [Sam's] the image of the arrested adolescent, entirely self-oriented, still intimidated by the women around him and attempting to prove himself superior to them. Through sexual conquest, he can, for a time, quell his constant fears of inferiority and failure. Indeed, the idea of a non-sexual relationship is completely foreign to him. As the years pass

and his physical attractiveness diminishes, he'll be doomed to a life of loneliness and despair, unable to give or receive love. [43]

Elsewhere in her paper, Diane writes, "His life is cheap and pathetic." These lines were written in season 4, and as *Cheers* goes along they become prophetic as Sam attempts to continue his previous lifestyle but finds it unfulfilling.

Sam Malone's aging has very literal physical impacts on his lifestyle in some episodes besides the emotional loneliness that is examined near the series finale. In the season 9 episode, "Sam Time Next Year," viewers learn that Sam has had a standing date for Valentine's Day for years and years that he has never missed (it is never addressed what this means for the years he was dating Diane and appeared to be faithful). Each year he meets the same woman, Lauren, at the same cabin for a night of passion. But this year, Sam hurts his back and can barely move. Even after forcing Woody to drive him to the cabin in a desperate attempt to meet his date, Sam can do little more than lie down in pain. After Lauren realizes what's wrong, they commiserate about growing old (loose skin under their arms, kidney stones, gray hair). [44]

But, the true point of realizing he may be getting too old for one-night stands comes in the final season. Rebecca tells Sam she is considering marrying the plumber, Don. Sam tells Rebecca she doesn't have to settle, and then tells her, "You know, I think there's a chance for you and me if . . . in the next couple of years, the right woman doesn't come along, you're on the top of a very short list." [45] In response to this charming offer, Rebecca tells Sam:

The woman that marries you will be the all-time four-star settler. . . . Take a look at yourself. Look at you. The only thing you ever think about is sex. You think you're gonna make some woman feel special just because she's just another notch in your sliver of a headboard? Sam, I mean, wise up! Do you ever hear women talk about you anymore? You're a cliché! You are pathetic! Women talk about you out there and they laugh at you like you're a joke. [46]

Minutes later, regarding the hypothetical idea of marrying him, even Carla tells Sam: "Sammy, that's a stupid question. Not in a million years. . . . Nobody loves you as much as I do, but I know you. You know we'd be taking our wedding vows and you'd be checking out the brides-

maid. You're a hound. I can't marry a hound."[47] It is after these ex-
changes with Rebecca and Carla that Sam decides to attend a sexual
addiction group recommended by Frasier. Diane had told Sam all these
things, he's know them for years, but Sam fought off the creeping advance of age for as long as possible. When sitting down with a therapist
and group of sex addicts, Sam admits out loud,

> Well, where to begin. I don't really have a problem, it's just my friends
> think I do. I've had a lot of sex in my life. . . . I don't know why they
> think I have a problem. So I have a healthy sex drive, what's the big
> deal about that? I mean, granted, it's a big part of my life, when I'm
> not having sex I'm thinking about it. I don't want you to think that I'm
> shallow, because I have other interests, too, you know. Like, my hair,
> the babes really love my hair. And I don't know what the big deal is.
> You know, when I was growing up, it was a sign of manhood how
> many women you shagged. I guess I just missed the announcement
> when they changed the rule, so I just kept on doing it. I suppose if I'm
> really honest, I'm not that happy anymore. I suppose I'm beginning to
> realize all that skirt chasing kept me from experiencing some of the
> good things in life. Some of the important things. Whew, maybe, uh,
> maybe I'm not here for my friends. Maybe I am here for myself.[48]

Sam Malone acknowledges to himself something viewers had been told
since the Diane years: his womanizing is fun, but hollow. It does not offer
him any fulfillment, and he now recognizes that his life is emptier than he
likes.

In a way, this monologue from Sam repositions many of the most
problematic aspects of the *Cheers* legacy. Before signing off for good,
Cheers says explicitly that Sam's sexual harassment, his constant innuen-
do, and his sleeping around are artifacts of a bygone era. What's more,
they're marks of a shallow, unhappy man. Sam's behavior, which embod-
ied the sexual liberation of the 1980s, did not bring him any legitimate or
lasting happiness. Sam Malone, the iconic womanizer of the 1980s,
sought out help because "I suppose I'm beginning to realize all that skirt
chasing kept me from experiencing some of the good things in life."[49]
This doesn't excuse his behavior of the previous hundreds of episodes,
but the final word from the series is explicitly that nobody should em-
brace Sam Malone as a role model. Perhaps this could be seen as the
series writers attempting to have their cake and eat it too. Deliver hun-

dreds of punchlines about Sam's promiscuity and allow him to sexually harass his employees, but condemn it in the end. But perhaps it's also the creators recognizing an evolution that happened while the show was on the air. When the series finale was looming, Glen Charles said in an interview, "I think it is a different time now . . . I think the Sam Malone character might not in this day and age be given the same latitude he was given."[50] The fact that Sam was launched on this trajectory in the second episode makes it feel like less of a last-minute change than a very natural but slowly developing character arc.

Danson said of closing the womanizing chapter of Sam's life, "The truth is he isn't happy anymore, which is a wonderful place to take Sam. . . . Basically, he has gotten to the point that at least he realizes his old lifestyle doesn't work anymore and he isn't happy. I kind of liked that the writers did that. I liked that they identified that he is alone, that he is sad. He has always had that alcoholic sadness which I really like."[51] In the pilot, we learn that Sam has conquered an alcohol addiction, and in the end we see him taking steps to address his sexually compulsive personality.

If Ted Danson had been willing, NBC was ready to bring *Cheers* back for a twelfth year. But Danson announced that he planned to leave the series. In discussing why, Danson said of Sam, "He got older, you know . . . [the writers] tried to make him Sammy again. But he's 45 now. I'm 45. It's OK to be chasing around when you're 37. But when you're 45, it's kind of sad to be chasing around that way."[52] Ken Levine continues this line of thought on why Danson decided to leave the show, causing its end: "I've never discussed this with him, but my feeling is he knew that at a certain age the character would border on sad. The slick player might seem very charming in his 30s but a little pathetic in his 40s. I think he left because he was protecting Sam Malone."[53]

It would be incredibly depressing to leave Sam realizing that his life had no meaning, which is why the finale makes the point that the bar and his friends are much more important than the string of women Sam dated. Despite his inability to form a lasting romantic relationship, Sam and the Cheers gang formed unbreakable bonds. Even when he sells the bar and buys a boat to sail around the world, even when the bar holds the worst memories of Diane, he finds his way back there. These are his employees and friends, and they are the family he would do anything for, which he shows time and time again. The time Cliff asked to come to his place for help with his date with Maggie O'Keefe, as Cliff kept going blind at the thought of commitment.[54] The time Frasier and Lilith fought, and Sam promised to help Frasier get her back.[55] The time Norm needed a job, and Sam hired him to be his accountant.[56] The time Sam danced with Carla because she wanted to win a competition.[57] The time he taught Lilith how to drive.[58] They all adore Sam, patrons and staff alike, but Sam needs them just as much as they need him.

This is perfectly demonstrated in the season 4 episode, "Relief Bartender," in which Sam believes he is full of great ideas, and hires another bartender so he can focus his time on managing the bar and implementing new ideas. Sam is a great many things, but a great businessman he is not, and his none of his ideas work out. Forced to return to the bar, he must let go of one of the bartenders. While Woody is a friend, and perhaps more like a brother at this point, the new bartender, Ken, has a wife and two kids and is also an extremely skilled bartender. The logical choice would be to keep Ken, but Sam needs Woody. Torn between choosing between the right thing and his heart, Sam decides to keep Ken and let Woody go. As a viewer you can feel the pain and sorrow Sam has as he tells Woody. As Woody is walking out, Ken informs Sam he has been given a better offer. The relief Sam showcases as he chases Woody down to tell him he can stay in the bar can be felt through the television.[59] Sam needs Woody by his side, just as he needs Carla, Norm, Cliff, and Frasier.

This family connection is why, in the series finale when Sam so casually announces he is moving to Los Angeles and Rebecca can take over the bar, the ending feels extra cruel—after eleven years, we know Sam and the bar go hand in hand. They are linked. Frustrated with the gang's lack of support for his decision to leave, Sam snaps back at them, "I am not your mother. This is not your home."[60] But it is. For both the gang and the Sam. Which is why it is so satisfying when Sam comes back and has a late night sitting around and chatting with the Cheers gang. Sam has learned that his love life is unfulfilling and shallow, but he has a firm foundation with which he can move forward. In the episode before the series finale, Sam comes to the melancholy realization that "I'm not that happy anymore,"[61] but Sam's penultimate line is, "Boy I tell ya, I'm the luckiest son of a bitch on Earth."[62] Thanks to Sam Malone's complexity and Ted Danson's nuanced acting, these seemingly contradictory sentiments are both true.

6

THE DEVOLUTION OF REBECCA HOWE

The No-Nonsense Businesswoman Becomes All Nonsense

Do you realize everything Rebecca has attempted in her life has resulted in failure?

At the end of season 5, the writers of *Cheers* faced a new challenge. Shelley Long had decided to leave the show, and they had to figure out how best to replace a female lead character. The creators had made America fall in love with "the corkscrew turns in the relationship of Sam the bar owner and ex-baseball player and Diane the pretentious waitress,"[1] but what would the show be without that dynamic?

It's a daunting task to step into the shoes of Shelley Long and Diane Chambers. Rebecca would need to be everything Diane was not. Every flaw Diane possessed, Rebecca would counter with an asset, and vice-versa. Pompous, entitled Diane would be replaced with hardworking businesswoman Rebecca. Or so we thought. Introduced as an anti-Diane, Rebecca Howe was clearly envisioned as a serious bar manager with no romantic interest in Sam Malone. From her opening scene, the audience could assume she would be professional, focused, and in charge. She would even be intimidating. But most of those attributes would not last.

Trying to define the character of Rebecca Howe is an odd exercise because of the transformation that occurs. Now, character evolutions are natural, and often lauded, especially over the course of six seasons. They typically are signs of growth and progression. In the case of Rebecca Howe, however, it is decidedly a regression.

There are two truths that should be acknowledged about Rebecca Howe: (1) Watching her emotional meltdowns is objectively funny, and (2) her transition from a professional, respectable career woman to . . . whatever her role is six years later is problematic for a show with only a few recurring female characters. The nature of her character change, contrasted with the other workers and patrons at Cheers, helps to identify why Rebecca Howe's journey stands out. While every other character has ups and downs during the run of *Cheers*, the other characters either end up more or less parallel from beginning to end in terms of life situation, or else their situation has improved—in some cases, dramatically.

Initially, we're presented with Sam Malone, an immature lothario who is a recovering alcoholic. His low point is his return to drinking at the beginning of season 3, but by the end of the series he has, of his own choice, begun to attend a sex addiction group because he has matured enough to realize the life he's leading is not healthy or geared toward long-term happiness. During the course of the series he goes from owner

Rebecca Howe (Kirstie Alley) and Sam Malone (Ted Danson)

of the bar, to bartender, and back to owner. While Sam has his down moments, things have a way of always swinging back in his favor.

Diane is a down-on-her-luck intellectual who has a rocky relationship with Sam, but in the end leaves Cheers to pursue a writing opportunity. When we next see her in the series finale, she is winning an award for writing a screenplay.

Carla doesn't change as much as Sam or Diane. When we meet her she's a single mother who is rude to customers, and that's pretty much where we leave her. There are more kids, and she is a widow, but in terms of her work status and personality, little has changed from the Carla in the season premiere to the Carla in the season finale. Norm has his ups and downs in terms of his employment (mostly nonexistent) and his relationship with Vera (mostly asexual), but in the end he's a man who drinks from the same barstool he always has. Similarly, Cliff gets into a spot of trouble occasionally with his job, and actually manages to have a romance or two, but remains a talkative know-it-all from beginning to end. Coach is the same lovably slow-on-the-uptake, grandfatherly figure from season 1 through season 3.

Woody has a major transformation in terms of life situation even as he remains the same naive, small-town boy who walked into Cheers looking for a job (and we're so thankful he never changed from that). When Woody first appears on the show, he's a fish out of water, a country rube from a farming town trying to find his way in the big city. When the show ends, he has married the fabulously wealthy, but equally naive, Kelly Gaines, with whom he has had a long and loving relationship. He has also been elected to the Boston city council but is still blissfully naive and earnest.

Frasier has significantly more alteration to his character, having arrived at Cheers while dating Diane to counsel Sam, but ends the series married to Lilith, with a son. This vitality is perhaps one reason Frasier was chosen to carry a spin-off, as beloved characters like Norm and Cliff definitely function as side characters and not central protagonists. Among the Cheers patrons, he is the closest to a downward spiral, similar to Rebecca's. After all, in the final season his wife, Lilith, cheats on him, and at one point he threatens to commit suicide by jumping out a building window. However, *Cheers* ends with Frasier and Lilith seemingly reconciled, and Frasier content. It's not until the first scene of the spin-off

Frasier that viewers learn that Frasier and Lilith have divorced, and Frasier Crane begins his own eleven-year evolution on that series.

Rebecca, however, starts off at the top of the mountain and just slides right on down for six years in a continual descent. What contributed massively to this change in defining the character is Alley's acting ability. Writer Cheri Steinkellner comments, "[Alley] started crying like nobody since Lucy Ricardo. That was the day we got our handle on Rebecca. We figured out she was not just another loser, she was the biggest, saddest loser in the bar."[2] While Rebecca is a self-proclaimed professional businesswoman, she is constantly eyeing advancement through marriage more than through merit. But after six years, she is undeniably all nonsense. The descent is a curious one, and it is a credit to Kirstie Alley's performance that the many roles Rebecca plays through her six seasons all work for comedy, even if they're inconsistent for a character.

In her first appearance, the audience is told in no uncertain terms that Rebecca is not someone to be messed with. Carla says that she "eats live sharks for breakfast," and Sam complains that she has taken away "all the charm, all the warmth" from his office by making it professional (but interestingly, more feminine). When Sam tells her she should lighten up, she coldly responds that "running a bar is hard work." And she immediately attacks Sam by tell him, "We only met a few seconds ago and I'm already tired of you. You're giving me a headache behind the eyes and it feels like a tiny little insect boring into my brain." These comments all take place within her opening scene on the show. Rebecca continues to inform Sam, "Mr. Malone, I've had a great deal of training and education to get to this point. And it's important to me that I succeed."[3] This version of Rebecca is clearly a hard worker, but quite quickly we see cracks in this armor she presents to Sam and the staff at Cheers.

Perhaps "no-nonsense" is not the perfect description of her first appearance, as she does fall apart a little bit at the mention of her boss, the silver-haired Evan Drake, played by Tom Skerritt. Although he doesn't appear in person until the tenth episode of season 6, his presence is felt from Rebecca's first episode. Drake calls the bar and Carla informs Rebecca he is on the line for her. She frantically scrambles back to take the call in her office. In a schoolgirl fluster, unable to open her office door, Rebecca mutters the line, "I've locked myself out. No I haven't."[4] This moment establishes what will ultimately become who her character is—a built-up facade of an empowered businesswoman but, deep down, a frivolous mess. Regarding this locked-door moment, there's a very telling quote from director James Burrows about discovering the comedy in the character of Rebecca Howe. While they were happy to have cast Alley as a new character replacing Long in the ensemble, the writers were struggling to hit the right notes with her in the first episode in which she appeared. Burrows explains that they couldn't seem to find the comedy:

> She wouldn't give Sam Malone the time of day. It wasn't working. She had to exit to her office, and somehow the office door got locked. An accident. She started wrestling with it, and we cracked up. It dawned on us that we had to make her a woman of the eighties and the nineties who thinks she's empowered but can't get through the day. The minute we found her frailty and vulnerability, then we had it. [5]

Les Charles on this same moment notes, "It's this little dithering moment. It was the first time we saw comedy potential."[6] To cast Alley without realizing her full comedic potential says a lot about her overall acting and the presence she would bring to the show. But it was this small gag that shaped the character of Rebecca to what we now know, as that small moment of frailty would balloon into emotional breakdowns and general incompetence. In order to appreciate this transformation, understanding her initial characterization is key.

It was always understood that another female character lead was necessary to counter Sam in Diane's absence. But the interesting idea was to reverse the relationship that had existed between Sam and Diane. Rather than have Sam be the boss and the woman be the waitress, what if the woman now owned or managed the bar, and Sam was a bartender working for her? James Burrows bluntly stated, "The one thing you won't see next year is a blonde waitress."[7] This created a brand-new setup that would lend itself to new scenarios never explored in the previous five seasons. To begin the process, the writers wrote a short scene for a "tough woman boss" and started auditioning potential actresses. [8]

When creating the character of Rebecca, the creators certainly went in a different direction in every possible way. Where Diane was blonde, Rebecca was brunette. Diane was delicate, graceful, and full of decorum; Rebecca was a booming presence where pratfalls abound. Diana had been an intellectual who in many ways thought she was better than the bar due to her education, while Rebecca was a professional brought in to manage the bar and who equated her success with the bar's success. Diane pursued every form of art studies in existence; Rebecca studied business. Diane wanted to create; Rebecca wanted status. Diane found her worth in her intellect; Rebecca found it in the men she pursued. Diane was infatuated with Sam; Rebecca barely gave him the time of day. Most significantly, Diane left her man to pursue a career. Rebecca married a man and gave up her career. Even the acting differed—where Long's strength rested in her eloquent monologues, Alley's brilliance is in her physical comedy. However, their similarities lie in their beauty, wealthy background, and expectations of an upper-class life.

This opposition extends into reality for the two actresses, as even their careers were opposite. The 1980s were a time when movie stars were considered to have a status high above television stars. Although film and television actors have become more equal today in status (in fact, it can be argued that it is heading toward just the opposite—television actors are given more fame and credit for their roles than in films), in a move typical of the time period, Long left a top-rated TV show to pursue a career in film. On the other hand, Alley had been doing movies, and took on the role, exclaiming, "I'm a movie star! They'd be lucky to have me."[9] Although she admits she hadn't seen the show, if she had, she may have been more nervous.

Despite all the differences, it is inevitable that Diane and Rebecca, and Long and Alley, would be compared. On one of the top-rated television shows in the country it would be foolish to think a series could get away with transitioning to a new main character without seeing comparisons. But Ted Danson claimed, "There will be comparisons made between Kirstie and Shelley, but in a while they'll all disappear."[10] And true to his prediction, it quickly became all about Kirstie Alley. And her six seasons on *Cheers* were a tremendous success.

Although it was known that Long would be leaving the show, there was secrecy about the auditioning process. Casting director Jeff Greenberg recalls casting Alley for Rebecca:

> We wanted to keep [her auditions] secret, because we didn't want to shove it in Shelley's face; it was only November, and she was going to be there until March. So we had all these secret meetings. My own assistants didn't even know it was happening. We had her come to the studio on a Saturday, when no one was on the *Cheers* set, and she did two scenes, one with Ted, and one with Rhea.[11]

Kirstie instantly seemed like the perfect fit and exactly what the show was looking for.

James Burrows elaborates about Kirstie Alley: "She was an unfamiliar face on television so we wouldn't be tilting the balance of the show by bringing in a known quantity. She had an incredible sexy voice that was perfect to drive Ted bananas. In the test scene, there was a line where she says she's not attracted to Sam. With Kirstie, you believed it."[12] But as easy as the casting process might have seemed, the difficulty lay with defining the role of Rebecca. Les Charles recalls, "We thought we'd cast her as a villainess. She'll be the dragon lady, Cruella de Vil, and make everyone else uncomfortable and funny."[13] And Burrows claims, "We thought of the part as a martinet, a bitch."[14] But that characterization wasn't working. On his blog, Ken Levine describes part of the evolution process of the character:

> The change came because Rebecca as the martinet just wasn't funny. Kirstie Alley was game and it wasn't her fault but the character as originally conceived just didn't pop. In one episode though, she had to fall apart for some reason and was hysterical. We realized that the more neurotic, insecure, and sexually frustrated she was—the funnier she was. So the character evolved in that direction.
>
> Side note: One of the hardest tricks to pull off is being able to cry while still being funny. You have to feel for the character and still feel it's okay to laugh. No one I've ever worked with is better at that than Kirstie.[15]

Those familiar with the show know that the initial descriptions of her are not the Rebecca Howe that existed over six seasons. Rebecca can be seen instantly as a sultry brunette, but a word continually used to describe her in those beginning, defining days is "vulnerable." Once they added in this side to her, the character took on a new form; as the writers poked holes in the privileged manager facade she presents, Rebecca reveals her true self.

Comparing Rebecca's initial scene on the show with her last reveals just how much change occurred. When we meet Rebecca for the first time, she descends the stairs to Cheers, the door being held open by Sam. Sam assumes he is going to instantly win her over with his charm, but he most assuredly does not. She walks in wearing a red jacket, pencil skirt, sheer black tights, and heels, with her hair down around her shoulders while holding a notepad, looking perfectly the part of a serious business-woman. She doesn't say a word before the screen fades to black indicating the commercial break, and the audience is left with her image alone in their mind for a few moments. Sam Malone, our endlessly, overly confident leading man is at a loss for words and is only able to mutter "booah" at the first sight of her. Even after Carla's introduction and Rebecca saying, "How do you do?" with her hand extended to him, Sam can still only mutter yet again, "booah."[16]

Sam is used to beautiful women, as we are shown and told repeatedly throughout the series. Therefore, with this interaction, we must infer there is something else about Rebecca affecting him. Her confidence and overall commanding presence overwhelms Sam. This is a harsh contrast to her final moment in season 11, where she is flitting around Cheers, having just married a plumber and claiming she will never work there again. The descent continues further through the spin-off, *Frasier*. Although Alley herself never appeared on the show to portray Rebecca, we are told through Sam that Rebecca's husband invented a crucial plumbing part, made lots of money, and left her, and that Rebecca is back at the Cheers. Not working, just back at Cheers.[17]

Ultimately, Rebecca regresses as a character because Cheers lets her. She has been in rigorous settings her whole life (army brat, business school, competitive corporation). Her father is an ex-Navy man, her mother a concert cellist, her sister Susan (played by Marcia Cross) is an actress, a former Miss San Diego who frequently stole Rebecca's boyfriends while growing up. Rebecca was forced to be the best or aim to be the best. She tells Sam, "I was taught to win. To strive. To achieve. To never ever settle."[18] Her background held her to a nearly impossible standard for most, but truly impossible for Rebecca. However, at Cheers, it is different. She doesn't have to be better than anyone (although, she automatically thinks she is), and she doesn't have to beat anyone. They let her be herself and accept her for it. In fact, she is loved and accepted more by the Cheers gang when she shows her true self, messy as it is, than when acting like the boss who has it all together.

Clearly, life does not take Rebecca where she expected it to. In the beginning of season 8, Sam tells her it has been three years of her managing the bar, and she cries, saying "Has it been that long."[19] Rebecca herself can't believe her lot in life, exclaiming, "How can somebody as beautiful as I am be such a loser?"[20] Rebecca hits ultimate rock bottom when Sam himself rejects her. Alley describes that moment as one of her favorites: "I had gotten drunk and realized I was basically worthless as a human being. I came on to [Sam] and he refused me. For the character of Sam to refuse any woman was a landmark in itself. I guess you could say I hit the all-time bottom when even Sam Malone rejected me."[21] However, Alley did win an Emmy for that very scene.[22]

Rebecca showing her "true self" through her time at Cheers is not an issue, except for the fact that there are times when she is a powerful, confident woman sprinkled throughout each season. There are times when she can handle running the bar, knows exactly what to do, and others rely on her. But then there are times when she can't do even the simplest of tasks. As a character Rebecca is at best inconsistent; at worst, hypocritical. She bounces back and forth between a confident business-woman and a complete disaster. Usually, this appears to be at the whim of the writers. Rebecca is there to give a ditzy moment for comedic effect or there to put Sam in his place for a dramatic scene. She makes mistakes with serious consequences, such as losing the bar's liquor license, flooding it, and then ultimately burning the bar down. And yet she is also the superintendent at her apartment building and runs private events at the bar. This inconsistency makes it hard to tell which Rebecca is the real Rebecca.

In season 11, Rebecca's father visits and tells her that because of all her failures, he is taking away her allowance and she needs to come home. Carla is quick to question the fact that a woman in her late 30s still receives an allowance from her father. Rebecca agrees, and in an increasingly high-pitched voice announces to the bar: "Everyone, I . . . I have something to say to you. I came here to this bar five years ago a strong, independent businesswoman, and now I'm going to go back home and move back in with mommy and daddy."[23] But in reality it is all a ploy to get more money out of her father, as he did not think she would actually come home and instead increases her allowance so she would stay in Boston. This makes Rebecca seem smarter than she presents herself to be. We commend the writers for making Rebecca a complicated character and not one dimensional, but the inconsistencies are perplexing. In the end, Rebecca is a mixture of typical female character characteristics: she's cool and sexy when the writers want her to be, and vulnerable and messy when it's funny. In some ways it is refreshing to see a female character behave this way, to have the gorgeous cool girl suddenly become not so cool, and then flip back to being confident—just as real women are never just one or the other. At the end of the series, Mike Duffy and Susan Stewart note about her character:

> Has any woman on TV ever worn her insecurities as flamboyantly as Rebecca Howe? Maybe one: Lucy. In an era of humorless exaltation of everything estrogen, Rebecca was a welcome breath of unfiltered air. (Yes, she smoked. Remember? She burned down the bar.) Rebecca knew what she was supposed to be—empowered, disciplined, caring—but she just couldn't be it. Drunk, bloated with pizza and putting clumsy moves on Sam after being dumped by her millionaire boyfriend, she was everybody's weaker half, which is why everybody loved her.[24]

But her downfall at times goes too far. All the strength of her character recedes as time goes by, leaving her with no respect from others. It is unfortunate that Rebecca ultimately becomes a female boss who is not respected by anyone at the bar or by the company as a whole, a woman who is boy crazy and whose career path is by way of demotions.

Speaking of boy crazy, if there is a wealthy man in Boston, Rebecca is, at some point, probably in love with him. For all her career goals, Rebecca's greatest aspiration in life is a husband. Or rather, a wealthy husband. Indeed, Rebecca is very interested in men, but only rich ones. At the end of the series, in a moment of self-reflection, Rebecca admits to Sam that when it comes to men she falls for their money, stating, "I allow myself to just fall all over him just because he's rich."[25] Aside from their wealth, Rebecca always seems to find herself romantically entangled with her bosses: Evan Drake, Martin Teal, and eventually, Sam Malone.

From her first introduction, we know of Rebecca's crush on Evan Drake, the very successful (and at the time, married) CEO of the company that bought Cheers from Sam after his final breakup with Diane at the end of season 5. Rebecca is obsessively in love with Drake, although it becomes evident that her love is more about the life he could give her rather than about the man himself. Does she truly love Evan Drake? Most likely not. Does she love the life he has? Most definitely. Over the course of season 6, Rebecca tries endlessly to get Drake's attention and tell him how she feels, resulting in many embarrassing (yet hilarious) situations. She kisses him at a holiday party, with Sam's encouragement.[26] She plots to win him over while on his yacht by pretending Sam is her date, forcing

Rebecca Howe (Kirstie Alley)

Sam's real date to pretend to be his sister, causing Drake to ultimately pursue Sam's real date.[27] Later in the season, Rebecca gets trapped in Drake's bedroom closet when she comes over to see the house while Norm paints the interiors, and Drake returns home early from a trip.[28] And then in the season 6 finale, Drake is promoted to run the company from the office in Japan, and Rebecca throws an impromptu goodbye party at Cheers. Refusing to let him leave the country without telling him how she feels, Rebecca locks Drake's driver in the coat closet with Sam's help, and she drives Drake to the airport. As she begins to tell him her feelings, Drake directs her to pick up Kristy, the woman who will be accompanying him to Japan. Distraught and heartbroken, Rebecca accidently crashes the car, thus ending for good any and all relationship potential with Evan Drake.[29]

It is a truth universally acknowledged that a single attractive woman on a television show must have a love interest. Since Evan Drake is no longer an option, in the premiere of season 7, Rebecca meets her new boss, Martin Teal, who immediately asks her out multiple times. Rebecca declines, but Teal is so aggressive in his pursuit that Rebecca ultimately fakes a relationship with Sam to avoid his advances as she fears losing her job if she continues declining him without a reason. It is a tragic reflection of the culture toward women (not that enough improvement has been made) that Rebecca felt her career was at stake and she must lie about being in a relationship so as to not offend her boss, rather than just telling him she is not interested. Thankfully, the Martin Teal storyline is short-lived.

In season 8, Robin Colcord appears as a new wealthy love interest. Robin is by far Rebecca's longest romantic relationship throughout the series. However, it is not a good one as he lies, cheats, and clearly doesn't really know her. Yet she stays with him through it all, simply because he is ridiculously wealthy. At the end of season 8 it is revealed that Robin is only dating Rebecca to get corporate secrets—yet she still stays with him because he is rich. Robin eventually goes to jail and loses all his money, but Rebecca stays with him, convinced he has money stashed somewhere. When she learns he truly has no money left, she leaves him for good.

Sam endlessly pursues and attempts to seduce Rebecca for years, crossing the border into harassment multiple times. It his behavior okay? No. It is one of the parts of the show that has aged the least well, but it is a part of the time period and forever a part of the show. Despite this, however, Sam and Rebecca clearly care deeply for one another and consistently provide the friendship each needs. Interestingly, having Rebecca in Sam's life brought out a new side to Sam that the writers might not have anticipated. Television critic Aljean Harmetz claims, "Characters are not always docile enough to obey their creators. To their surprise, the Charles brothers discovered that the reversed situation loosened Sam up and made him a little more carefree."[30] And Les Charles notes, "Where he was straight man to Shelley, now he can be more of a goof-off."[31] Whether this was due to the new character of Rebecca, or due to Ted Danson's different chemistry with Kirstie Alley versus Shelley Long, is unclear and will never be known, but it is evident there is a new, lighter side to Sam explored in the later seasons of the series.

Through many ups and downs of their relationship, Sam proves to be a great friend to Rebecca. Perhaps most significant is when he tries to stop her wedding to Robin after Rebecca drunkenly admits that she doesn't love him and shouldn't marry him. Rebecca wakes up the next morning with no memory of what she said. Sam, knowing the truth, rushes to the city hall wedding to make sure it doesn't happen. This is an interesting parallel to the season 3 wedding in which Diane was going to marry Frasier; Sam flew to Italy in an attempt to stop their wedding (but does not find them). That action was not about caring for Diane, but rather selfishly wanting her all for himself regardless of what she wanted. (Turns out, however, she did want Sam and not Frasier.) Sam stops Rebecca's wedding for purely selfless reasons and for her benefit.

In one of the last episodes of the series, a plumber named Don comes to make a repair at Cheers and immediately falls for Rebecca. Where other men were aggressive and dismissive, Don is respectful and caring toward Rebecca, and the pair quickly become engaged. Well, sort of. Rebecca desperately wants to say yes when Don proposes, but cannot bring herself to do so because he is a plumber and therefore not wealthy. She cannot believe that she would end up with him, yet loves him. Eventually they return to Cheers one afternoon, having just been married. Tragically, as mentioned earlier in the chapter, we are told on *Frasier* that Rebecca's happiness was short-lived: Don got rich and divorced Rebecca.

Despite all these love interests, none were an actual option. Yes, Robin proposed and came back for her multiple times, but it was clear he didn't really know her, and she didn't really love him. What she loved was his money. And the same can be said for all the men Rebecca was interested in, aside from Sam and Don. While none of Rebecca's romantic storylines reflect highly on Rebecca and on women in general, it is clear they were written in for the comedy they established. *New York Times* TV critic Josh Wolk comments on Alley's performance after discovering Robin had been seeing another woman: "While her character began as brusque and (mostly) self-assured, the writers quickly discovered she was much more fun as a hapless, gold-digging mess. She is positively Lucille Ball-like in the final scene as she swings between faux-bravado and blubbering: Nobody cries funnier than Kirstie Alley."[32] Kirstie is phenomenal in this role and, as we stated before, watching her meltdowns is objectively funny. But does the laugh justify the downward spiral of the character? Each viewer may have a different answer to that question.

THE WOMEN OF CHEERS

For a show about a bar in the 1980s, *Cheers* features very powerful female characters. While there are flaws in the way they are presented at times, the women of *Cheers* are consistently much more motivated in life than are the male characters. As Norm, Cliff, and, by the end, even Frasier seem to be content in hanging out at the bar each night (or day) to drink beer, Rebecca, Diane, Carla, and Lilith all either continuously work hard or aspire for more.

The four main female characters on *Cheers* represent very different types of women. Carla, the only female character to appear in all eleven seasons (not to mention every single episode) is the single mom, forced to work full time and carry her family on her own, accepting that her life is hard and that it probably will never change. Diane, Rebecca, and Lilith are each educated, professional women. A relatively new representation of woman—as Diane states, "I'm so proud of us. We women have taken our place in society as never before. Working, doing, rising on merit through the ranks. We are taking our place alongside of, and in many cases above men. Once exploited. Now we are equal."[33] Diane seems to have endless educational pursuits and ends the show having won an award for her writing. Rebecca lived a life of privilege, went to school, and was a manager of a bar. She initially had career goals and aspirations and was on track to achieve them. And Lilith, perhaps the most liberated (but simultaneously buttoned-up) of them all, had a very successful career, a happy (for a time) marriage, and a son. She even convinced Frasier to be the primary caregiver to their son, Frederick, because her career was more successful and therefore, important. All four women are dynamic, interesting, powerful characters. But they are, for the most part, still merely side characters whose lives and stories are dictated by the men of *Cheers*.

There are two episodes that particularly dwell on the main characters' physical appearances to drive the plot. Lilith and Rebecca each receive makeovers, which greatly alter the reactions they receive from men. There is also another episode in which Cliff's neighbor receives a makeover, falling into the well-worn cliché of removing the glasses, adding some makeup, and poof, she's a whole new beautiful girl.[34] There are zero episodes featuring a male character receiving a makeover, although Sam's vanity and interest in hair products does bridge that gap somewhat.

In the season 5 episode, "Abnormal Psychology," Frasier and Lilith appear on a psychology television show together. At this time they are not dating, previously having gone on a terrible date, and neither is thrilled to have to work with the other. Diane takes it upon herself to convince Lilith that Frasier's hostility toward her is a mark of attraction, and that she can be the type of woman Frasier wants if she would simply soften the edges and "perhaps loosen the bun a bit to release some of the tension in [her] face"[35] and, of course, add a little makeup. Lilith, typically buttoned up to the top button of her blouse with her hair pulled back in a tight bun, appears on the show with her hair down, the top buttons undone on her blouse, and wearing makeup, earrings, and a pearl necklace. This new "alluring" look has the immediate desired effect on Frasier, and the two share an innuendo-filled interview on the television show.

In the season 7 episode, "The Gift of the Woodi," it is Lilith giving the makeover as Rebecca turns to her for fashion advice for a woman in business. Rebecca asks, "Lilith, I love that way you look . . . I love the way you dress. I admire your style. Do you think that you could help me develop a more businesslike appearance?"[36] Needing to attend a corporate meeting, Rebecca wants to be taken more seriously, resulting in this conclusion:

> I have just about had it up to here with this corporation. I get invited to
> my first power lunch meeting, and nobody even notices me. As usual, I

am just ignored. And I finally figured out why. I am just too darned attractive. You know, the problem is that everybody just sees me as a sex kitten. I hate that. I think I need to find a new role model. If only I knew one successful career woman with an image that invites no sexual appeal whatsoever.

The result is an exact reversal of Diane's previous advice to Lilith. Rebecca emerges with her hair slicked back in a bun, buttoned to the top button blouse, covered by a suit jacket with a skirt, complete with ace bandage strapped around her breasts. She, hilariously, also mimics Lilith stiff walk. Lilith explains to Rebecca the reason behind her appearance:

Lilith: There are two approaches a woman can take in turning her look to her advantage. The first is to play upon the male sexual drive and turn yourself into an object of desire. I have opted for the second.

Rebecca: What's that?

Lilith: Scaring them stupid.

Lilith tells Carla that they are going to "show those executives what a real no-nonsense businesswoman looks like." Carla responds, "Oh. A man."[37] Both these makeovers highlight unfortunate television and cultural ideals around women; the need to take away a women's sexual appeal in order to be taken seriously at work is just as problematic as the need to add makeup and jewelry to a woman just to appeal more to a man.

While there are strong female characters on *Cheers*, the show consistently demeans and objectifies women and displays moments of sexual harassment. We recognize that *Cheers* is a product of its time and a reflection of the culture of the 1980s and early 1990s; however, watching and analyzing parts of the show from today's perspective is nothing short of jarring and slightly horrifying. *Cheers* is not alone among sitcoms in using sexual harassment and comments toward women for humor as this has been commonplace since the beginning of television. However, notably, some believe this has become less common since the early 1990s when Anita Hill accused her former boss, then U.S. Supreme Court nominee Clarence Thomas, of sexual harassment. This highly publicized event brought the issue of workplace sexual harassment to society's attention.[38] Robert Thompson, director of the Bleier Center for Television & Popular

Culture at Syracuse University, states, "I think television and 'Hollywood' did respond to that. Hollywood may not have responded to it in how they actually behave as we're finding out, but I think there was a consciousness about it. I don't think the first three seasons of 'M*A*S*H' would have been made after Anita Hill."[39] And Amanda Lotz, author of the book, "Redesigning Women: Television after the Network Era," notes, "The late 1990s is when those jokes stopped being funny,"[40] particularly on network television. However, cable shows did not show as much of a decline.

Aside from sexual harassment being morally wrong behavior, there are major issues with the portrayal of it on television. Shortly after *Cheers* went off the air, in a 1994 article titled "TV Sitcoms Are Rife with Sexual Harassment, Study Says," James Hannah states that "lewd remarks, suggestive touches and other forms of sexual harassment can trigger lawsuits in the real world. But a research team has found that it's routine in the world of sitcoms."[41] Hannah also notes that a major problem is that in sitcoms, sexual harassment is "presented in such a way to make it seem acceptable," as "the behavior was reinforced by laugh tracks and by the lack of consequences for characters who harassed."[42] The continual witnessing of such actions, particularly when received with a laugh, marks it as fine and acceptable and can promote and encourage such behavior in real life.

Understandably, it is not helpful, nor productive, to list the times in which the show portrays sexual harassment or physical assault (yes, there was the time Sam slapped Diane. And she slapped him right back. And then he slapped her. And she slapped him. In fact, this slap volley back and forth pretty much sums up their entire relationship).[43] At the unavoidable surface level is the fact that Sam relentlessly pursues his employee or employer (Diane or Rebecca) throughout all eleven seasons. This is so standard in *Cheers* that the portrayal of harassment can be made to seem acceptable or simply part of everyday life. We can't change any of this. These moments and dialogues exist, the writers wrote them and the actors portrayed them, and they reflect the time in which *Cheers* was created and set.

At the time of writing this book, 2018, sexual harassment and assault is a commanding topic. This is the power that comes with watching a show thirty years after it aired—we have the hindsight of seeing how wrong something actually is, as society has (hopefully) progressed. Was this behavior wrong thirty years ago? Yes. But was it culturally accept-able? Yes. Or, at least much more so than now. Which is why these scenarios were not only allowed on network television but also used as jokes and punchlines that the audience went along with. In light of the #MeToo movement and a cultural reckoning with the pervasiveness of sexual harassment, it is less likely this type of behavior will be allowed on television in the future. But this is a cultural history, and what is portrayed on television is often either a reflection of or a reaction to what society really is.

While there are offensive, belittling, sexual comments and harass-ments made throughout the series, there are two episodes that stand out, as their storylines center around a main character being sexually harassed. In the finale of season 7, Frasier's former colleague, Dr. Lawrence Cran-dell, comes to Boston to promote his latest book on marriage fidelity, titled *The Forever Couple: The Joy of Loving One Person for the Rest of Your Life.* Crandell claims ten months of celibacy, as he has been away from his wife on a book tour. After meeting everyone at the bar, Dr. Crandell needs to make a copy of a review of his book and uses the copier in Rebecca's office. Rebecca enters the office as he is just finishing, and he lags behind to ask her a question. This is their exchange:

Dr. Crandell: I hope you won't take this the wrong way, but my field is human sexual dynamics, and just now I had the strangest impres-sion . . . please tell me if I'm wrong . . . that something happened when you and I were introduced. I sensed some spark, some flicker of re-sponse on your part, very subtle, but unmistakable. Was I imagining that?

Rebecca: I think so.

Dr. Crandell: Well, my mistake. I'm sure you understand.

Rebecca: Of course.

Dr. Crandell: You are aware I wasn't being judgmental.

Rebecca: Of course.

Dr. Crandell: It's the response itself that interested me, purely as a scientist. And you are quite sure that on some very basic level you didn't experience an undeniable attraction?

Rebecca: Positive.

Dr. Crandell: Well, I'm glad we cleared that up. Still I can't keep wondering whether your subconscious may not be trying to tell us something.

Rebecca: I swear to you . . .

Dr. Crandell [interrupting her]: When I hear such facile denial, it always sets off a little alarm in my head.

Rebecca: Dr. Crandell.

Dr. Crandell: Call me Lawrence.

Rebecca: Let me make this as clear as I know how. There was no attraction when we met or since. I felt nothing. I feel nothing. Zero. Nada. Zip.

Dr. Crandell: "Zip." Interesting unconscious choice of word.[44]

It is then Dr. Crandell finally leaves the office. It is important to note this took place in Rebecca's office, her private space. Where she should feel safe. And that despite Rebecca's insistence on not being attracted to him, he continues to question and pressure her—"Are you quite sure?"— as though she couldn't possibly understand what it is to be attracted to someone and therefore she must be wrong and needs him to explain it to her.

Later, Rebecca brushes Dr. Crandell off after he asks for a couple of drinks. Sam and Frasier approach Rebecca, asking why she was so rude to Dr. Crandell. As she tries to explain the interaction, Frasier and Sam actually convince Rebecca that she was wrong and should apologize. Rebecca remarks, "Gee, I guess I could have been wrong. What if he was just being psychological or something. I should apologize to him, huh?" And then she runs over to apologize to Dr. Crandell for getting upset and hopes he doesn't think she is rude. Yes, he didn't do anything physically wrong. But that's not all sexual harassment is—it is a feeling of helplessness, of being trapped as unwanted sexual advances are made. As Rebecca apologizes, Dr. Crandell switches the narrative to play the victim himself—claiming to be awkward and uncomfortable around women, while rubbing his foot along her leg. "I'm sorry, I thought it was a table leg. A supple, quivering table leg that goes on forever," he claims. It's a tragically common move to convince victims that what has happened is somehow their fault. Frasier and Sam still don't believe Rebecca when she tells them, "He toed my calf." Frasier defends his colleague, telling Rebecca, "Do you realize that you're impugning the reputation of the man that literally wrote the book on fidelity in marriage. You've insulted him and frankly you've insulted me." And Sam attempts to explain to her what her real problem is: "No, you know, I see what's going on here. You've just projected your frustrations onto somebody else because it's been too long since you've had your tires rotated."

What is written for laughs is a scenario far too many women have faced at some point in their lives. This episode perfectly captures the helplessness women feel in these situations, especially as her closest friends won't listen to her or understand how Dr. Crandell is making her feel. It's a grim episode, but it is strengthened because Rebecca does not back down. For all her flightiness, for all her nonsense and, at times, ditziness, Rebecca can handle herself with men. Sure, she caters to their every desire when she is in love with them, but she always stands up to them when she doesn't. She has brushed off advances for years. She doesn't give in to her boss, Martin Teal, when he attempts to date her. And she insistently attempts to make Dr. Crandell admit to what he has done.

In the seventeenth episode of season 8, Woody finally meets his girlfriend Kelly's mother. He is extremely nervous and desperately wants Kelly's mother to like him, as he admits the rest of Kelly's family hates him. While attending a large dinner party, Kelly's mother is alone with Woody and aggressively kisses him on the couch after telling him Kelly is too young for him, and that he has the maturity to appreciate older women, like herself. Woody forces her off of him, but she continually and frequently touches him inappropriately through the night as she pinches his butt, holds his hand, adjusts his napkin on his lap, uses her feet on him underneath the table, tells him of her "coconut cracking thighs" and coquettishly says to him, "Is there something about me that makes you nervous." All of this causes Woody to have an outburst at dinner in front of the other guests, yelling, "I won't have sex with you. I won't! I won't! I won't! No sex. Do you hear me?"[45] Kelly apologizes to Woody for her mother, justifying it by saying that her mother just likes to flirt and it was all just "innocent fun." An older, more powerful individual goes after a younger, innocent individual who doesn't want to cause a problem or make a fuss. Woody needs Kelly's mother to like him as she is his last hope in the Gaines family.

On October 5, 2017, the *New York Times* published a breaking story in which actress Ashley Judd accused media mogul Harvey Weinstein of sexual harassment. The article alone triggered a domino effect in which dozens of high-profile individuals from all industries have been accused of sexual harassment. Ten days after the article was published, actress Alyssa Milano tweeted the following: "If you've been sexually harassed or assaulted write 'me too' as a reply to this tweet" along with an image of text stating, "Me Too. Suggested by a friend: 'If all the women who have been sexually harassed or assaulted wrote "Me too." as a status, we might give people a sense of the magnitude of the problem.'"[46] This tweet is credited with turning the accusations into a movement. The downfalls of careers were immediate—CEOs were fired, actors replaced, political leaders disgraced. For the first time it felt like no powerful man was safe from the consequences of his unethical and immoral actions.

At the time of the writing of this book, we are deep in and yet still at the very start of the #MeToo movement. It is just beginning to unfold. Accusations and revelations are still pouring in as women and men alike stand up to their abusers. We don't know what this means for the future; in a year's time we could be looking at a completely different landscape. What we do know is that this movement changes how we view the past—how we look at our own culture as portrayed in popular culture, such as on *Cheers*. Noel Murray, in his analysis of an episode in which Diane is sexually assaulted by Norm's boss until Norm intervenes and is then fired, notes, "I also always find TV's evolving attitudes toward sexual assault fascinating. In this case, I doubt that a sitcom today could have a scene like the one between Diane, Norm, and Norm's boss in the pool room, because who would believe that Norm could be fired for what happened there?"[47] As we watch and study past television shows, we should note where they are representative of an unfortunate past that can serve as a marker of where society has evolved. In turn, we should consider contemporary entertainment and examine what values are being normalized as unquestioned truths, presented regularly in the art and diversions we consume.

7

SAM AND DIANE

Will They, Won't They, They Did,
They Don't, Now What?

Breaking up has always been the cornerstone of our relationship.

There are many notable achievements that *Cheers* pulled off to earn its hallowed status in popular culture. It went from the least watched show on television to the most watched. It juggled a shifting roster of actresses and actors without losing its comedic touch. It drew a huge audience as essentially two different shows. There's the Diane era with Shelley Long and the Rebecca era with Kirstie Alley. Pulling off that transition while maintaining its quality and devoted fans is one of the greatest success stories in sitcom history. But, in terms of long-term impact on the sitcom in American television, the Sam and Diane relationship is the most significant aspect of the *Cheers* legacy. Television (and *Cheers*) writer David Isaacs argues, "The best comedies are constructed around a core relationship," and "Diane Chambers (Shelley Long) and Sam Malone (Ted Danson), in particular, are the alpha and omega of romantic comedy."[1]

Diane's seasons, which originally aired from 1982 to 1987, are remembered for the Sam and Diane relationship. In these years, the series was much more of a romantic comedy, with the ups and downs of the core relationship defining the show. Over and over you can find references of the creators to the "Hepburn and Tracy" dynamic they wanted to explore with Ted Danson and Shelley Long. During the Rebecca seasons

(1987–1993), there is some romantic tension as Sam pursues her—they eventually even try to have a kid together—but the Sam-Rebecca dynamic never defined the series in the same way Sam and Diane had.

It was not a surprise to producers that Shelley Long would not be renewing her initial five-year contract. But for fans and media critics, an actress leaving a popular series in the middle of its run was a cause for concern and speculation. Numerous theories about just why Long left have been presented over the years. Generally, the reasons presented fall into three camps. First, Shelley Long was ready to move on from television to pursue a film career. Second, there was tension on the set and it was becoming uncomfortable for everyone. Third, the Sam-and-Diane dynamic was overdone, and Long didn't see where it could go in a creatively satisfying direction.

In an oral history of *Cheers* by Brian Raftery that was published in 2012, Long addresses all of these versions of her departure. First, she notes that "I was getting movie offers, which made people think, 'Oh, she's so snooty. She thinks she's going to do movies.'"[2] During her time on *Cheers*, Long did stay busy with film projects. She was in *Losin' It* with Tom Cruise; *Irreconcilable Differences*, for which she was nominated for a Golden Globe for Best Actress; *The Money Pit* with Tom Hanks; and *Outrageous Fortune* with Bette Midler. While none of these films were massive hits, Long was consistently working in Hollywood.

Second, Long addresses the reports of on-set tension. Even at the time of her departure there were articles that noted "well-publicized differences" between Long and Danson. For his part, Danson said, "I ain't gonna say anything bad about my partner. . . . I mean, my wife and I have terrible arguments sometimes, and they're kind of our business. Our relationship, Shelley's and mine, has included not being happy with each other and being happy with each other."[3] In Raftery's oral history, Long acknowledges that she did not fit in as smoothly as the rest of the cast, and by the fifth year it was more apparent:

> I'd gotten into a routine of going into my dressing room and meditating at lunch. I needed to rest, just let go of all of it. Because I really felt sometimes like I was physically pulling the plot, and it was heavy. I'm sure it didn't look great that I was going into my dressing room at lunch. I wish I could've hung out with the cast and got lunch. But it's not restful for me to be in a public dining room and eat. It's just not.

And I was exhausted by the end of the morning because I tried to deliver as much of a performance as I could for each run-through.[4]

In defense of Long's methods, Glen Charles said, "Shelley liked to discuss things. It was never a tantrum. But it did take a lot of talking, and I think the biggest problem was with the rest of the cast . . . [it] created a schism between Shelley and the rest of the cast."[5] Danson also makes it clear that "Shelley's process would have infuriated you if it had been mean or if it hadn't been purposeful. But it was purposeful—it was her way of being Diane—and there's not a mean bone in Shelley's body."[6]

And finally, concerning whether the Sam and Diane relationship had simply run its course, Long recalled that "I felt like I was repeating myself; it bothered me a little bit."[7] While fans likely had concerns about how the show would continue after Long's departure, Danson agreed with Long's assessment about their famous characters' romance. In between seasons 4 and 5, Danson had told a television critic, "I just hope Sam becomes a more dimensional character. Enough already about his dumbness where bad women are concerned. I'd like some of the heat off the Sam/Diane thing so they can follow other story lines. But I'm not the writer, just the actor."[8] And, in an interview leading up to Long's exit from the series, Danson concluded, "The [Sam and Diane] relationship was beginning to slow down. . . . I think it's wonderfully appropriate on all levels that Shelley decided to leave. I think the relationship had been done."[9] Any fan who had watched the first five seasons knew that their relationship had been deeply mined for comedy and drama.

Danson and Long's admission that there didn't feel like new variations were left doesn't seem like an indictment of the writing staff but a recognition of how much had already been done. Writers had presented both couples as the pursuer and the pursuee at different points, they had each had serious relationships with other people, they had been together and bickered and then been apart and desired one another for five seasons. Long was not wrong to question what was left for the characters, short of marriage, which did not fit the plans for the series.

In all likelihood, there was no singular reason for Long's departure; all the reasons that have been given were factors in her decision. Additionally, Long had a young child (the show had hidden her pregnancy from viewers in season three while writing Rhea Perlman's simultaneous pregnancy into the show), and she wanted to spend more time with her family.

In any event, despite fan outcry and concerns when she was leaving, it should be recognized that Long honored her original contract. Long did not quit and she wasn't fired; she chose to depart after five years, which is exactly how long she had committed to work on the series. In any event, the show had to completely redefine itself if it hoped to continue its successful run, which it did.

And yet, the Sam and Diane relationship remains an iconic part of *Cheers. Cheers* had a brilliant ensemble cast, but the beating heart of the show was definitely Sam and Diane. In a retrospective at the time *Cheers* was heading off the air, George Wendt recalled that his favorite episodes were "in the romantic comedy years, the first two or three years where the stories were about Sam and Diane. Coach would have a nice little scene, Cliff had some wacky thing and Norm had a little entrance and a teaser. Everything sort of fit into the pegs they were supposed to."[10] Wendt also noted that the episodes focusing on the side characters felt off. And he's right, they often do, because the show is so clearly about Sam and Diane in those early years. As James Burrows identifies, it was after Shelley Long left that the other characters were elevated: "When [Long] left, we had to do shows about the rest of the people in the bar, because we didn't want to do Rebecca and Sam in a romance."[11] In the first five seasons, the show was set up and running like a finely tuned watch, but when the focus shifted off of Sam and Diane, it felt imbalanced. This is not to say that the episodes with a strong A-plot focusing on Cliff, Norm, Carla, or Coach were bad; they just lack the iconic feeling of an early *Cheers* episode.

Strangely enough for how quickly Sam and Diane took center stage on *Cheers*, the creators did not set out with the intention of creating a will-they-won't-they romance. *Cheers* was already a few weeks into production before Sam and Diane became the focus. David Isaacs, a writer and producer, states, "Jim [Burrows] came up to eat lunch with us and said, 'Sam and Diane is our money. We have to go back to them, regardless of what the story is, [every] episode.'"[12] And with that, the focus of the series was born, and sitcoms would never be the same.

What is it about Sam that attracts Diane? Martin Gitlin points out a certain shallowness to Diane's interest, as she is "wildly attracted to his Cro-Magnon good looks and recoils at his Cro-Magnon intellect."[13] There is some truth to that; Diane is undoubtedly attracted physically to Sam but makes frequent aspersions about his intelligence. Yet there must be more for Diane and the audience to want to see her get together with Sam. One underrated aspect of Sam is that he is intensely faithful to Diane. This cuts against his reputation as a womanizer and his inability to let go of his little black book of phone numbers, but Sam never once cheats while they're together. And there are ample tests that he passes on this front.

Sam also allows Diane to be herself. Part of her elitist intellectualism is undoubtedly performative, and the only person we ever see make Diane drop that mask is Sam, both positively and negatively. She is filled with childlike giddiness in the beginning of season 2 when they first get together. Imagine the prim and proper Diane with her stack of classics, giggling as she runs around a room with a water pistol, but that's exactly how "Sumner's Return" opens.[14] And it feels honest and true for her in that moment. Conversely, when she and Sam have a fight that ends in nose pulling, she cries out, "We have sunk as low as human beings can sink. There's no degradation left."[15] Both the giddy playfulness and the ugly nose pulling are something separate from the Diane we normally see on *Cheers*, but there is a truth to those moments that is lacking when Diane forces a Dostoevsky reference into a casual conversation (even if forcing literary references is an iconically Diane thing to do).

If there is something more to pull Diane toward Sam, there must also be something about Diane that intrigues Sam. First, it's quickly established that Diane is more intellectual than most women Sam has dated. While his girlfriends' (and one-night stands') lack of intellectual prowess never bothered Sam before he met Diane, it does after. In "Sam's Women," Sam can't bring himself to pursue a woman because he now sees she's "dumb as a stump." He sees this not because Diane tells him, but because he compares her to Diane. Well before Sam and Diane begin dating, just meeting Diane inspires Sam to change his standards. For a man with a well-earned reputation for shallowness like Sam to change so dramatically requires a spark of intrigue that he can't ignore. Simply put, Diane is better than most women he has dated and he knows it, which is why he goes to such fruitless efforts to prove he has dated smart women, such as staging a scene for Diane's benefit in which Sam discusses a Mozart concert that he and a date supposedly attended.[16]

Diane Chambers (Shelley Long) and Sam Malone (Ted Danson)

*You love each other. And you hate each other. And you hate yourselves
for loving each other.*

Very quickly, Glen and Les Charles and James Burrows deliberately
focused on the potential romance between the former jock and the aspir-
ing intellectual as the creative spark that would drive the show. The
inspiration was taken both from what they wanted the show to be and
what they wanted to avoid it becoming. Burrows said they harkened back
to a "Katharine Hepburn/Spencer Tracy–type relationship" in envisioning
the core relationship of the series. [17]

The fast-talking banter with a simmering attraction from several films
of the Golden Age of Hollywood are clearly narrative antecedents to
Cheers. But, this was also an era of sitcom television, often with little
long-term plot development or evolution in characters, such that the episodes could practically be watched out of order with nothing gained or
lost. Glen and Les Charles insisted on long-term plots that would see
some characters change from the beginning of the series to the end. [18] Not
all the characters—Norm and Cliff are still Norm and Cliff from beginning to end—but enough change would occur in relationships to get a
sense of the beats and motions of a real relationship. Sam and Diane will

start apart and come together; Frasier and Lilith will fight in their first appearance, yet get married; Carla and Edie will find a way to get married, and then he'll die in a Zamboni accident. Evolution, change, ups and downs, that was what viewers tuning in to *Cheers* would find from week to week. The setting would remain comfortably familiar, and the status of the main characters would be flexible.

There is, of course, the fabled "*Moonlighting* curse." When a show is built around a will-they-won't-they chemistry, well, when they do, what is there to keep the story interesting? Particularly in a culture saturated with a happily-ever-after, pseudo-wish-fulfillment narrative, when it comes to portrayals of romance, the journey seems to be over if the characters get together. That's when the credits roll, after all, so who's staying to see what's next? *Cheers* managed to avoid this curse with the same couple driving the series for five years.

One way that *Cheers* prevented stagnation was by never allowing any status quo in the Sam and Diane relationship to linger for too long. Even with the ever-changing nature of their relationship, the primacy of Sam and Diane is readily apparent. The writers and showrunners clearly knew that this was the hook to draw viewers in, even after long breaks. Seasons 1 through 4 each end on a cliffhanger, and what is meant to ensure that fans make an appointment to see the next season's premiere is uncertainty about Sam and Diane.

Season 1 ends with a fight that transforms into a kiss. But will that kiss quickly turn back into a fight? Is it a one-time kiss, or the beginning of a long-term relationship? You had to tune in to the second season premiere to find out.

This pattern continued in each subsequent Diane season. In the season 2 finale, Sam and Diane have a fight, and it's a doozy. Will they ever get back together? Will Diane quit working at Cheers? What will the new status quo for the sitcom pairing look like?

In season 3, Diane was prepared—well, at least scheduled—to marry Frasier Crane, when Sam flew to Europe to stop the wedding. Viewers were left in the dark about the results of Sam's quest until the next season began.

Season 4 ends most provocatively of all. Sam has been dating a woman, Janet Eldridge, and it is presented as a serious and mature relationship. Janet asks Sam to fire Diane from Cheers so that Diane can move on with her life, but also because Janet is jealous of Diane's past relationship. The jealousy is not presented as petty, but natural, and Janet acknowledges that is part of her reasoning. At the end of the episode, Sam picks up a phone and dials a number and asks the woman who answers the phone to marry him. But it's not revealed whom Sam has asked.

On a series that saw Diane become engaged to marry Frasier Crane, it's not impossible to imagine an opening to season 5 in which Sam has proposed to Janet Eldridge. But viewers learn it was Diane who answered the call, setting the stage for a madcap final season of Sam and Diane's protracted dance. The creators, for the first five years of the show, were trusting that curiosity about how the next chapter of Sam and Diane would turn out would be sufficient to bring the audience back each year.

The two of you have a relationship whose best moments were full of anguish and self-loathing.

It is important to keep in mind that although Sam and Diane remains an iconic pairing in popular culture, this was never presented as a fairy-tale romance. While the skilled writers and talented cast could obviously have crafted a story that ended up with Sam and Diane blissfully together, watching the journey closely it rarely feels like a happily-ever-after is just around the corner. There's too much volatility, too much simmering tension, too much raw emotion to believe these characters were meant to be together. Which is one reason that watching them try so desperately to make it work is fascinating. A viewer will root for Sam and Diane to get together, even though they so clearly should not.

Though great for viewers, Sam and Diane were horrible for each other. That may seem odd to say about "the most famous sparring lovebirds in sitcom history,"[19] but it's undeniable once you start to examine their relationship with any kind of depth. Though it is almost inevitable for Sam and Diane to appear on online lists of greatest TV couples, Kevin Fitzpatrick included Sam and Diane as number 2 in his list of "The Most Absolutely Awful TV Couples," falling only behind the ill-fated pairing of Joey and Rachel from *Friends*.[20]

The coyly flirtatious dance in season 1 is a classic Hollywood will-they-won't-they dynamic. Even if you don't consider it the definitive version of that type of relationship, it is undeniably the star-crossed pairing that codified that storytelling device into a standard of American television network sitcoms. But when analyzing the ways in which Sam and Diane grate against each other, what is supposed to be an up-and-down relationship is revealed to be a roller coaster that is almost all down, with too little up. Taffy Brodesser-Akner concluded that Sam and Diane, in real life, would "tend to suck all the joy out of the room as we debate if their insults and bickering and overall disdain for each other is something enjoyable to be around. It is not."[21] Fortunately, we're engaging with these characters through the soothing glow of the television screen, because none of the characters on *Cheers* would be likable in real life.

Five years is a long time to tease out and play with a romantic relationship. It still is, but it was even more so by the standards of 1980s television storytelling. So, what exactly was the structure of the Sam and Diane romance?

Season 1: Constant fighting with obvious romantic subtext, they finally kiss in the season finale.

Season 2: They're together, but there are signs of discontent until it all blows up in the finale.

Season 3: Trouble the romance by introducing a new romantic interest (Frasier Crane), but hint that there may still be feelings between Sam and Diane until a choice must be made in the season finale.

Season 4: Slowly mend fences and rekindle the romance, building to a proposal in the finale.

Season 5: Reveal that Diane rejected Sam's proposal and Sam is through with this relationship, but Diane insists they can make it work and it all builds up to a wedding in the season finale that never takes place.

Essentially, (1) Will they, won't they? (2) They did. (3) Now they don't. (4) Now they do. (5) Once more, will they, won't they? Maybe . . . nope.

By the time the relationship had been stretched to its fifth year without a commitment, developments were beginning to be notably thin. Many of the season 5 episodes move the relationship to the back burner, which was probably for the best. Not only does the audience feel a bit yanked back and forth after more than one hundred episodes of Sam and Diane's relationship never really cooling off entirely, nor committing to a permanent on setting such as marriage, there wasn't much room left to cover. To even have the characters become engaged in the 108th episode of the series, absurd lengths that strain credulity had to be reached. Earlier in the season, Sam had proposed and Diane had said no, and Sam insisted he never would have a relationship with her again. After a convoluted series of events, they are in court, and a judge orders Sam to propose again. Obviously television viewers are well-trained to suspend their disbelief, but this plotline makes that practice impossible. Sam laments before proposing, "You want me to propose to you. I propose to you. You say, 'No.' I say, 'Fine. I never want to see you again.' You drive me nuts telling me you want me to propose again. I do. You turn me down. Next thing I know I'm in a court of law where I've gotta propose to you or I'll go to jail. It's the classic American love story."[22] Sam does propose and Diane accepts, and Sam shifts very quickly to excitement about his pending nuptials. This whole episode is the messy muddle in the middle of the season-long storyline that leads to their supposed wedding day, but it's a shame a more plausible reason wasn't found for their engagement.

If they were so terrible for each other, was it good that Sam and Diane got together? Absolutely. Their relationship changed them each for the better. Diane was a pseudo-intellectual who lived in the abstract, desperately needing grounding and a solid foundation. Sam was lecherous womanizer who objectified women and needed someone to come along and shock him out of an outdated mindset. Through the fighting and loving and pushing away and drawing near, they changed each other for the better.

Diane left to write her book, and that was the best way for her to leave. When she came to Cheers, she was a teaching assistant being manipulated and used by her older professor. She was naive and entitled, and she needed a dose of the blue-collar wisdom that Sam could offer. Of course, the blue-collar wisdom came laced with too many insults. Brodesser-Akner writes, "I would submit that only the girls with the lowest self-esteem end up with their insulters-in-chief, and only a show written from the sole point of view of a man would allow that any great woman would still want a man who had lurched the kinds of insults that Sam had onto Diane."[23] It should be noted that many of the very best episodes of the Sam and Diane era were written or cowritten by women. In fact, almost a quarter of the episodes in the first five seasons were written by women, most prominently Heide Perlman and Cheri Eichen. But, Brodesser-Akner's assertion stands that too much toxicity had been heaped upon Diane from Sam for theirs to be a healthy relationship. However, the show does not leave them together. At Sam's insistence, Diane moves on to bigger and better things than being a barmaid. She becomes an award-winning writer, fulfilling one of her dreams, thanks to a combination of her skill and education and Sam pushing her in that direction.

Sam was a ladies man whose personal identity was wrapped up in how many women he could sleep with. His evolution begins immediately, as he can't date the "bimbos" he used to after meeting Diane.[24] Diane doesn't only elevate his taste in women; she makes Sam care about things he never cared about before.

Also, though their relationship was far from ideal, they never cheated on each other. For Sam, based on the reputation he has burnished as *the* ladies' man who cannot and will not say no to a late-night meeting, this demonstrates a fidelity to be lauded even while it's unexpected.

I'm sorry I haven't been in touch.

And then she was gone. Yes, there are references to Diane after she leaves—it would be weird for Frasier and Sam in particular to never mention her again. In the season 6 premiere, "Home Is the Sailor," when Sam comes back after a failed sailing adventure and sees the bar redecorated, he tells Rebecca, the new manager, "See, I was, uh, I was afraid that I was gonna walk in here today and see her everywhere I look, but instead what I saw was all these silly changes you made."[25]

Of course, Diane had to come back for the finale. Well, she didn't *have* to. Shelley Long "was not contractually obligated to do so,"[26] but was willing to come back after six years away to help complete the story of *Cheers*. Long's willingness to circle back to her character for "One for the Road" does suggest that despite rumors of on-set tension being a reason she left the show, it was never the primary reason. Add in the fact that Long was willing to come back in character on *Frasier* several times—as a brief cameo,[27] as a full guest star in an episode devoted to Diane writing a play based on her time at Cheers,[28] and as a figment of Frasier's imagination as he attempts to figure out his own messed-up romantic life[29]—and it seems clear that Long harbored no animosity regarding her time on *Cheers*. Add in the fact that her appearances on *Frasier* were directed by James Burrows and Kelsey Grammer, and there is ample evidence that Long held no bitterness toward the character or the creators and cast.

Knowing that season 11 was the last one after Ted Danson announced he would not be coming back for a twelfth, producers brought back many identifiable guests from the previous eleven years. These included not only semi-recurring characters like Nick and Loretta Tortelli[30] and Esther Clavin[31] but also smaller characters from the early seasons such as the unhinged Andy Andy,[32] the con man Harry "The Hat" Gittes[33] (who had disappeared from *Cheers* when the actor Harry Anderson was cast as the star of *Night Court*), and Cliff's antagonistic fellow postal worker, Walter Q. Twitchell.[34] With so many nostalgic callbacks occurring, Long's absence would have been felt even more.

The long storytelling championed by Burrows and the Charles brothers wasn't only in the form of season-long arcs. In the case of *Cheers*, it would be series-long, and for that they needed Diane to make another appearance. It's handled well; as expected, Sam and Diane begin antagonistically, move toward a romance, but realize they're not right for each other. "One for the Road" is a microcosm of the Sam and Diane years played out in a series finale, and it is the perfect coda to the most famous sitcom couple in television history.

Diane Chambers (Shelley Long) and Sam Malone (Ted Danson)

THE POP CULTURE CHILDREN OF SAM AND DIANE

In the modern era of on-demand viewing, long-running plots are the norm. In the era when *Cheers* was produced, character evolution, significant changes in relationships, and continuing plots were eschewed in favor of iconic and static characters who would get into a situation, comedically resolve, and return to their original status quo. The illusion of change only lasted twenty-four minutes before everything reverted to its platonic ideal. Perhaps accidentally—and certainly not initially—*Cheers* revealed that an audience will tune in week after week to watch characters change and evolve. And they will also hang onto the twists and turns of a romantic couple falling in and out and back in love.

It is likely that without *Cheers*, other sitcoms would have discovered this formula, but *Cheers* was there first. Therefore, all the subsequent sitcoms that have relied on a will-they-won't-they dynamic to ensure fan engagement owe a debt to the writers, directors, and actors on *Cheers*. Though Sam and Diane never got together to have the family they dreamed of on *Cheers*, in pop culture, they have many progeny. James Burrows calls Sam and Diane's first kiss one of his favorite moments in his lengthy career, and it's a moment that has coined a shorthand in television. Burrows, who has worked on many more shows than the average director, says, "'Sam and Diane' has become vernacular in the writing business. I've been on a number of shows where someone says, 'At this point, we need for them to have a Sam and Diane relationship.'"[35]

Cheers popularized a formula that has become a staple of the sitcom format. Ross and Rachel on *Friends*. Niles and Daphne on *Frasier*. Elliot and J.D. on *Scrubs*. Jim and Pam on *The Office*. Leonard and Penny on *The Big Bang Theory*. And the list includes hour-long dramas as well. Outside of sitcoms, you have Maddy and David from *Moonlighting*, Josh and Donna from *The West Wing*, Booth and Brennan from *Bones*, and Castle and Beckett from *Castle*. Dragging out a teased romance is expected at this point.

Viewers who have never seen an episode of *Cheers* have seen the patterns established and popularized on the series played out over and over again. Josh Bell concludes that "the uncouth bartender and the uppity waitress became the template for countless future sitcom couples whose relationships were fraught with sexual tension."[36] This is not to claim that these subsequent series are plagiarizing *Cheers*. It is a natural part of storytelling to stand on the foundations that came before, and *Cheers* has become a foundation text for sitcoms.

CONCLUSION

"We're Closed"

Even if someone has not watched any episode of *Cheers*, the show still permeates our culture to such a degree that some familiarity is inevitable. Through simple cultural osmosis, anyone who consumes narrative entertainment made after its popularity rose has seen or heard references to *Cheers*. Even decades after it has gone off the air, the allusions keep coming. *Cheers* is pervasive, and references to the show abound in subsequent entertainment. There is a 2005 episode of the NBC sitcom *Scrubs* in which the protagonist, J.D., imagines his life in a four-camera sitcom after treating a fictional *Cheers* writer (Charles James, a blending of Glen and Les Charles and James Burrows) that used the *Cheers* theme song to incredible emotional effect.[1] Unfortunately, the *Cheers* theme only appeared when the show originally aired; due to rights issues and prohibitive costs, the episode inserted a generic song in syndication, DVD releases, and streaming. In 2013, an episode of Cartoon Network's animated series *Adventure Time* had a character begin reenacting a scene from *Cheers* for another character.[2] In the 2017 blockbuster superhero film, *Guardians of the Galaxy, Vol. 2*, Peter Quill compares his relationship with Gamora to that of Sam and Diane.[3] In 2018, the Internet had a moment when the NBC sitcom *The Good Place* put Ted Danson behind a bar for a single scene.[4] Finding references in sources as disparate as an NBC sitcom, a children's cartoon, and a summer blockbuster movie demonstrates that *Cheers* can show up anywhere.

As embedded as *Cheers* has become in popular culture, there are inevitably questions that arise about the show after decades of repeat viewings and fan discussions. What exactly are the operating hours for this bar? How do the characters leave to go watch a basketball game after closing up? Why does Carla always complain about Diane not working and leaving her with too much to do, but then there's never a mention of hiring another waitress after Diane leaves? So, Norm's tab . . . ? But the thing is, none of this matters.

Well, it could matter to some viewers. *Cheers* exists and is out there, and viewer reaction is out of the hands of its creators. The interesting thing about popular culture is that it also reflects the individual viewing it. You can see *Cheers* as a show about a group of sad, unmotivated individuals who choose to waste their time drinking at a bar. You can watch it looking for how unrealistic the work environment is. You can see the

From left, back row: Carla Lozupone Tortelli LeBec (Rhea Perlman), Woodrow Tiberius "Woody" Boyd (Woody Harrelson), Dr. Frasier W. Crane (Kelsey Grammer), Dr. Lilith Sternin-Crane (Bebe Neuwirth); front row: Hilary Norman "Norm" Peterson (George Wendt), Rebecca Howe (Kirstie Alley), Sam "Mayday" Malone (Ted Danson), Clifford C. "Cliff" Clavin Jr. (John Ratzenberger)

show as being about a group of great friends who would rather hang out with one another than all the other options life presents. Whichever way you see it says a lot more about you, the viewer, than about the actual show.

Any viewer coming to *Cheers* for verisimilitude will be disappointed, but if they're coming to be entertained, *Cheers* provided that for 275 episodes and more than a decade. Watching *Cheers* from beginning to end with no break would take almost six days,[5] and, despite all the changes and different chapters, *Cheers* would provide a remarkably steady six days of entertainment. As Ken Bloom and Frank Vlastnik concluded, "A seminal show in terms of its smart writing, expert acting and all-around class, *Cheers* has become exactly like its setting: a warm, comfortable place into which to pop your head and have a few laughs with familiar faces."[6]

After writing a book about one of the greatest television shows of all time, one thing has become clear: There remains much that can be said about *Cheers*. Hopefully this text becomes a part of a larger conversation analyzing this popular culture artifact. *Cheers* stands out not only as a self-contained masterpiece but also as a transformational text that altered the course of the television sitcom. As such, there's simply too much to cover in a single book. But we also hope that what was covered in this volume was illuminating and of value.

In the era of DVDs and on-demand viewing, there is an interesting aspect to finishing watching a series that could not have been anticipated in 1982. As Sam Malone wistfully announces, "We're closed," and exits stage right to the pool room at the back of the bar, the audience can appreciate the incredible journey the cast and crew produced across 275 episodes. And then, if they want, without missing a beat, they can switch out the disc or select the pilot episode to start the series over again and see a decade-younger Sam Malone walk out from the back room and prep Cheers for opening.

Or maybe viewers take a break, watch other shows, and then years later decide they want to go back to where they know everybody's name. Starting over, they realize they missed the Diane years, even if they were happy to see Rebecca arrive during their last viewing of the series. They fondly realize Coach is back, and his sweetness is endearing. They begin looking forward to Frasier and Woody arriving in the bar. Now, thanks to new methods of engaging television shows, it's possible for Cheers to be open whenever you want and to see that underage drinker sidle up to the bar, try to pull one over on Sam Malone, and launch one of the greatest stories in American entertainment when he asks, "How 'bout a beer, Chief?"

THE EPISODES

An Opinionated Compendium

In the end, any rating system regarding the quality of a television episode is subjective. Certainly there are objective issues that can be identified, such as poor camera work, plot holes, or uncharacteristic behavior, but in general *Cheers* doesn't suffer from those problems. We're using a four-star system to rate every episode of *Cheers*, with four stars representing a great episode, three stars a very good episode, two stars an okay episode, and one star a flawed episode. Undoubtedly, fans of *Cheers* will have differing opinions, and by no means can we assume our ratings are definitive statements about how one should consider each episode. A brief reason is provided for any episode that received a four-star rating or a one-star rating.

Episode 1.1: "Give Me a Ring Sometime" (September 30, 1982)
****

Diane waits at the bar for a love interest to come back and pick her up, but he abandons her. Sam offers her a job. *Why four stars:* The behind-the-scenes and in-front-of-camera talent came together from the very beginning to create one of the most perfect television pilots ever filmed. Setting, character, tone, and quality are all perfectly on display.

Episode 1.2: "Sam's Women" (October 7, 1982) ***

Diane mocks the shallow women Sam dates and asserts a sophisticated woman would never fall for his pickup lines. Sam tricks her into falling for one.

Episode 1.3: "The Tortelli Tort" (October 14, 1982) **

Carla attacks a Yankees fan who was mocking Boston sports, and he threatens to sue Sam.

Episode 1.4: "Sam at Eleven" (October 21, 1982) ***

A sportscaster asks to interview Sam for the news, but the interviewer leaves in the middle of the interview when a more current sports figure agrees to come on.

Episode 1.5: "Coach's Daughter" (October 28, 1982) ** (but with a four-star scene)

Coach meets his daughter's fiance but tries to convince her she is too good for him. *Note:* The scene between Coach and his daughter is special—one of the highlights of the series—but the episode as a whole doesn't quite reach that quality.

Episode 1.6: "Any Friend of Diane's" (November 4, 1982) ***

Sam attempts to date Diane's friend, Rebecca, but finds her boring.

Episode 1.7: "Friends, Romans, Accountants" (November 11, 1982) ***

Norm's boss is sexually aggressive toward Diane; Norm stops him and is fired.

Episode 1.8: "Truce or Consequences" (November 18, 1982)
***

Carla convinces Diane that Sam is the father of one of her children.

Episode 1.9: "Coach Returns to Action" (November 25, 1982)
**

Coach begins a flirtatious relationship with his new neighbor.

Episode 1.10: "Endless Slumper" (December 2, 1982) ****

When Sam fears he'll fall off the wagon, Diane stays with him to help. *Why four stars:* This was the first episode that clearly declared there is more happening on this show than you have come to expect from a network sitcom. Depths of pathos can be delivered within the confines of this bar along with the laughs.

Episode 1.11: "One for the Book" (December 9, 1982) ***

A man considering entering a monastery is questioning his decision until he witnesses a "miracle" in the bar.

Episode 1.12: "The Spy Who Came in for a Cold One" (December 16, 1982) **

A stranger in the bar claims to have led a mysterious life, but Diane refuses to believe him.

Episode 1.13: "Now Pitching, Sam Malone" (January 6, 1983)
***

Sam begins dating an advertising agent who gets him into commercials.

Episode 1.14: "Let Me Count the Ways" (January 13, 1983) ***

Diane's cat dies, and nobody cares.

Episode 1.15: "Father Knows Last" (January 20, 1983) *

Carla is pregnant and tries to trick a respectable bar patron into believing he is the father. *Why one star:* Carla is lovably prickly, but attempting to trick a respectable man into believing he's the father of her child is so morally repugnant, it's hard to watch.

Episode 1.16: "The Boys in the Bar" (January 27, 1983) ***

One of Sam's old teammates comes out as gay, and the patrons of Cheers worry about it becoming a gay bar.

Episode 1.17: "Diane's Perfect Date" (February 10, 1983) ****

Sam accidentally sets up Diane on a blind date with a potential murderer. *Why four stars:* One of the early forays into absurdity and broad comedy, this episode demonstrates the breadth of comedic styles that can be displayed within a single setting.

Episode 1.18: "No Contest" (February 17, 1983) **

Sam enters Diane into a Miss Boston Barmaid contest.

Episode 1.19: "Pick a Con . . . Any Con" (February 24, 1983) ***

Coach recruits a conman, Harry the Hat, to help recover money from an unscrupulous gambler.

Episode 1.20: "Someone Single, Someone Blue" (March 3, 1983) **

Diane's family will lose their wealth unless Diane marries the next day.

Episode 1.21: "Showdown, Part 1" (March 24, 1983) ***

Sam's too-perfect brother comes into town, making Sam jealous.

Episode 1.22: "Showdown, Part 2" (March 31, 1983) ****

Sam and Diane argue, then recognize their mutual attraction. *Why four stars:* The moment that audiences (and bar patrons) have been waiting for comes in an emotionally charged season finale.

Episode 2.1: "Power Play" (September 29, 1983) ***

When Sam makes fun of Diane's stuffed animals, the romantic mood sours.

Episode 2.2: "Li'l Sister Don't Cha" (October 13, 1983) **

Carla goes into labor and her sister takes over at the bar. Cliff falls in love with her.

Episode 2.3: "Personal Business" (October 20, 1983) ***

Diane explores employment outside the bar but ends up returning to her role as a barmaid.

Episode 2.4: "Homicidal Ham" (October 27, 1983) ****

Andy Andy returns and performs a Shakespeare scene with Diane. *Why four stars:* Guest star Derek McGrath finds the comedy in a dramatic scene from *Othello*.

Episode 2.5: "Sumner's Return" (November 3, 1983) ****

Sumner returns, and Sam tries to impress him by reading *War and Peace*. *Why four stars:* Expertly demonstrating the contrast between Sam Malone and Sumner Sloane allows a comedic exploration of the Sam and Diane relationship.

Episode 2.6: "Affairs of the Heart" (November 10, 1983) ***

A patron is attracted to Carla, but his heart condition prohibits a physical relationship.

Episode 2.7: "Old Flames" (November 17, 1983) ***

One of Sam's old buddies wants Sam to return to his womanizing ways.

Episode 2.8: "Manager Coach" (November 24, 1983) **

Coach manages a little league baseball team and becomes a tyrant.

Episode 2.9: "They Call Me Mayday" (December 1, 1983) ****

Sam is encouraged to write his life story, much to Diane's dismay. *Why four stars:* Anytime Sam enters Diane's world, it's delightful.

Episode 2.10: "How Do I Love Thee, Let Me Call You Back" (December 8, 1983) ***

Sam casually tells Diane he loves her, sparking a much deeper conversation than he hoped for.

Episode 2.11: "Just Three Friends" (December 15, 1983) **

Diane's old friend visits, and it's unclear if she's coming on to Sam.

Episode 2.12: "Where There's a Will" (December 22, 1983) *

A wealthy patron leaves the gang money, but the promise of wealth destroys relationships. *Why one star:* The plot is the wrong kind of stereotypical sitcom fare.

Episode 2.13: "Battle of the Exes" (January 5, 1984) *

Carla's ex-husband is getting married, and she borrows Sam as a date to make him jealous. *Why one star:* Sam's moment with Carla is as close to cheating on Diane as he ever comes, and it's too much.

Episode 2.14: "No Help Wanted" (January 12, 1984) ***

Sam hires Norm as his accountant but doesn't entirely trust his work.

Episode 2.15: "And Coachie Makes Three" (January 19, 1984) ***

Coach becomes a constant companion to Sam and Diane, crimping their romantic relationship.

Episode 2.16: "Cliff's Rocky Moment" (January 26, 1984) **

A patron is annoyed with Cliff and challenges him to a fight.

Episode 2.17: "Fortune and Men's Weight" (February 2, 1984) ***

When Coach buys a scale that dispenses fortunes, the messages cause unexpected stress.

Episode 2.18: "Snow Job" (February 9, 1984) ***

Sam tries to dupe Diane so that he can go on an annual party weekend with his baseball friends.

Episode 2.19: "Coach Buries a Grudge" (February 16, 1984) ***

Coach finds out a recently deceased baseball player made a pass at his wife years ago.

Episode 2.20: "Norman's Conquest" (February 23, 1984) *

Norm has a new client, and she may be romantically interested in him. *Why one star:* The patrons in the bar demonstrate inexcusable toxic masculinity in their behavior toward Norm.

Episode 2.21: "I'll Be Seeing You, Part 1" (May 3, 1984) ****

Sam forbids Diane from sitting for an artist who wants to paint her portrait. *Why four stars:* The creators know how to end a season to ensure that viewers come back again next season.

Episode 2.22: "I'll Be Seeing You, Part 2" (May 10, 1984) ***

After Diane sits for a portrait, Sam and Diane have a highly charged fight.

Episode 3.1: "Rebound, Part 1" (September 27, 1984) ****

Sam is drinking again and Diane has her new boyfriend, Frasier Crane, help him. *Why four stars:* The introduction of Frasier Crane makes a love triangle that injects new tension into the series, and seeing Sam's alcoholism adds permanent pathos to the character.

Episode 3.2: "Rebound, Part 2" (October 4, 1984) ****

Diane is convinced to return to work at Cheers. *Why four stars:* Coach's manipulation of Sam, Diane, and Frasier is executed for maximum comedy.

Episode 3.3: "I Call Your Name" (October 18, 1984) **

Sam believes Diane still has feelings for him.

Episode 3.4: "Fairy Tales Can Come True" (October 25, 1984) **

At a Halloween costume party, Cliff finds love while dressed as Ponce de Leon.

Episode 3.5: "Sam Turns the Other Cheek" (November 1, 1984) ****

A jealous husband confronts Sam. *Why four stars:* Sam Malone shoots himself in the butt. It's not only highbrow literary references that can be hilarious.

Episode 3.6: "Coach in Love, Part 1" (November 8, 1984) ***

When Coach's girlfriend wins the lottery, she forgets that Coach proposed to her.

Episode 3.7: "Coach in Love, Part 2" (November 15, 1984) *

As Coach prepares for his wedding, his fiancee becomes more distant. *Why one star:* Coach not believing or accepting that his fiancee has left him takes his dim-wittedness a little too far.

Episode 3.8: "Diane Meets Mom" (November 22, 1984) *

Diane meets Frasier's mother, Hester, and it does not go well. *Why one star:* The portrayal of Frasier's mother is inexcusably broad.

Episode 3.9: "An American Family" (November 29, 1984) **

Carla's ex-husband returns and attempts to take one of his children from Carla.

Episode 3.10: "Diane's Allergy" (December 6, 1984) ****

Diane and Frasier plan to move in together, until Diane has an allergic reaction. *Why four stars:* Shelley Long's physical comedy is underrated, and this episode is an example of her excellence.

Episode 3.11: "Peterson Crusoe" (December 13, 1984) ***

After a health scare, Norm announces his plans to move to a tropical island.

Episode 3.12: "A Ditch in Time" (December 20, 1984) ***

Sam is interested in one of Diane's friends, but Diane knows a secret about her.

Episode 3.13: "Whodunit?" (January 3, 1985) **

Carla starts dating Frasier's mentor.

Episode 3.14: "The Heart Is a Lonely Snipe Hunter" (January 10, 1985) ****

Frasier tries to become one of the boys at Cheers. *Why four stars:* Frasier becomes part of the gang, and the combination of comedy and emotion elevates the episode.

Episode 3.15: "King of the Hill" (January 24, 1985) ***

Sam accepts an invitation to play in a charity baseball game, but he takes it too seriously.

Episode 3.16: "Teacher's Pet" (January 31, 1985) **

Sam and Coach take a night class to receive their high school degrees.

Episode 3.17: "The Mail Goes to Jail" (February 7, 1985) ***

When Cliff is sick, Norm offers to deliver his last few pieces of mail.

Episode 3.18: "Bar Bet" (February 14, 1985) **

When Sam was drinking, he made a bet that may cost him his bar.

Episode 3.19: "Behind Every Great Man" (February 21, 1985) ****

A misunderstanding makes Diane thinks Sam is interested in rekindling things with her. *Why four stars:* Diane's begrudging interest and vulnerability reinvests viewers in Sam and Diane.

Episode 3.20: "If Ever I Would Leave You" (February 28, 1985) **

Carla's ex-husband starts working at the bar after he's dumped by his new wife.

Episode 3.21: "The Executive's Executioner" (March 7, 1985) **

Norm learns he is being promoted to a job requiring him to fire other employees.

Episode 3.22: "Cheerio, Cheers" (April 11, 1985) ***

Frasier is asked to be a visiting professor in Europe and asks Diane to go with him.

Episode 3.23: "The Bartender's Tale" (April 18, 1985) ***

Sam hires a new waitress to replace Diane, and an unexpected romantic entanglement ensues.

Episode 3.24: "The Belles of St. Clete's" (May 2, 1985) *

Carla is obsessed with the idea of revenge against her old school head-mistress. *Why one star:* Even for Carla, this is an unusually petty and vindictive episode.

Episode 3.25: "Rescue Me" (May 9, 1985) ****

When Frasier proposes to Diane, Sam considers flying to Europe to stop the wedding. *Why four stars:* Sam takes his most assertive move yet, and the cliffhanger leaves the audience on edge.

Episode 4.1: "Birth, Death, Love and Rice" (September 26, 1985) ***

Sam finds out Diane left Frasier at the altar.

Episode 4.2: "Woody Goes Belly Up" (October 3, 1985) ***

Sam and Diane fly Woody's old girlfriend from Indiana to visit him.

Episode 4.3: "Someday My Prince Will Come" (October 17, 1985) ***

Diane is more attracted with to the idea of a man than she is attracted to his appearance.

Episode 4.4: "The Groom Wore Clearasil" (October 24, 1985) **

Carla's son wants to get engaged to his girlfriend; Sam tries to convince him the single life is fun.

Episode 4.5: "Diane's Nightmare" (October 31, 1985) ****

Diane dreams that Andy Andy is back, then dreams that Sam is suddenly sophisticated. *Why four stars:* While dream episodes are hard to pull off well, the writers make this one work.

Episode 4.6: "I'll Gladly Pay You Tuesday" (November 7, 1985) ****

Sam loans Diane $500 so that she can buy a rare Hemingway book. *Why four stars:* Sam becoming legitimately interested in Diane's interests, but screwing it up always works as a plot point.

Episode 4.7: "2 Good to Be 4 Real" (November 14, 1985) **

After Carla is depressed about her love life, the gang writes fake responses to her personal ad.

Episode 4.8: "Love Thy Neighbor" (November 21, 1985) **

Norm is worried Vera might be having an affair.

Episode 4.9: "From Beer to Eternity" (November 28, 1985) ****

The Cheers gang challenges its rivals to a bowling tournament. *Why four stars:* A great beginning to a multi-season episode arc that unites the gang with a common enemy.

Episode 4.10: "The Barstoolie" (December 5, 1985) **

Cliff reconnects with his long-lost father; Sam suspects Diane is sabotaging his date.

Episode 4.11: "Don Juan Is Hell" (December 12, 1985) ****

Diane studies Sam for a psychology paper. *Why four stars:* Diane's powerful analysis of Sam continues to shape his character for the rest of the series.

Episode 4.12: "Fools and Their Money" (December 19, 1985) ***

Sam tries to protect Woody when he makes a risky bet.

Episode 4.13: "Take My Shirt . . . Please" (January 9, 1986) ***

Sam donates his old Red Sox jersey for an auction on television.

Episode 4.14: "Suspicion" (January 16, 1986) ****

Diane plays a prank on everyone at the bar and becomes paranoid thinking they will prank her back. *Why four stars:* Beautifully showcases Diane's desire for acceptance at the bar.

Episode 4.15: "The Triangle" (January 23, 1986) ***

Diane forces Sam to go to Frasier to help with fake depression.

Episode 4.16: "Cliffie's Big Score" (January 30, 1986) **

Cliff asks both Diane and Carla to go to the postman's ball.

Episode 4.17: "Second Time Around" (February 6, 1986) ***

Sam sets up Frasier with one of his many women.

Episode 4.18: "The Peterson Principle" (February 13, 1986) ***

Norm is up for a promotion at work.

Episode 4.19: "Dark Imaginings" (February 20, 1986) ****

Sam suffers a hernia as he tries to prove he's not getting old. *Why four stars:* Sam grappling with his age is an important theme that *Cheers* manages to weave in seamlessly to storylines.

Episode 4.20: "Save the Last Dance for Me" (February 27, 1986) **

Carla and Sam compete in a dance competition against Nick and Loretta.

Episode 4.21: "Fear Is My Co-Pilot" (March 13, 1986) *

Sam and Diane have a near-death experience on an airplane. *Why one star:* Something is off about this episode, resulting in it not feeling like *Cheers*.

Episode 4.22: "Diane Chambers Day" (March 20, 1986) ****

Feeling guilty about how much they tease her, the guys at Cheers take Diane to the opera. *Why four stars:* A great episode showcasing the depth of the Cheers gang's friendships with one another.

Episode 4.23: "Relief Bartender" (March 27, 1986) ***

Sam hires a new bartender.

Episode 4.24: "Strange Bedfellows, Part 1" (May 1, 1986) ****

Sam begins dating a city councilwoman running for reelection. *Why four stars:* A new side to the Sam and Diane drama still proves it to be the driving force of the show.

Episode 4.25: "Strange Bedfellows, Part 2" (May 8, 1986) ****

Sam's relationship with the city councilwoman becomes more serious. *Why four stars:* Tension mounts in the Sam/Diane/Janet love triangle.

Episode 4.26: "Strange Bedfellows, Part 3" (May 15, 1986) ****

Sam must choose between Diane and the city councilwoman. *Why four stars:* An excellent cliffhanger leaves the audience anticipating the next season.

Episode 5.1: "The Proposal" (September 25, 1986) ****

Sam proposes to Diane, but she says no. But she then demands another chance. *Why four stars:* The moment that fans have been waiting for: Sam proposes to Diane, and it goes quite badly.

Episode 5.2: "The Cape Cad" (October 2, 1986) ****

Sam takes a date to an inn, but Diane follows them there and ruins things. *Why four stars:* A new status quo is established.

Episode 5.3: "Money Dearest" (October 9, 1986) **

Cliff tries to get his mother to date a wealthy older man.

Episode 5.4: "Abnormal Psychology" (October 16, 1986) ****

Frasier is on a TV talk show with a fellow psychiatrist, Dr. Lilith Sternin. *Why four stars:* Frasier and Lilith on screen together is always phenomenal, and their television interview is one of their most memorable moments.

Episode 5.5: "House of Horrors with Formal Dining and Used Brick" (October 30, 1986) **

Cliff finds a house on his mail route that Carla could afford, but she worries it's haunted.

Episode 5.6: "Tan 'n' Wash" (November 6, 1986) ****

Norm has a new business, and the regulars at Cheers become investors. *Why four stars:* A memorable episode that results in one of Woody's best lines of the show.

Episode 5.7: "Young Dr. Weinstein" (November 13, 1986) ****

Sam impersonates a doctor to get into an exclusive restaurant and make Diane jealous. *Why four stars:* Sam pretending to be someone he's not is always hilarious.

Episode 5.8: "Knights of the Scimitar" (November 20, 1986) ***

Cliff gets Norm to join his lodge, while Diane tries to make Sam jealous.

Episode 5.9: "Thanksgiving Orphans" (November 27, 1986) ****

The Cheers gang gets together for Thanksgiving. *Why four stars:* Food. Fight.

Episode 5.10: "Everyone Imitates Art" (December 4, 1986) ****

Diane's poetry is rejected by a publisher, but Sam's submission is accepted. *Why four stars:* Long gives a phenomenal performance of Diana's downward spiral of jealousy.

Episode 5.11: "The Book of Samuel" (December 11, 1986) *

Woody tries to get a date from Sam's little black book but accidentally calls his cleaning lady. *Why one star:* The cleaning lady plotline feels out of character for Woody, and cruel.

Episode 5.12: "Dance, Diane, Dance" (December 18, 1986) *

Diane's dream of becoming a dancer goes poorly. *Why one star:* The whole scenario feels unnecessarily cruel.

Episode 5.13: "Chambers vs. Malone" (January 8, 1987) *

Diane and Sam end up in court, then agree to be engaged to be married. *Why one star:* Diane filing charges against Sam and then forcing the court to have them be engaged is the worst storyline of the series.

Episode 5.14: "Diamond Sam" (January 15, 1987) ***

Sam buys a cheap ring for Diane, but spends a lot to cover up his cheapness.

Episode 5.15: "Spellbound" (January 22, 1987) **

Nick and Loretta bring their marital troubles to Cheers.

Episode 5.16: "Never Love a Goalie, Part 1" (January 29, 1987) ***

Carla begins dating a hockey goalie, Eddie LeBec.

Episode 5.17: "Never Love a Goalie, Part 2" (February 5, 1987) ***

Carla is superstitious about her relationship with Eddie.

Episode 5.18: "One Last Fling" (February 12, 1987) ***

Diane allows Sam one last day to have a fling.

Episode 5.19: "Dog Bites Cliff" (February 19, 1987) **

Cliff tries to sue the owner of a dog that bit him.

Episode 5.20: "Dinner at Eight-ish" (February 26, 1987) ****

Frasier and Lilith invite Sam and Diane over for dinner. *Why four stars:* Dinner parties are always great for comedy.

Episode 5.21: "Simon Says" (March 5, 1987) **

A relationship expert predicts a sad outcome for Sam and Diane.

Episode 5.22: "The Godfather, Part III" (March 19, 1987) **

Woody starts dating Coach's goddaughter.

Episode 5.23: "Norm's First Hurrah" (March 26, 1987) ***

Norm has a new job, and Diane tries to coach him into being more aggressive.

Episode 5.24: "Cheers: The Motion Picture" (April 2, 1987) **

The gang at Cheers makes a video for Woody's parents.

Episode 5.25: "A House Is Not a Home" (April 30, 1987) **

Sam and Diane try to buy a house together.

Episode 5.26: "I Do, Adieu" (May 7, 1987) ****

The day of Sam and Diane's wedding, Diane learns of a new opportunity. *Why four stars:* Sam and Diane's parting moment is one of the highlights of the series.

Episode 6.1: "Home Is the Sailor" (September 24, 1987) ****

Sam sold the bar and it's now managed by Rebecca Howe. *Why four stars: Cheers* manages to gracefully navigate into a new season filled with changes.

Episode 6.2: "I on Sports" (October 1, 1987) ***

Sam takes over the sports desk on a newscast for a week.

Episode 6.3: "Little Carla, Happy at Last: Part 1" (October 15, 1987) **

Carla and Eddie plan their wedding.

Episode 6.4: "Little Carla, Happy at Last: Part 2" (October 22, 1987) **

Because of their superstitions, Carla and Eddie struggle with their wedding plans.

Episode 6.5: "The Crane Mutiny" (October 29, 1987) ***

Frasier dumps Lilith to pursue a relationship with Rebecca.

Episode 6.6: "Paint Your Office" (November 5, 1987) ***

Rebecca hires Norm to paint her office.

Episode 6.7: "The Last Angry Mailman" (November 12, 1987) *

Cliff tries to stop his mom's house from being demolished. *Why one star:* Cliff chaining himself to a pillar to stop demolition is an overused sitcom trope that doesn't fit with *Cheers*.

Episode 6.8: "Bidding on the Boys" (November 19, 1987) **

Rebecca hosts a bachelor auction at Cheers.

Episode 6.9: "Pudd'n Head Boyd" (November 26, 1987) **

Woody dresses as Mark Twain because he's an understudy for a community play.

Episode 6.10: "A Kiss Is Still a Kiss" (December 3, 1987) ***

Sam tricks Rebecca into kissing him in front of Mr. Drake.

Episode 6.11: "My Fair Clavin" (December 10, 1987) **

Cliff convinces his plain-looking girlfriend to get a makeover.

Episode 6.12: "Christmas Cheers" (December 17, 1987) ***

Sam hunts for a Christmas gift for Rebecca after he realizes she has gifts for all the employees.

Episode 6.13: "Woody for Hire Meets Norman of the Apes" (January 7, 1988) **

Cliff won't pay Norm for painting his apartment, and Woody insists he met a famous actor.

Episode 6.14: "And God Created Woodman" (January 14, 1988) ***

Rebecca accidentally breaks a valuable vase, but Woody takes the fall for it.

Episode 6.15: "Tale of Two Cuties" (January 21, 1988) **

A new cocktail waitress causes unexpected drama.

Episode 6.16: "Yacht of Fools" (February 4, 1988) ****

Mr. Drake, believing Sam and Rebecca are dating, invites them onto his yacht. *Why four stars:* Highly entertaining farce episode.

Episode 6.17: "To All the Girls I've Loved Before" (February 11, 1988) ***

Frasier and Lilith fight and then reconcile as their wedding approaches.

Episode 6.18: "Let Sleeping Drakes Lie" (February 18, 1988) **

Norm is hired to paint Mr. Drake's house and sneaks Rebecca in to see where her crush lives.

Episode 6.19: "Airport V" (February 25, 1988) **

Carla's fear of flying prevents her from visiting Eddie when he's on tour with the ice show.

Episode 6.20: "The Sam in the Gray Flannel Suit" (March 3, 1988) ***

Sam is hired as a corporate executive, but only so he can help the corporate baseball team.

Episode 6.21: "Our Hourly Bread" (March 10, 1988) ***

A raffle is held to increase sales at the bar, but Woody messes up the prizes.

Episode 6.22: "Slumber Party Massacred" (March 24, 1988) **

When Carla finds out she's going to be a grandma, she panics.

Episode 6.23: "Bar Wars" (March 31, 1988) **

A prank war between Cheers and Gary's Old Towne Tavern escalates.

Episode 6.24: "The Big Kiss-Off" (April 28, 1988) ***

Sam and Woody make a bet about who can kiss Rebecca first.

Episode 6.25: "Backseat Becky, Up Front" (May 5, 1988) ***

Rebecca tries to make her feelings for Mr. Drake clear, but it's too late.

Episode 7.1: "How to Recede in Business" (October 27, 1988) ***

With Mr. Drake's departure, Rebecca attempts to further her career.

Episode 7.2: "Swear to God" (November 3, 1988) **

A woman informs Sam he is possibly the father of her child.

Episode 7.3: "Executive Sweet" (November 10, 1988) **

Rebecca is asked out by her new boss.

Episode 7.4: "One Happy Chappy in a Snappy Serape" (November 17, 1988) **

Rebecca convinces Sam to pretend to date her so she can avoid the advances from her boss.

Episode 7.5: "Those Lips, Those Ice" (November 24, 1988) **

Carla is concerned Eddie is having an affair.

Episode 7.6: "Norm, Is That You?" (December 8, 1988) ***

Norm redecorates Frasier and Lilith's home.

Episode 7.7: "How to Win Friends and Electrocute People" (December 15, 1988) ***

Cliff has surgery, but only Frasier comes to visit him at the hospital.

Episode 7.8: "Jumping Jerks" (December 22, 1988) ****

Sam, Woody, Norm, and Cliff go skydiving. *Why four stars:* A great episode displaying the friendship in the Cheers gang.

Episode 7.9: "Send in the Crane" (January 5, 1989) *

Sam is interested in a woman he use to date and her now grown up daughter. *Why one star:* Sam's behavior is too gross, even for a sexual compulsive we've come to like.

Episode 7.10: "Bar Wars II: The Woodman Strikes Back" (January 12, 1989) **

Cheers competes in a Bloody Mary contest against Gary's Olde Towne Tavern.

Episode 7.11: "Adventures in Housesitting" (January 19, 1989) ***

Rebecca is asked to house-sit for a VP of the company and loses his dog.

Episode 7.12: "Please Mr. Postman" (February 2, 1989) ***

Cliff is assigned to train a new postal employee.

Episode 7.13: "Golden Boyd" (February 9, 1989) ***

Rebecca throws a party for a VP's daughter and hires Sam and Woody to bartend.

Episode 7.14: "I Kid You Not" (February 16, 1989) ***

Frasier and Lilith spend time with Carla's son, Ludlow, to see if they want to be parents.

Episode 7.15: "Don't Paint Your Chickens" (February 23, 1989) ***

Sam dates an athletic young woman and pretends to be more active than he is.

Episode 7.16: "The Cranemakers" (March 2, 1989) ****

Lilith relishes being pregnant. *Why four stars:* Bebe Neuwirth. She's generally great, but particularly brilliant in this episode.

Episode 7.17: "Hot Rocks" (March 16, 1989) **

Sam and Rebecca each get stood up by their date.

Episode 7.18: "What's Up, Doc?" (March 30, 1989) ***

Sam asks out a woman in the bar, but she turns him down.

Episode 7.19: "The Gift of the Woodi" (April 6, 1989) ****

Rebecca turns to Lilith for fashion advice as a woman in the business world. *Why four stars:* Again, Bebe Neuwirth is particularly fantastic in this episode.

Episode 7.20: "Call Me Irresponsible" (April 13, 1989) ***

Sam runs betting in the bar, and Rebecca reluctantly participates.

Episode 7.21: "Sisterly Love" (April 27, 1989) ***

Rebecca's sister Susan visits Cheers.

Episode 7.22: "The Visiting Lecher" (May 4, 1989) ***

Frasier's colleague is promoting his new book on marital fidelity, but he hits on Rebecca.

Episode 8.1: "The Improbable Dream, Part 1" (September 21, 1989) ***

Rebecca can't sleep because of a recurring erotic dream about Sam.

Episode 8.2: "The Improbable Dream, Part 2" (September 28, 1989) ***

The extremely wealthy businessman, Robin Colcord, begins dating Rebecca.

Episode 8.3: "A Bar Is Born" (October 12, 1989) ***

Sam finds a new place where he can open his own bar.

Episode 8.4: "How to Marry a Mailman" (October 19, 1989) ***

Cliff wants to date Maggie, but has psychological issues before asking her out.

Episode 8.5: "The Two Faces of Norm" (October 26, 1989) **

Norm hires painters to help him with his jobs but has difficulty managing them.

Episode 8.6: "The Stork Brings a Crane" (November 2, 1989) ***

Lilith goes into labor.

Episode 8.7: "Death Takes a Holiday on Ice" (November 9, 1989) ****

Carla's husband Eddie dies in a freak accident, and she discovers he had a second wife. *Why four stars:* The unexpected plot twist of Eddie having a second wife makes an okay episode into a great episode.

Episode 8.8: "For Real Men Only" (November 16, 1989) **

Carla tries to get Eddie's number retired as a memorial to him.

Episode 8.9: "Two Girls for Every Boyd" (November 23, 1989) ***

Sam, Cliff, Norm, and Frasier have a beard-growing contest.

Episode 8.10: "The Art of the Steal" (November 30, 1989) ***

Rebecca attempts to surprise Robin by waiting for him at his apartment naked.

Episode 8.11: "Feeble Attraction" (December 7, 1989) ***

Norm has to fire his secretary at work; however, she misinterprets his feelings toward her.

Episode 8.12: "Sam Ahoy" (December 14, 1989) **

Sam sails Robin's boat in a race in an attempt to earn money to buy the bar back.

Episode 8.13: "Sammy and the Professor" (January 4, 1980) ***

Rebecca's old college professor visits, and Sam turns to her for advice.

Episode 8.14: "What Is . . . Cliff Clavin?" (January 18, 1990) ****

Cliff is on *Jeopardy*, and a kid steals Sam's black book. *Why four stars:* It's unexpectedly fun to see Cliff succeed at a trivia game but blow it all in the end.

Episode 8.15: "Finally! Part 1" (January 25, 1990) ***

Robin invites Rebecca and Sam to a charity dinner.

Episode 8.16: "Finally! Part 2" (February 1, 1990) ***

Sam finds out Robin is seeing a woman other than Rebecca.

Episode 8.17: "Woody or Won't He" (February 8, 1990) ****

Woody is nervous to meet Kelly's mother for the first time. *Why four stars:* Woody's outburst at the dinner is a highlight moment for Woody Harrelson.

Episode 8.18: "Severe Crane Damage" (February 15, 1990) ****

Lilith appears on TV to promote her new book, *Good Girls/Bad Boys*. *Why four stars:* Sam and Frasier are excellent foils when allowed to be contrasted so clearly.

Episode 8.19: "Indoor Fun with Sammy and Robby" (February 22, 1990) ***

Robin takes the day off to spend time with Rebecca, but he ends up competing with Sam all day.

Episode 8.20: "50-50 Carla" (March 8, 1990) **

Eddie's life insurance money causes Carla stress.

Episode 8.21: "Bar Wars III: The Return of Tecumseh" (March 15, 1990) ***

Cheers patrons think they are being pranked by Gary's Olde Towne Tavern for St. Patrick's Day.

Episode 8.22: "Loverboyd" (March 29, 1990) **

Kelly's father is sending her off to Europe because he doesn't want her to date Woody.

Episode 8.23: "The Ghost and Mrs. LeBec" (April 12, 1990) **

Carla goes on a date, but is haunted by Eddie's ghost.

Episode 8.24: "Mr. Otis Regrets" (April 19, 1990) ***

Rebecca knows Robin is seeing another woman.

Episode 8.25: "Cry Hard" (April 26, 1990) ****

Rebecca discovers Robin is stealing company secrets through her. *Why four stars:* An unexpected reveal that makes sense and forces you to reconsider the past season.

Episode 8.26: "Cry Harder" (May 3, 1990) ***

Sam reports Robin for what he has done and gets the bar back as his reward.

Episode 9.1: "Love Is a Really, Really Perfectly Okay Thing" (September 20, 1990) **

Rebecca and Sam lie to Robin, saying that nothing happened between them.

Episode 9.2: "Cheers Fouls Out" (September 27, 1990) **

Cheers gets Kevin McHale to help win a basketball game.

Episode 9.3: "Rebecca Redux" (October 4, 1990) ***

Rebecca works as a car show girl.

Episode 9.4: "Where Nobody Knows Your Name" (October 11, 1990) ***

One of Robin's mistresses is in the news.

Episode 9.5: "Ma Always Liked You Best" (October 18, 1990) **

Woody lets Cliff's mother stay with him.

Episode 9.6: "Grease" (October 25, 1990) **

Norm tries to save a favorite restaurant, the Hungry Heifer, from closing.

Episode 9.7: "Breaking In Is Hard to Do" (November 1, 1990) ***

Frasier and Lilith debate who should stay home with Frederick.

Episode 9.8: "Cheers 200th Anniversary Special, Part 1" (November 8, 1990)

John McLaughlin hosts a special retrospective of *Cheers*.

Episode 9.9: "Cheers 200th Anniversary Special, Part 2" (November 8, 1990)

John McLaughlin hosts a special retrospective of *Cheers*.

Episode 9.10: "Bad Neighbor Sam" (November 15, 1990) ****

John Hill is the new owner of Melville's, and he drives Sam nuts. *Why four stars:* John Hill brings in a hilarious new dynamic to the bar.

Episode 9.11: "Veggie-Boyd" (November 22, 1990) ***

Woody plays a bartender in a commercial.

Episode 9.12: "Norm and Cliff's Excellent Adventure" (December 6, 1990) ****

Norm and Cliff are bored and start a fight between Frasier and Sam. *Why four stars:* In some instances, seeing two characters fight makes you realize what good friends they are.

Episode 9.13: "Woody Interruptus" (December 13, 1990) ***

Kelly returns from France with a Frenchman who wants to steal her away.

Episode 9.14: "Honor Thy Mother" (January 3, 1991) *

Carla's mother has the "death" dream and asks Carla to continue a particular family tradition. *Why one star:* The storyline feels forced compared to the rest of the series.

Episode 9.15: "Achilles Hill" (January 10, 1991) ***

As a means of getting back at John Hill, Sam tries to date his daughter.

Episode 9.16: "The Days of Wine and Neuroses" (January 24, 1991) ***

Robin is getting out of jail and asks Rebecca to marry him.

Episode 9.17: "Wedding Bell Blues" (January 31, 1991) ***

Rebecca can't decide if she wants to marry Robin.

Episode 9.18: "I'm Getting My Act Together and Sticking It in Your Face" (February 7, 1991) **

Rebecca has a hard time handling her break up from Robin.

Episode 9.19: "Sam Time Next Year" (February 14, 1991) ****

No one's Valentine's day goes according to plan. *Why four stars:* Ted Danson's performance adds excellent depth and pathos to Sam Malone's character.

Episode 9.20: "Crash of the Titans" (February 21, 1991) *

Rebecca tries to buy the bar from Sam but buys the pool room from John Allen Hill. *Why one star:* Just a bit icky.

Episode 9.21: "It's a Wonderful Wife" (February 28, 1991) ***

The gang at Cheers throws Frasier a party for his birthday but makes him do all the work.

Episode 9.22: "Cheers Has Chili" (March 14, 1991) ***

Rebecca attempts to open a tearoom in the pool room at Cheers.

Episode 9.23: "Carla Loves Clavin" (March 21, 1991) **

Carla competes in the annual Miss Boston Barmaid.

Episode 9.24: "Pitch It Again, Sam" (March 28, 1991) **

Sam takes on an old baseball nemesis, Dutch Kincaid, in a baseball game.

Episode 9.25: "Rat Girl" (April 4, 1991) ***

Lilith mourns the death of her favorite lab rat.

Episode 9.26: "Home Malone" (April 25, 1991) ****

Frasier and Lilith ask Sam to babysit Frederick. *Why four stars:* A key episode in Sam's evolution, and it's great to see him bested by a child.

Episode 9.27: "Uncle Sam Wants You" (May 2, 1991) **

Sam decides he wants a child and asks Rebecca to be the mother.

Episode 10.1: "Baby Talk" (September 19, 1991) ***

Sam and Rebecca each get advice from Frasier and Lilith.

Episode 10.2: "Get Your Kicks on Route 666" (September 26, 1991) ***

Frasier, Sam, Norm, and Cliff take a road trip together.

Episode 10.3: "Madame LaCarla" (October 3, 1991) **

Carla's spiritualist retires, and Carla wants to become a spiritualist as well.

Episode 10.4: "The Norm Who Came to Dinner" (October 10, 1991) ***

Norm gets injured while painting at the Cranes' and overstays his welcome.

Episode 10.5: "Ma's Little League" (October 17, 1991) **

Cliff's girlfriend, Margaret, meets his mother.

Episode 10.6: "Unplanned Parenthood" (October 24, 1991) **

Sam and Rebecca babysit Carla's children.

Episode 10.7: "Bar Wars V: The Final Judgment" (October 31, 1991) ***

On Halloween, everyone at Cheers pranks Sam along with Gary's Olde Towne Tavern.

Episode 10.8: "Where Have All the Floorboards Gone" (November 7, 1991) ***

The gang debates how many bolts are in the Madison Square Garden floor.

Episode 10.9: "Head over Hill" (November 14, 1991) ***

Carla falls for Sam's nemesis, John Hill.

Episode 10.10: "A Fine French Whine" (November 21, 1991) ***

Henri's visa is expiring, and he convinces Kelly to marry him so he can stay in America.

Episode 10.11: "I'm Okay, You're Defective" (December 5, 1991) **

Sam and Rebecca worry about Sam's fertility.

Episode 10.12: "Go Make" (December 12, 1991) **

Neither Sam or Rebecca want to have a baby anymore.

Episode 10.13: "Don't Shoot . . . I'm Only the Psychiatrist" (January 2, 1992) **

Woody gives Sam a haircut, and Frasier brings a group of socially awkward patients to the bar.

Episode 10.14: "No Rest for the Woody" (January 9, 1992) ***

Woody gets a second job to pay for Kelly's engagement ring.

Episode 10.15: "My Son, the Father" (January 16, 1992) ***

One of Carla's sons decides to become a priest, and Sam and John Hill continue to feud.

Episode 10.16: "One Hugs, the Other Doesn't" (January 30, 1992) ****

Frasier discovers his first wife is now a popular children's performer named Nanny Gee. *Why four stars:* Emma Thompson is a scene-stealing guest star.

Episode 10.17: "A Diminished Rebecca with a Suspended Cliff" (February 6, 1992) ****

Woody's cousin visits Boston and falls in love with Rebecca. *Why four stars:* Just as Emma stole the show in the previous episode, Harry Connick Jr. is another fantastic guest star.

Episode 10.18: "License to Hill" (February 13, 1992) ****

The guys throw a poker game at Cheers and Rebecca forgot to mail in the bar's liquor license. *Why four stars:* Kirstie Alley's episode-long desperation is a great bit of acting.

Episode 10.19: "Rich Man, Wood Man" (February 20, 1992) ***

Woody comes back from a trip to London with Kelly's family and has changed.

Episode 10.20: "Smotherly Love" (February 27, 1992) **

Lilith's mother comes to visit and insists Frasier and Lilith renew their vows.

Episode 10.21: "Take Me out of the Ball Game" (March 26, 1992) **

Sam attempts a comeback in baseball.

Episode 10.22: "Rebecca's Lover . . . Not" (April 23, 1992) ***

Rebecca considers rekindling the romance with her first boyfriend, only to find out he's gay.

Episode 10.23: "Bar Wars VI: This Time It's for Real" (April 30, 1992) ***

The gang starts a prank war with a mob boss.

Episode 10.24: "Heeeeere's . . . Cliffy!" (May 7, 1992) *

Cliff submits a joke to *The Tonight Show Starring Johnny Carson*. *Why one star:* The overall premise doesn't work and feels off compared to the rest of the series.

Episode 10.25: "An Old-Fashioned Wedding, Part 1" (May 14, 1992) ****

Everything goes wrong just before Woody and Kelly's wedding. *Why four stars:* Weddings always make for great episodes.

Episode 10.26: "An Old-Fashioned Wedding, Part 2" (May 14, 1992) ****

Everything goes wrong just before Woody and Kelly's wedding. *Why four stars:* Weddings always make for great episodes.

Episode 11.1: "The Little Match Girl" (September 24, 1992) ***

Rebecca vows to quit smoking but accidentally burns down part of Cheers.

Episode 11.2: "The Beer Is Always Greener" (October 1, 1992) **

It's the grand reopening of Cheers after the repairs.

Episode 11.3: "The King of Beers" (October 8, 1992) ***

A slot machine is accidentally sent to the bar, and Rebecca never wins.

Episode 11.4: "The Magnificent Six" (October 22, 1992) ****

Henri competes with Sam to see who can get the most phone numbers from women. *Why four stars:* Sam turns his charm on full force.

Episode 11.5: "Do Not Forsake Me, O' My Postman" (October 29, 1992) ***

Margaret returns to Cheers pregnant, but Cliff is not the father.

Episode 11.6: "Teaching with the Enemy" (November 5, 1992) ****

Lilith admits to Frasier that she has been having an affair with her colleague. *Why four stars:* Kelsey Grammer excels in this episode.

Episode 11.7: "The Girl in the Plastic Bubble" (November 12, 1992) ****

Lilith tells Frasier she is leaving him. Frasier does not handle it well. *Why four stars:* Kelsey Grammer again is fantastic.

Episode 11.8: "Ill-Gotten Gaines" (November 19, 1992) ***

Everyone decides to have Thanksgiving at Cheers. Woody stands up to his father-in-law.

Episode 11.9: "Feelings . . . Whoa, Whoa, Whoa" (December 3, 1992) ***

John Hill has a heart attack, and Carla considers their relationship.

Episode 11.10: "Daddy's Middle-Aged Girl" (December 10, 1992) ***

Rebecca's father comes to Boston to visit.

Episode 11.11: "Love Me, Love My Car" (December 17, 1992) **

Sam attempts to get his car back from the new owner's widow.

Episode 11.12: "Sunday Dinner" (January 7, 1993) **

Frasier, now separated from Lilith, decides to pursue a relationship with his secretary.

Episode 11.13: "Norm's Big Audit" (January 14, 1993) **

Norm is audited and tries to flirt his way out of it.

Episode 11.14: "It's a Mad, Mad, Mad, Mad Bar" (January 21, 1993) **

Robin Colcord returns to Cheers completely poor.

Episode 11.15: "Loathe and Marriage" (February 4, 1993) **

Carla's daughter Serafina is pregnant and gets married.

Episode 11.16: "Is There a Doctor in the Howe?" (February 11, 1993) ****

Lilith writes to Frasier, telling him she wants a divorce. Everyone tries to comfort Frasier. *Why four stars:* Everyone comes together for one of their best performances.

Episode 11.17: "The Bar Manager, the Shrink, His Wife and Her Lover" (February 18, 1993) ***

Lilith returns from the eco-pod.

Episode 11.18: "The Last Picture Show" (February 25, 1993) ***

The boys head to a drive-in movie theater that's about to be demolished.

Episode 11.19: "Bar Wars VII: The Naked Prey" (March 18, 1993) ***

The pranks with Gary's Old Towne Tavern reach new heights.

Episode 11.20: "Look before You Sleep" (April 1, 1993) **

Sam locks his keys in the bar and approaches the Cheers regulars, looking for a place to crash.

Episode 11.21: "Woody Gets an Election" (April 22, 1993) ***

Woody decides to run for city council.

Episode 11.22: "It's Lonely on the Top" (April 29, 1993) ***

Carla sleeps with Paul, and Sam reveals a secret shame of his own to make her feel better.

Episode 11.23: "Rebecca Gaines, Rebecca Loses, Part 1" (May 6, 1993) ***

Rebecca thinks that Kelly's rich father, Walter, is interested in her.

Episode 11.24: "Rebecca Gaines, Rebecca Loses, Part 2" (May 6, 1993) ***

Rebecca is wrong in her assumption that Kelly's rich father is interested in her.

Episode 11.25: "The Guy Can't Help It" (May 13, 1993) ****

Sam joins a help group for sexual compulsives. *Why four stars:* A necessary and brilliantly handled endpoint for the character of Sam Malone.

Episode 11.26: "One for the Road, Part 1" (May 20, 1993) ****

Diane is back. *Why four stars:* After six years, seeing Diane back is a reminder of the strengths of the earliest version of *Cheers*.

Episode 11.27: "One for the Road, Part 2" (May 20, 1993) ****

Diane and Sam decide to get married. *Why four stars:* Even while a savvy viewer knows the series will not end with Sam angrily leaving the bar and his friends, it still works to make you realize how important these bonds have become.

Episode 11.28: "One for the Road, Part 3" (May 20, 1993) ****

Sam does not marry Diane, and the gang talks about the meaning of life. *Why four stars:* The gang sitting together at the end of the episode is a wonderful capstone to the series, and "We're closed" is one of the most perfect closing lines in television history.

NOTES

"HOW 'BOUT A BEER, CHIEF?"

1. Jessica Stahl, "Is 'Cheers' Still Funny?" *Washington Post*, March 7, 2014. https://www.washingtonpost.com/news/arts-and-entertainment/wp/2014/03/07/is-cheers-still-funny/?noredirect=on&utm_term=.fd4e070ee0de.

2. Quoted in Brian Raftery, "The Best TV Show That's Ever Been," *GQ*, September 27, 2012. http://www.gq.com/story/cheers-oral-history-extended.

3. Marc Evan Jackson, "Ch. 26: Michael Schur, Creator," *The Good Place: The Podcast*. Podcast audio, September 21, 2018. https://www.nbc.com/the-good-place/exclusives/tgp-podcast.

4. Quoted in Raftery, "The Best TV Show."

5. Nat Hentoff, "'Cheers': No Blacks at the Bar," *Washington Post*, August 24, 1984. https://www.washingtonpost.com/archive/politics/1984/08/24/cheers-no-blacks-at-the-bar/b4490fe5-d9e0-487d-8fae-bb075a525a4c/?utm_term=.01eef5121437.

6. Spencer Buell, "Michael Che Made Another Boston Joke, This Time at the Emmys," *Boston Magazine*, September 18, 2018. https://www.bostonmagazine.com/news/2018/09/18/michael-che-boston-emmys/.

7. Ken Levine, "The *Cheers* Episode We Wrote That Is Now Very Timely," *. . . by Ken Levine* (blog), May 5, 2013. http://kenlevine.blogspot.com/2013/05/the-cheers-episode-we-wrote-that-is-now.html.

1. A JEW AND TWO MORMONS
WALK INTO A BAR

1. Warren Littlefield, with T. R. Pearson, *Top of the Rock: Inside the Rise and Fall of Must See TV* (New York: Doubleday, 2012), 21.

2. Marley Brant, *Happier Days: Paramount Television's Classic Sitcoms 1974–1984* (New York: Billboard Books, 2006), 140.

3. Ibid.

4. "Glen Charles: Writer/Producer," *The Television Academy Foundation: The Interviews*, December 8, 2003. https://interviews.televisionacademy.com/interviews/glen-charles.

5. Ibid.

6. "Les Charles: Writer/Producer," *The Television Academy Foundation: The Interviews*, December 8, 2003. https://interviews.televisionacademy.com/interviews/les-charles.

7. "Glen Charles: Writer/Producer."

8. Ibid.

9. Vince Waldron, *Classic Sitcoms: A Celebration of the Best in Prime-Time Comedy* (New York: Macmillan, 1987), 469.

10. Waldron, *Classic Sitcoms*, 470.

11. Ibid.

12. Brant, *Happier Days*, 140.

13. Brant, *Happier Days*, 471.

14. Littlefield, *Top of the Rock*, 21.

15. "James Burrows," Directors Guild of America, December 23, 2014. https://www.dga.org/News/Guild-News/2015/Jan2015/Awards-Jim-Burrows-LATV.aspx.

16. Brant, *Happier Days*, 141.

17. "James Burrows," Directors Guild of America.

18. Brian Raftery, "The Best TV Show That's Ever Been," *GQ*, September 27, 2012.

19. Ibid.

20. Ibid.

21. Ibid.

22. Littlefield, *Top of the Rock*, 19.

23. Ibid.

24. Paul L. Klein, "Why You Watch What You Watch When You Watch," *TV Guide*, July 24, 1971, 7.

25. Klein, "Why You Watch," 8.

26. Ibid.

27. Littlefield, *Top of the Rock*, 21.

28. Littlefield, *Top of the Rock*, 23.

29. Quoted in Littlefield, *Top of the Rock*, 24.

30. Waldron, *Classic Sitcoms*, 469.

31. Brian Welk, "'Cheers' Finale at 25: 12 Best Moments from 'One for the Road,'" *The Wrap*, May 20, 2018. https://www.thewrap.com/cheers-finale-25th-anniversary-best-moments-from-one-for-the-road/

32. Dennis Bjorklund, *Toasting Cheers: An Episode Guide to the 1982–1993 Comedy Series with Cast Biographies and Character Profiles* (Jefferson, NC: McFarland Press, 1997), 3.

33. Arnie Reisman, "Where Everybody Borrows Your Name," *Vineyard Gazette*, March 25, 2016.

34. Dan McCarthy, "The *Cheers* Conspiracy," *Boston Magazine*, March 20, 2018.

35. Ken Levine, "The *Cheers* Conspiracy," . . . *by Ken Levine, The World as Seen by a TV Comedy Writer* (blog), March 27, 2018.

36. Ibid.

37. Vikram Murthi, "When *Cheers* Became *Cheers*: An Appreciation of 'Endless Slumper,'" *Vulture*, December 6, 2017.

38. Bill Carter, "The Tonic That Keeps 'Cheers' Bubbling Along," *New York Times*, April 29, 1990.

39. "Glen and Les Charles on Casting 'Cheers'—EMMYTVLEGENDS.org," YouTube, December 12, 2012. https://www.youtube.com/watch?v=TbaaM_l0baw.

40. Martin Gitlin, *The Greatest Sitcoms of All Time* (Lanham, MD: Scarecrow Press, 2014), 45.

41. Littlefield, *Top of the Rock*, 24.

42. Littlefield, *Top of the Rock*, 25.

43. Bjorklund, *Toasting Cheers*, 7.

44. Littlefield, *Top of the Rock*, 26.

45. "Setting the Bar: A Conversation with Ted Danson," *Cheers Season 1*, DVD Special Features, Disc 4 (Paramount, 2003).

46. "Glen and Les Charles on Creating the Characters on 'Cheers'—EMMYTVLEGENDS.org." YouTube, December 12, 2012. https://www.youtube.com/watch?v=g7oe7wI_kas.

47. Ibid.

48. Bjorklund, *Toasting Cheers*, 107.

49. Josh Kurp, "The Greatest TV Writers Room Ever," *Vulture*, June 2011. http://www.vulture.com/2011/06/the-greatest-tv-writers-rooms-ever.html.

50. Dave Nemetz, "How Gary Portnoy Made 'Cheers' the Place Where Everybody Knows Your Name," Yahoo.com, April 3, 2013. https://www.yahoo.

com/entertainment/news/how-gary-portnoy-made--cheers--the-place--where-everybody-knows-your-name---230349578.html.

51. Ibid.

52. Ken Levine, "The Story behind the *Cheers* Theme," . . . *by Ken Levine, The World as Seen by a TV Comedy Writer* (blog), September 21, 2014. http://kenlevine.blogspot.com/2014/09/the-story-behind-cheers-theme.html.

53. Ibid.

54. "The Story behind the Cheers Theme," Garyportnoy.com, n.d. https://www.garyportnoy.com/cheers-story/.

55. Ibid.

56. Nemetz, "How Gary Portnoy Made 'Cheers.'"

57. "The Story behind the Cheers Theme."

58. Nemetz, "How Gary Portnoy Made 'Cheers.'"

59. Stephen Coles, "*Cheers* Logo and Opening Titles," Fonts in Use, October 29, 2013. https://fontsinuse.com/uses/5067/cheers-logo-and-opening-titles.

60. "Glen and Les Charles on the 'Cheers' Theme Song - EMMYTVLEGNEDS.org," YouTube, December 12, 2012. https://www.youtube.com/watch?v=zi3EsEvuJuE.

61. Coles, "*Cheers* Logo and Opening Titles."

62. Bjorklund, *Toasting Cheers*, 82.

63. Ibid.

64. "Reviews of New Television Shows," *Variety*, October 6, 1982.

65. Harry Castleman and Walter J. Podrazik, *Watching TV: Six Decades of American Television*, (Syracuse, NY: Syracuse University Press, 2010), 309.

66. Ibid.

67. Alan Sepinwall and Matt Zoller Seitz, *TV (The Book): Two Experts Pick the Greatest American Shows of All Time* (New York: Grand Central Publishing, 2016), 202.

68. Gary Susman, "10 Greatest TV Pilot Episodes," *Time*, September 8, 2013. http://entertainment.time.com/2013/09/09/10-greatest-tv-pilot-episodes/slide/ready-for-takeoff/

69. A.V. Club Staff, "*Cheers*: 'Give Me a Ring Sometime'/'Sam's Women,'" A.V. Club, November 11, 2011. https://tv.avclub.com/cheers-give-me-a-ring-sometime-sam-s-women-1798170424

70. "Give Me a Ring Sometime," *Cheers*, S1E1. Directed by James Burrows; written by Glen Charles and Les Charles. NBC, September 1982.

71. Josh Wolk, "*Parks and Recreation* Showrunner Michael Schur Gives a Masterclass on *Cheers*," *Vulture*, September 1, 2011. http://www.vulture.com/2011/09/cheers_parks_and_recreation_mi.html.

72. Ken Levine, "The 'Lost' *Cheers* Scene," . . . *by Ken Levine, The World as Seen by a TV Comedy Writer* (blog), February 5, 2017. http://kenlevine.blogspot.com/2018/02/the-lost-cheers-scene.html.

73. Ibid.

74. Brian Cronin, "Did the United States Government Create a Special Never-Broadcast Episode of *Cheers*?" LegendsRevealed.com, October 18, 2017. http://legendsrevealed.com/entertainment/2016/10/18/did-the-united-states-government-create-a-special-never-broadcast-episode-of-cheers/.

75. Rick Mitz, *The Great TV Sitcom Book*, expanded ed. (New York: Perigree Books, 1983), 2.

76. Mitz, *Great TV Sitcom Book*, 449.

77. Ibid.

78. David Bianculli, *The Platinum Age of Television: From* I Love Lucy *to* The Walking Dead, *How TV Became Terrific* (New York: First Anchor Books, 2017), 299.

79. Ibid.

80. Ibid.

81. Fred Rothenberg, "Ask Why NBC . . . ," *Lewiston Journal*, September 24, 1983. https://news.google.com/newspapers?id=3Q8gAAAAIBAJ&sjid=imUFAAAAIBAJ&dq=cheers%20television%20%7C%20tv&pg=1347%2C3808893.

2. WHEN EVERYBODY KNOWS YOUR NAME

1. Bill Carter, "The Tonic That Keeps 'Cheers' Bubbling Along," *New York Times*, April 29, 1990.

2. Vince Waldron, *Classic Sitcoms: A Celebration of the Best in Prime-Time Comedy* (New York: Macmillan, 1987), 473.

3. "Strictly Top Shelf: The Guys behind the Bar," *Cheers Season 2*, DVD Special Features, Disc 4 (Paramount, 2004).

4. Ibid.

5. Waldron, *Classic Sitcoms*, 473.

6. Dennis Bjorklund, *Toasting Cheers: An Episode Guide to the 1982–1993 Comedy Series with Cast Biographies and Character Profiles* (Jefferson, NC: McFarland Press, 1997), 8.

7. Warren Littlefield, with T. R. Pearson, *Top of the Rock: Inside the Rise and Fall of Must See TV* (New York: Doubleday, 2012), 31.

8. David Bianculli, *The Platinum Age of Television: From* I Love Lucy *to* The Walking Dead, *How TV Became Terrific* (New York: First Anchor Books, 2017), 298.

9. Ibid.

10. Littlefield, *Top of the Rock,* 31.

11. Martin Gitlin, *The Greatest Sitcoms of All Time* (Lanham, MD: Scarecrow Press, 2014), 43.

12. Gitlin, *Greatest Sitcoms,* 45.

13. Waldron, *Classic Sitcoms,* 473.

14. "Give Me a Ring Sometime," *Cheers,* S1E1. Directed by James Burrows; written by Glen Charles and Les Charles. NBC, September 1982.

15. "Sam's Women," *Cheers,* S1E2. Directed by James Burrows; written by Earl Pomerantz. NBC, October 1982.

16. Ibid.

17. "Coach's Daughter," *Cheers,* S1E5. Directed by James Burrows; written by Ken Estin. NBC, October 1982.

18. "Showdown, Part 2," *Cheers,* S1E22. Directed by James Burrows; written by Glen and Les Charles. NBC, March 1982.

19. Vikram Murthi, "When *Cheers* Became *Cheers*: An Appreciation of 'Endless Slumper,'" *Vulture,* December 6, 2017.

20. "Endless Slumper," *Cheers,* S1E10. Directed by James Burrows; written by Sam Simon. NBC, December 1982.

21. "Coach's Daughter," *Cheers.*

22. "Showdown, Part 2," *Cheers.*

23. "Power Play," *Cheers,* S2E1. Directed by James Burrows; written by Glen and Les Charles. NBC, September 1983.

24. "Homicidal Ham," *Cheers,* S2E4. Directed by James Burrows; written by David Lloyd. NBC, October 1983.

25. "Sumner's Return," *Cheers,* S2E5. Directed by James Burrows; written by Michael J. Weithorn. NBC, November 1983.

26. "I'll Be Seeing You, Part 2," *Cheers,* S2E22. Directed by James Burrows; written by Glen and Les Charles. NBC, May 1984.

27. Ryan McGee, Meredith Blake, Todd VanDerWerff, Noel Murray, Phil Dyess-Nugent, Erik Adams, and Donna Bowman, "*Cheers*: 'I'll Be Seeing You,'" A.V. Club, April 26, 2012. https://tv.avclub.com/cheers-i-ll-be-seeing-you-1798172563.

28. Waldron, *Classic Sitcoms,* 501.

29. Associated Press, "Splitting Up Takes Nights for Sam, Diane of 'Cheers.'" *Toledo Blade,* May 3, 1984. https://news.google.com/newspapers?id=4VZQAAAAIBAJ&sjid=LA4EAAAAIBAJ&pg=6868%2C2662620.

30. Joseph J. Darowski and Kate Darowski, *Frasier: A Cultural History* (Lanham, MD: Rowman & Littlefield, 2017), 11.

31. "Rescue Me," *Cheers,* S3E25. Directed by James Burrows; written by Ken Estin. NBC, May 1985.

32. Ken Levine, "How to Hide the Miracle of Life," . . . *by Ken Levine, The World as Seen by a TV Comedy Writer* (blog), April 3, 2007. http://kenlevine. blogspot.com/2007/04/how-to-hide-miracle-of-life.html.

33. Ibid.

34. "Don Juan Is Hell," *Cheers*, S4E11. Directed by James Burrows; written by Phoef Sutton. NBC, December 1985.

35. "Dark Imaginings," *Cheers*, S4E19. Directed by James Burrows; written by David Angell. NBC, February 1986.

36. "Diane Chambers Day," *Cheers*, S4E22. Directed by James Burrows; written by Kimberly Hill. NBC, March 1986.

37. "Strange Bedfellows, Part 3," *Cheers*, S4E26. Directed by James Burrows; written by David Angell. NBC, May 1986.

38. Waldron, *Classic Sitcoms*, 487.

39. "Chambers vs. Malone," *Cheers*, S5E13. Directed by James Burrows; written by David Angell. NBC, January 1987.

40. "Dinner at Eight-ish," *Cheers*, S5E20. Directed by James Burrows; written by Phoef Sutton. NBC, February 1987.

41. "I Do, Adieu," *Cheers*, S5E26. Directed by James Burrows, written by Glen Charles and Les Charles. NBC, May 1987.

42. "Home Is the Sailor," *Cheers*, S6E1. Directed by James Burrows; written by Glen and Les Charles. NBC, September 1987.

43. "The Crane Mutiny," *Cheers*, S6E5. Directed by James Burrows; written by David Angell. NBC, October 1987.

44. "Yacht of Fools," *Cheers*, S6E16. Directed by Thomas Lofaro; written by Cheri Eichen and Bill Steinkellner. NBC, February 1988.

45. "Backseat Becky, Up Front," *Cheers*, S6E25. Directed by James Burrows; written by Cheri Eichen and Bill Steinkellner. NBC, May 1988.

46. "The Visiting Lecher," *Cheers*, S7E22. Directed by James Burrows; written by David Lloyd. NBC, May 1989.

47. "Norm, Is That You?" *Cheers*, S7E6. Directed by James Burrows; written by Cheri Eichen and Bill Steinkellner. NBC, November 1988.

48. "Jumping Jerks," *Cheers*, S7E8. Directed by James Burrows; written by Ken Levine and David Isaacs. NBC, December 1988.

49. "The Cranemakers," *Cheers*, S7E16. Directed by Andy Ackerman; written by Phoef Sutton. NBC, March 1989.

50. "The Stork Brings a Crane," *Cheers*, S8E6. Directed by Andy Ackerman; written by David Lloyd. NBC, November 1989.

51. "What Is . . . Cliff Clavin?" *Cheers*, S8E14. Directed by Andy Ackerman; written by Dan O'Shannon and Tom Anderson. NBC, January 1990.

52. "Cry Harder," *Cheers*, S8E26. Directed by James Burrows; written by Cheri Eichen, Bill Steinkellner, and Phoef Sutton. NBC, May 1990.

53. "Uncle Sam Wants You," *Cheers*, S9E27. Directed by James Burrows; written by Dan Staley and Rob Long. NBC, May 1991.

54. "An Old-Fashioned Wedding," *Cheers*, S10E25–26. Directed by James Burrows; written by David Lloyd. NBC, May 1992.

55. "Teaching with the Enemy," *Cheers*, S11E6. Directed by James Burrows; written by Tom Anderson. NBC, November 1992.

56. "One for the Road," *Cheers*, S11E26–28. Directed by James Burrows; written by Glen and Les Charles. NBC, May 1993.

57. Bjorklund, *Toasting Cheers*, 188.

58. "Never Love a Goalie, Part 1," *Cheers*, S5E17. Directed by James Burrows; written by Ken Levine and David Isaacs. NBC, January 1987.

59. "Death Takes a Holiday on Ice," *Cheers*, S8E7. Directed by James Burrows; written by Ken Levine and David Isaacs. NBC, November 1989.

60. Brian Cronin, "TV Legends Revealed: Why You Don't Mess with Carla on *Cheers*," *Comic Book Resources*, January 10, 2013. http://spinoff. comicbookresources.com/2013/01/10/tv-legends-revealed-why-you-dont-mess-with-carla-on-cheers/.

61. Ken Levine, "The Kiss of Death for Eddie LeBec," . . . *by Ken Levine: The World as Seen by a TV Comedy Writer*, July 21, 2006. http://kenlevine. blogspot.com/2006/07/kiss-of-death-for-eddie-lebec.html.

62. Brian Raftery, "The Best TV Show That's Ever Been," *GQ*, September 27, 2012. http://www.gq.com/story/cheers-oral-history-extended.

63. Ibid.

64. Levine, "The Kiss of Death for Eddie LeBec."

65. Ibid.

66. "Death Takes a Holiday on Ice," *Cheers*.

67. Reuters, "Leno Calls Telecast on 'Cheers' 'a Mistake': Drunken Cast Members Ruined 'Tonight' Broadcast from Boston Bar, He Says," *Los Angeles Times*, May 28, 1993.

68. *EW* Staff, "The Year That Was," *Entertainment Weekly*, December 24, 1993. http://www.ew.com/article/1993/12/24/year-was.

69. John J. O'Connor, "Critic's Notebook: 'Cheers' Is Dead, but There's Always the Wake . . . " *New York Times*, May 21, 1993.

70. A.V. Club, *Inventory: 16 Films Featuring Manic Pixie Dream Girls, 10 Great Songs Nearly Ruined by Saxophone, and 100 More Obsessively Specific Pop-Culture Lists* (New York: Scribner, 2009), 61.

71. Littlefield, *Top of the Rock*, 41.

72. Ibid.

3. THE POWER OF THE BAR

1. Peter Kerr, "NBC Comedy 'Cheers' Turns into a Success," *New York Times*, November 29, 1983. https://www.nytimes.com/1983/11/29/arts/nbc-comedy-cheers-turns-into-a-success.html.

2. Daniel J. Flynn, "Cheers to the Bull & Finch," *American Spectator*, March 24, 2014. https://spectator.org/57725_cheers-bull-finch/.

3. Ken Levine, "The *Cheers* Set," . . . *by Ken Levine, The World as Seen by a TV Comedy Writer* (blog), February 12, 2017. http://kenlevine.blogspot.com/2017/02/the-cheers-set.html.

4. Flynn, "Cheers to the Bull & Finch."

5. Dennis A. Bjorklund, *Toasting Cheers: An Episode Guide to the 1982–1993 Comedy Series with Cast Biographies and Character Profiles* (Jefferson, NC: McFarland Press, 1997), 7.

6. Georgia Dullea, "'Cheers' Has Brewed Trouble for Patrons of the Real Boston Watering Hole," *Chicago Tribune*, October 6, 1985. https://www.chicagotribune.com/news/ct-xpm-1985-10-06-8503080137-story.html.

7. Ibid.

8. Ibid.

9. Flynn, "Cheers to the Bull & Finch."

10. "Bar Tour," *Cheers Season 3*, DVD Special Features, Disc 4 (Paramount, 2004).

11. Levine, "The *Cheers* Set."

12. Brian Raftery, "The Best TV Show That's Ever Been," *GQ*, September 27, 2012. http://www.gq.com/story/cheers-oral-history-extended.

13. Ken Levine, "Re: Questions about Cheers," personal e-mail, March 3, 2018.

14. Mark Lewisohn, *Radio Times Guide to TV Comedy* (London: BBC Worldwide, 2012), 152.

15. Levine, "The *Cheers* Set."

16. Vikram Murthi, "When *Cheers* Became *Cheers*: An Appreciation of 'Endless Slumper,'" *Vulture*, December 6, 2017. https://www.vulture.com/2017/12/cheers-an-appreciation-of-the-endless-slumper-episode.html.

17. Ken Levine, "How to Be a Good Showrunner," . . . *By Ken Levine, The World as Seen by a TV Comedy Writer* (blog), November 10, 2012. https://kenlevine.blogspot.com/2012/11/how-to-be-good-showrunner.html.

18. Jeremy G. Butler, *Television: Critical Methods and Applications*, 4th ed. (London: Routledge, 2011), 262.

19. Levine, "Re: Questions about Cheers."

20. "Diane's Perfect Date," *Cheers*, S1E17. Directed by James Burrows; written by David Lloyd. NBC, February 1983.

21. "Thanksgiving Orphans," *Cheers*, S5E9. Directed by James Burrows; written by Cheri Eichen and Bill Steinkellner. NBC, November 1986.

22. Marc Freeman, "'Cheers' Finale at 25: Untold Stories from inside the Writers Room," *Hollywood Reporter*, May 20, 2018. https://www. hollywoodreporter.com/amp/live-feed/cheers-at-25-untold-stories-inside-writers-room-1113428.

23. Levine, "Re: Questions about Cheers."

24. Quoted in Raftery, "The Best TV Show That's Ever Been."

25. Freeman, "'Cheers' Finale at 25."

26. Alan Sepinwall and Matt Zoller Seitz, *TV (The Book): Two Experts Pick the Greatest American Shows of All Time* (New York, Grand Central Publishing, 2016), 43.

27. Quoted in Freeman, "'Cheers' Finale at 25."

28. Ryan McGee, Meredith Blake, Todd VanDerWerff, Noel Murray, Phil Dyess-Nugent, Erik Adams, Donna Bowman, and Keith Phipps, "*Cheers*: 'Coach Returns to Action'/'Endless Slumper,'" A.V. Club, December 15, 2011. https://tv.avclub.com/cheers-coach-returns-to-action-endless-slumper-1798170877.

29. "The Show Where Diane Comes Back," *Frasier*, S3E14. Directed by James Burrows; written by Christopher Lloyd. NBC, February 1996.

30. Chris Jones, "'Cheers' to Sam and Diane, a Pair Whose Names You Know," *Chicago Tribune*, September 23, 2016. https://www.chicagotribune. com/entertainment/theater/reviews/ct-cheers-live-review-ent-0923-20160922-column.html.

31. "It's Lonely on the Top," *Cheers*, S11E22. Directed by James Burrows; written by Heide Perlman. NBC, April 1993.

32. "Home Is the Sailor," *Cheers*, S6E1. Directed by James Burrows; written by Glen and Les Charles. NBC, September 1987.

33. Aljean Harmetz, "Television: Can Kirstie Alley Keep the 'Cheers' Bar Open?" *New York Times*, September 20, 1987. https://www.nytimes.com/1987/ 09/20/arts/television-can-kirstie-alley-keep-the-cheers-bar-open.html.

34. "Home Is the Sailor," *Cheers*.

35. Raftery, "The Best TV Show That's Ever Been."

36. Susan King, "Decades Later and We Still Remember Their Names: The Cast of 'Cheers' Reflects on the Beloved Series," *Los Angeles Times*, May 16, 1993. https://www.latimes.com/entertainment/tv/la-et-st-cheers-end-19930516-snap-story.html.

37. Jay Winston, "The Designated Driver Campaign: Why It Worked," *Huffington Post*, March 18, 2010; updated May 25, 2011. https://www. huffingtonpost.com/jay-winston/designated-driver-campaig_b_405249.html.

38. Ibid.

39. "Rebound, Part 1," *Cheers*, S3E1. Directed by James Burrows; written by Glen and Les Charles. NBC, September 1984.

40. Ken Levine, "How Did We Handle Drinking on *Cheers*," . . . *by Ken Levine, The World as Seen by a TV Comedy Writer* (blog), December 23, 2010. http://kenlevine.blogspot.com/2010/12/how-did-we-handle-drinking-on-cheers. html.

41. Tim Delaney and Tim Madigan, *The Sociology of Sports: An Introduction* (Jefferson, NC: McFarland Press, 2009), 81.

42. Ibid.

43. "Cliff's Rocky Moment," *Cheers*, S2E16. Directed by James Burrows; written by David Lloyd. NBC, January 1984.

44. "The Stork Brings a Crane," *Cheers*, S8E6. Directed by Andy Ackerman; written by David Lloyd. NBC, November 1989.

45. A.V. Club Staff, *"Cheers*: 'Give Me a Ring Sometime'/'Sam's Women,'" A.V. Club, November 11, 2011. https://tv.avclub.com/cheers-give-me-a-ring-sometime-sam-s-women-1798170424.

46. "Sam's Women," *Cheers*, S1E2. Directed by James Burrows; written by Earl Pomerantz. NBC, October 1982.

47. Freeman, "'Cheers' Finale at 25."

48. Levine, "Re: Questions about Cheers."

49. See "Homicidal Ham," *Cheers*, S2E4; "Sam Turns the Other Cheek," *Cheers*, S3E5; "Diane Meets Mom," *Cheers*, S3E8 (all directed by James Burrows and written by David Lloyd); "Birth, Death, Love and Rice," *Cheers*, S4E1 (directed by Burrows and written by Heide Perlman); "One Happy Chappy in a Snappy Serape," *Cheers*, S7E4 (directed by Burrows and written by Cheri Eichen and Bill Steinkellner); and "Sisterly Love," *Cheers*, S7E21 (directed by Burrows and written by David Lloyd).

50. "Give Me a Ring Sometime," *Cheers*, S1E1. Directed by James Burrows; written by Glen and Les Charles. NBC, September 1982.

51. Kerr, "NBC Comedy 'Cheers' Turns into a Success."

52. Freeman, "'Cheers' Finale at 25."

53. "The Book of Samuel," *Cheers*, S5E11. Directed by James Burrows; written by Phoef Sutton. NBC, December 1986.

54. "The Spy Who Came in for a Cold One," *Cheers*, S1E12. Directed by James Burrows; written by David Lloyd. NBC, November 1982.

55. Ibid.

56. Ibid.

4. THE ALCOHOLIC GREEK CHORUS AND THE STAFF THAT SERVES THEM

1. Quoted in Marc Freeman, "'Cheers' Finale at 25: Untold Stories from inside the Writers Room," *Hollywood Reporter*, May 20, 2018. https://www.hollywoodreporter.com/amp/live-feed/cheers-at-25-untold-stories-inside-writers-room-1113428.

2. Ibid.

3. "Let Me Count the Ways," *Cheers*, S1E14. Directed by James Burrows; written by Heide Perlman. NBC, January 1983.

4. "Bidding on the Boys," *Cheers*, S6E8. Directed by Thomas Lofaro; written by David Lloyd. NBC, November 1987.

5. "Death Takes a Holiday on Ice," *Cheers*, S8E7. Directed by James Burrows; written by Ken Levine and David Isaacs. NBC, November 1989.

6. Gary Hoppenstand, "Re: Cheers," personal e-mail, August 22, 2016.

7. Josh Wolk, "*Parks and Recreation* Showrunner Michael Schur Gives a Master Class on *Cheers*," *Vulture*, September 1, 2011. https://www.vulture.com/2011/09/cheers_parks_and_recreation_mi.html.

8. Andy Greenwald, "Men in Black: The Show?" *Grantland*, January 23, 2013. http://grantland.com/features/tv-mailbag-time/.

9. Brett White, "'Cheers' Has the Greatest (and Messiest) Thanksgiving Episode of All Time," *Decider*, November 23, 2017. https://decider.com/2017/11/23/cheers-thanksgiving-episode/.

10. Quoted in Freeman, "'Cheers' Finale at 25."

11. Ryan McGee, Meredith Blake, Todd VanDerWerff, Noel Murray, Phil Dyess-Nugent, Erik Adams, Donna Bowman, and Keith Phipps, "*Cheers*: 'Friends, Romans, Accountants'/'Truce or Consequences,'" A.V. Club, December 8, 2011. https://tv.avclub.com/cheers-friends-romans-accountants-truce-or-conseq-1798170817.

12. "Friends, Romans, Accountants," *Cheers*, S1E7. Directed by James Burrows; written by Ken Levine and David Isaacs. NBC, November 1982.

13. "House of Horrors with Formal Dining and Used Brick," *Cheers*, S5E5. Directed by James Burrows; written by David Angell. NBC, October 1986.

14. "Fools and Their Money," *Cheers*, S4E12. Directed by James Burrows; written by Heide Perlman. NBC, December 1985.

15. "Someone Single, Someone Blue," *Cheers*, S1E20. Directed by James Burrows; written by David Angell. NBC, March 1983.

16. Ryan McGee, Meredith Blake, Todd VanDerWerff, Phil Dyess-Nugent, Erik Adams, and Donna Bowman, "*Cheers*: 'Pick a Con, Any Con'/'Someone Single, Someone Blue,'" A.V. Club, January 26, 2012. https://tv.avclub.com/cheers-pick-a-con-any-con-someone-single-someone-1798171308.

17. "Li'l Sister Don't Cha," *Cheers*, S2E2. Directed by James Burrows; written by Heide Perlman. NBC, October 1983.

18. "Thanksgiving Orphans," *Cheers*, S5E9. Directed by James Burrows; written by Cheri Eichen and Bill Steinkellner. NBC, November 1986.

19. Ibid.

20. Quoted in Freeman, "'Cheers' Finale at 25."

21. Dave Nemetz, "Food Fight! The Messy True Story behind the Classic 'Cheers' Episode, 'Thanksgiving Orphans,'" Yahoo.com, November 24, 2015. https://www.yahoo.com/entertainment/news/cheers-thanksgiving-orphans-episode-true-story-054056375.html.

22. Ibid.

23. "From Beer to Eternity," *Cheers*, S4E9. Directed by James Burrows; written by Peter Casey and David Lee. NBC, November 1985.

24. "Bar Wars," *Cheers*, S6E23; "Bar Wars II: The Woodman Strikes Back," *Cheers*, S7E10; "Bar Wars III: The Return of Tecumseh," *Cheers*, S8E21; "Cheers Fouls Out," *Cheers*, S9E2; "Bar Wars V: The Final Judgment," *Cheers*, S10E7; "Bar Wars VI: This Time It's for Real," *Cheers*, S10E23; "Bar Wars VII: The Naked Prey," *Cheers*, S11E19. All seven were directed by James Burrows; "Cheers Fouls Out" was written by Larry Balmagia, and the rest were written by Ken Levine and David Isaacs.

25. Ken Levine, "The Story behind the *Cheers* Bar War Episodes," . . . *by Ken Levine, The World as Seen by a TV Comedy Writer* (blog), July 18, 2010. http://kenlevine.blogspot.com/2010/07/story-behind-cheers-bar-war-episodes.html.

26. Ibid.

27. Alex McLevy, "Gary's Olde Town Tavern Gave *Cheers* a Nemesis—and a Perfect Foil." A.V. Club, April 5, 2016. https://tv.avclub.com/gary-s-olde-town-tavern-gave-cheers-a-nemesis-and-a-per-1798245924.

28. Harry Castleman and Walter J. Podrazik, *Watching TV: Six Decades of American Television*, 2nd ed. (Syracuse, NY: Syracuse University Press, 2010), 309.

29. "Setting the Bar: A Conversation with Ted Danson," *Cheers Season 1*, DVD Special Features, Disc 4 (Paramount, 2003).

30. Brian Raftery, "The Best TV Show That's Ever Been," *GQ*, September 27, 2012. http://www.gq.com/story/cheers-oral-history-extended.

31. StarTrek.com Staff, "Mark Allen Shepherd Was Born to be Morn—Part 1," Star Trek Discovery, April 11, 2011. http://www.startrek.com/article/mark-allen-shepherd-was-born-to-be-morn-part-1.

32. Steve Olenski, "Is Norm the New Norm? The 'Cheers' Effect on Marketing," *Forbes*, August 16, 2018. https://www.forbes.com/sites/steveolenski/2018/08/16/is-norm-the-new-norm-the-cheers-effect-on-marketing/#9ac5fef682e8.

33. Quoted in Freeman, "'Cheers' Finale at 25."

34. Ibid.

35. Ken Levine, "Re: Questions about Cheers," personal e-mail, March 3, 2018.

36. Raftery, "The Best TV Show That's Ever Been."

37. "Snow Job," *Cheers*, S2E18. Directed by James Burrows; written by David Angell. NBC, February 1984.

38. "Tan 'n' Wash," *Cheers*, S5E6. Directed by James Burrows; written by Cheri Eichen and Bill Steinkellner. NBC, November 1986.

39. "Bar Wars II: The Woodman Strikes Back," *Cheers*.

40. "Bar Wars III: The Return of Tecumseh," *Cheers*.

41. "The Norm Who Came to Dinner," *Cheers*, S10E4. Directed by Tom Moore; written by Dan O'Shannon and Tom Anderson. NBC, October 1991.

42. "Sam's Women," *Cheers*, S1E2. Directed by James Burrows; written by Earl Pomerantz. NBC, October 1982.

43. "The Norm Who Came to Dinner," *Cheers*.

44. "Crash of the Titans," *Cheers*, S9E20. Directed by James Burrows; written by Dan Staley and Rob Long. NBC, February 1991.

45. "The Two Faces of Norm," *Cheers*, S8E5. Directed by Andy Ackerman; written by Eugene B. Stein. NBC, October 1989.

46. "Norm's First Hurrah," *Cheers*, S5E23. Directed by Thomas Lofaro; written by Andy Cowan and David S. Williger. NBC, March 1987.

47. Janis D. Froelich, "George Wendt: Norm Reflects on His TV Series, Life and Drinking," *Deseret News*, October 16, 1990. https://www.deseretnews.com/article/127517/GEORGE-WENDT--NORM-REFLECTS-ON-HIS-TV-SERIES-LIFE-AND-DRINKING.html.

48. "Crash of the Titans," *Cheers*.

49. Raftery, "The Best TV Show That's Ever Been."

50. "Tan 'n' Wash," *Cheers*.

51. "Swear to God," *Cheers*, S7E2. Directed by James Burrows; written by Tom Reeder. NBC, November 1988.

52. "Don't Shoot . . . I'm Only the Psychiatrist," *Cheers*, S10E13. Directed by James Burrows; written by Kathy Ann Stumpe. NBC, January 1992.

53. "Glen and Les Charles on Creating the Characters on 'Cheers'—EMMYTVLEGENDS.org," YouTube, December 12, 2012. https://www.youtube.com/watch?v=g7oe7wI_kas.

54. "How to Win Friends and Electrocute People," *Cheers*, S7E7. Directed by James Burrows; written by Phoef Sutton. NBC, December 1988.

55. Ibid.

56. Susan King, "Decades Later and We Still Remember Their Names: The Cast of 'Cheers' Reflects on the Beloved Series," *Los Angeles Times*, May 16,

1993. https://www.latimes.com/entertainment/tv/la-et-st-cheers-end-19930516-snap-story.html.

57. Jordan Zakarin, "'Cheers' Turns 30, and Cliff Clavin Delivers His Memories," *Hollywood Reporter*, October 1, 2012. https://www.hollywoodreporter.com/news/cheers-30th-anniversary-john-ratzenberger-ted-danson-375263.

58. Raftery, "The Best TV Show That's Ever Been."

59. Freeman, "'Cheers' Finale at 25."

60. Ibid.

61. Ibid.

62. "Bio Channel: Kelsey Grammer (Full Documentary)," YouTube, February 28, 2018. https://www.youtube.com/watch?v=hepVnn_fm6g.

63. Raftery, "The Best TV Show That's Ever Been."

64. Quoted in Freeman, "'Cheers' Finale at 25."

65. "Birth, Death, Love and Rice," *Cheers*, S4E1. Directed by James Burrows; written by Heide Perlman. NBC, September 1985.

66. "The Heart Is a Lonely Snipe Hunter," *Cheers*, S3E14. Directed by James Burrows; written by Heide Perlman. NBC, January 1985.

67. Ibid.

68. Quoted in Raftery, "The Best TV Show That's Ever Been."

69. "Second Time Around," *Cheers*, S4E17. Directed by Thomas Lofaro; written by Cheri Eichen and Bill Steinkellner. NBC, February 1986.

70. Quoted in Freeman, "'Cheers' Finale at 25."

71. Ibid.

72. "Second Time Around," *Cheers*.

73. Quoted in Raftery, "The Best TV Show That's Ever Been."

74. Ibid.

75. Jerry Buck, "Actress Bebe Neuwirth Brings Flexibility to Her Rigid Role on NBC's 'Cheers,'" *Tulsa World*, May 24, 1992. https://www.tulsaworld.com/archives/actress-bebe-neuwirth-brings-flexibility-to-her-rigid-role-on/article_68b484f7-1f16-5bf3-8012-3bc22c3de825.html.

76. "Give Me a Ring Sometime," *Cheers*, S1E1. Directed by James Burrows; written by Glen and Les Charles. NBC, September 1982.

77. Raftery, "The Best TV Show That's Ever Been."

78. Bill Carter, "The Tonic That Keeps 'Cheers' Bubbling Along," *New York Times*, April 29, 1990. https://www.nytimes.com/1990/04/29/arts/television-the-tonic-that-keeps-cheers-bubbling-along.html?pagewanted=all.

79. "Suspicion," *Cheers*, S4E14. Directed by James Burrows; written by Tom Reeder. NBC, January 1986.

80. Raftery, "The Best TV Show That's Ever Been."

81. Ibid.

82. Carrie Weiner, "11 Years Ago 'Cheers' Bid Farewell to Shelley Long," *Entertainment Weekly*, May 1, 1998. https://ew.com/article/1998/05/01/11-years-ago-cheers-bid-farewell-shelley-long/.

83. Carter, "The Tonic That Keeps 'Cheers' Bubbling Along."

84. Freeman, "'Cheers' Finale at 25."

85. "2 Good to Be 4 Real," *Cheers*, S4E7. Directed by James Burrows; written by Peter Casey and David Lee. NBC, November 1985.

86. Freeman, "'Cheers' Finale at 25."

87. Ibid.

88. Ibid.

89. Raftery, "The Best TV Show That's Ever Been."

90. Freeman, "'Cheers' Finale at 25."

91. "Whodunit?" *Cheers*, S3E13. Directed by James Burrows; written by Tom Reeder. NBC, January 1985.

92. Heather Hundley, "Sex, Society, and Double Standards in *Cheers*," in *Transmitting the Past: Historical and Cultural Perspectives on Broadcasting*, ed. J. Emmett Winn and Susan L. Brinson (Tuscaloosa: University of Alabama Press, 2005), 207.

93. "Slumber Party Massacred," *Cheers*, S6E22. Directed by James Burrows; written by Phoef Sutton. NBC, March 24, 1988.

94. Freeman, "'Cheers' Finale at 25."

95. Ibid.

96. "The Tortelli Tort," *Cheers*, S1E3. Directed by James Burrows; written by Tom Reeder. NBC, October 14, 1982.

97. "Battle of the Exes," *Cheers*, S2E13. Directed by James Burrows; written by Ken Estin and Sam Simon. NBC, January 5, 1984.

98. Tom Shales, "Coach Really 'Got 'Em,' and He Will Be Missed," *Chicago Tribune*, February 19, 1985. https://www.chicagotribune.com/news/ct-xpm-1985-02-19-8501100295-story.html.

99. Castleman and Podrazik, *Watching TV*, 309.

100. "Whodunit?" *Cheers*.

101. "Coach Returns to Action," *Cheers*, S1E9. Directed by James Burrows; written by Earl Pomerantz. NBC, November 1982.

102. Jerry Buck, "Colasanto Strayed from Directing to Take Role as 'Cheers' Bartender," *Schenectady Gazette*, August 4, 1984. https://news.google.com/newspapers?id=SRMhAAAAIBAJ&sjid=YHMFAAAAIBAJ&dq=cheers%20coach%20worldly%20wise&pg=2377%2C1168140.

103. "Nick Colasanto: His Final Season," *Cheers Season 3*, DVD Special Features, Disc 4 (Paramount, 2004).

104. "Coach's Daughter," *Cheers*, S1E5. Directed by James Burrows; written by Ken Estin. NBC, October 1982.

105. Levine, "Re: Questions about Cheers."

106. Shales, "Coach Really 'Got 'Em.'"

107. Heather Keets, "Remembering Nicholas Colasanto as Coach on 'Cheers,'" *Entertainment Weekly*, February 11, 1994. https://ew.com/article/1994/02/11/remembering-nicholas-colasanto-coach-cheers/.

108. Raftery, "The Best TV Show That's Ever Been."

109. "Setting the Bar: A Conversation with Ted Danson."

110. Keets, "Remembering Nicholas Colasanto as Coach."

111. Ibid.

112. "Nick Colasanto: His Final Season."

113. "Cheerio, Cheers," *Cheers*, S3E22. Directed by James Burrows; written by Sam Simon. NBC, April 1985.

114. "Birth, Death, Love and Rice," *Cheers*.

115. Raftery, "The Best TV Show That's Ever Been."

116. Ibid.

117. Ibid.

118. Sara K. Eskridge, "'There Goes Old Gomer': Rural Comedy, Public Persona, and the Wavering Line between Fiction and Reality," *Southern Cultures*, December 2014.

119. "Tan 'n' Wash," *Cheers*.

120. Dave Nemetz, "How 'Cheers' Replaced Coach: James Burrows Looks Back, 30 Years Later," Yahoo.com, February 12, 2015. https://www.yahoo.com/entertainment/blogs/tv-news/cheers-james-burrows-coach-woody-010936771.html.

121. Jane Mulkerrins, "In the Mood for Danson," *The Telegraph*, February 25, 2013. https://www.telegraph.co.uk/culture/tvandradio/9883086/In-the-mood-for-Danson.html.

122. Raftery, "The Best TV Show That's Ever Been."

123. Jon E. Lewis and Penny Stempel, *Cult TV: The Comedies* (London: Pavilion Books, 1998), 54.

124. Freeman, "'Cheers' Finale at 25."

125. "Pudd'n Head Boyd," *Cheers*, S6E9. Directed by James Burrows; written by Cheri Eichen and Bill Steinkellner. NBC, November 26, 1987.

126. "Woody Goes Belly Up," *Cheers*, S4E2. Directed by James Burrows; written by Heide Perlman. NBC, October 1985.

5. THE EVOLUTION OF SAM MALONE

1. "Give Me a Ring Sometime," *Cheers*, S1E1. Directed by James Burrows; written by Glen and Les Charles. NBC, September 1982.

2. "One for the Road, Part 3," *Cheers*, S11E28. Directed by James Burrows; written by Glen and Les Charles. NBC, May 1993.

3. "Give Me a Ring Sometime," *Cheers*.

4. "Bar Tour," *Cheers Season 3*, DVD Special Features, Disc 4 (Paramount, 2004).

5. "Showdown, Part 1," *Cheers*, S1E21. Directed by James Burrows; written by Glen and Les Charles. NBC, March 1983.

6. "The Crane Mutiny," *Cheers*, S6E5. Directed by James Burrows; written by David Angell. NBC, October 1987.

7. "Dark Imaginings," *Cheers*, S4E19. Directed by James Burrows; written by David Angell. NBC, February 1986.

8. "Endless Slumper," *Cheers*, S1E10. Directed by James Burrows; written by Sam Simon. NBC, December 1982.

9. "Rebound, Part 1," *Cheers*, S3E1. Directed by James Burrows; written by Glen and Les Charles. NBC, September 1984.

10. "The Days of Wine and Neuroses," *Cheers*, S9E16. Directed by James Burrows; written by Brian Pollack and Mert Rich. NBC, January 1991.

11. "Young Dr. Weinstein," *Cheers*, S5E7. Directed by James Burrows; written by Phoef Sutton. NBC, November 1986.

12. Patrice M. Buzzanell and Suzy D'Enbeau, "Aging Masculinity in Popular Culture: The Case of *Mad Men*'s Roger Sterling," in *Aging Heroes: Growing Old in Popular Culture*, ed. Norma Jones and Bob Batchelor (Lanham, MD: Rowman & Littlefield, 2015), 131.

13. Ibid.

14. Alan Sepinwall and Matt Zoller Seitz, *TV (The Book): Two Experts Pick the Greatest American Shows of All Time* (New York: Grand Central Publishing, 2016), 42.

15. "Dark Imaginings," *Cheers*.

16. Ibid.

17. Ibid.

18. "Knights of the Scimitar," *Cheers*, S5E8. Directed by James Burrows; written by Jeff Abugov. NBC, November 1986.

19. Ibid.

20. "It's Lonely on the Top," *Cheers*, S11E22. Directed by James Burrows; written by Heide Perlman. NBC, April 1993.

21. "Give Me a Ring Sometime," *Cheers*.

22. "It's Lonely on the Top," *Cheers*.

23. "Ted Danson, on Life (and 'Death') after 'Cheers,'" *Fresh Air*, NPR, September 16, 2009. https://www.npr.org/templates/transcript/transcript.php?storyId=112884242.

24. "Give Me a Ring Sometime," *Cheers*.

25. "Sam at Eleven," *Cheers*, S1E4. Directed by James Burrows; written by Glen and Les Charles. NBC, October 1982.

26. "King of the Hill," *Cheers*, S3E15. Directed by James Burrows; written by Elliot Shoenman. NBC, January 1985.

27. Ibid.

28. "*I* on Sports," *Cheers*, S6E2. Directed by James Burrows; written by Ken Levine and David Isaacs. NBC, October 1987.

29. "Take Me out of the Ball Game," *Cheers*, S10E21. Directed by James Burrows; written by Kathy Ann Stumpe. NBC, March 1992.

30. Ibid.

31. "Give Me a Ring Sometime," *Cheers*.

32. "Sam's Women," *Cheers*, S1E2. Directed by James Burrows; written by Earl Pomerantz. NBC, October 1982.

33. "Sam Turns the Other Cheek," *Cheers*, S3E5. Directed by James Burrows; written by David Lloyd. NBC, November 1984.

34. "Send in the Crane," *Cheers*, S7E9. Directed by James Burrows; written by David Lloyd. NBC, January 1989.

35. "Love Me, Love My Car," *Cheers*, S11E10. Directed by James Burrows; written by David Lloyd. NBC, December 1992.

36. "Now Pitching, Sam Malone," *Cheers*, S1E13. Directed by James Burrows; written by Heide Perlman. NBC, January 1983.

37. "Don Juan Is Hell," *Cheers*, S4E11. Directed by James Burrows; written by Phoef Sutton. NBC, December 1985.

38. "Send in the Crane," *Cheers*.

39. "Love Is a Really, Really Perfectly OK Thing," *Cheers*, S9E1. Directed by James Burrows; written by Phoef Sutton. NBC, September 1990.

40. "Send in the Crane," *Cheers*.

41. "Sam's Women," *Cheers*.

42. "The Groom Wore Clearasil," *Cheers*, S4E4. Directed by James Burrows; written by Peter Casey and David Lee. NBC, October 1985.

43. "Don Juan Is Hell," *Cheers*.

44. "Sam Time Next Year," *Cheers*, S9E19. Directed by James Burrows; written by Larry Balmagia. NBC, February 1991.

45. "The Guy Can't Help It," *Cheers*, S11E25. Directed by James Burrows; written by David Angell, Peter Casey, and David Lee. NBC, May 1993.

46. Ibid.

47. Ibid.

48. Ibid.

49. Ibid.

50. Susan King, "The Creative Brew: Glen and Les Charles, James Burrows," *Los Angeles Times*, May 16, 1993. https://articles.latimes.com/1993-05-16/news/tv-35836_1_glen-charles.

51. Susan King, "Decades Later and We Still Remember Their Names: The Cast of 'Cheers' Reflects on the Beloved Series," *Los Angeles Times*, May 16, 1993. https://www.latimes.com/entertainment/tv/la-et-st-cheers-end-19930516-snap-story.html.

52. David Zurawik, "Last Call for Cheers: The Boston Bar Is Just a Sitcom Set, but for Viewers It Has Become a Real Place, Where Friends Hang Out," *Baltimore Sun*, May 16, 1993. https://www.baltimoresun.com/news/bs-xpm-1993-05-16-1993136158-story.html.

53. Ken Levine, "May Day (Malone)," *. . . by Ken Levine, The World as Seen by a TV Comedy Writer* (blog), May 1, 2016. http://kenlevine.blogspot.com/2016/05/may-day-malone.html.

54. "How to Marry a Mailman," *Cheers*, S8E4. Directed by James Burrows; written by Brian Pollack and Mert Rich. NBC, October 1989.

55. "Bidding on the Boys," *Cheers*, S6E8. Directed by Thomas Lofaro; written by David Lloyd. NBC, November 1987.

56. "No Help Wanted," *Cheers*, S2E14. Directed by James Burrows; written by Max Tash. NBC, January 1984.

57. "Save the Last Dance for Me," *Cheers*, S4E20. Directed by James Burrows; written by Heide Perlman. NBC, February 1986.

58. "How to Win Friends and Electrocute People," *Cheers*, S7E7. Directed by James Burrows; written by Phoef Sutton. NBC, December 1988.

59. "Relief Bartender," *Cheers*, S4E23. Directed by James Burrows; written by Miriam Trogdon. NBC, March 1986.

60. "One for the Road," *Cheers*, S11E26–28. Directed by James Burrows; written by Glen and Les Charles. NBC, May 1993.

61. "The Guy Can't Help It," *Cheers*.

62. "One for the Road," *Cheers*.

6. THE DEVOLUTION OF REBECCA HOWE

1. Aljean Harmetz, "Television: Can Kirstie Alley Keep the 'Cheers' Bar Open?" *New York Times*, September 20, 1987. https://www.nytimes.com/1987/09/20/arts/television-can-kirstie-alley-keep-the-cheers-bar-open.html.

2. Quoted in Marc Freeman, "'Cheers' Finale at 25: Untold Stories from inside the Writers Room," *Hollywood Reporter*, May 20, 2018. https://www.hollywoodreporter.com/amp/live-feed/cheers-at-25-untold-stories-inside-writers-room-1113428.

3. "Home Is the Sailor," *Cheers*, S6E1. Directed by James Burrows; written by Glen and Les Charles. NBC, September 1987.

4. Ibid.

5. Warren Littlefield, with T. R. Pearson, *Top of the Rock: Inside the Rise and Fall of Must See TV* (New York: Doubleday, 2012), 39.

6. Freeman, "'Cheers' Finale at 25."

7. Harmetz, "Television: Can Kirstie Alley Keep the 'Cheers' Bar Open?"

8. Ibid.

9. Brian Raftery, "The Best TV Show That's Ever Been," *GQ*, September 27, 2012. http://www.gq.com/story/cheers-oral-history-extended.

10. Joanne Kaufman, "A Great Mixer, Kirstie Alley Is the Toast of Cheers— Where Nobody Gives a Dram about Her Predecessor," *People*, November 30, 1987. https://people.com/archive/a-great-mixer-kirstie-alley-is-the-toast-of-cheers-where-nobody-gives-a-dram-about-her-predecessor-vol-28-no-22/.

11. Raftery, "The Best TV Show That's Ever Been."

12. Harmetz, "Television: Can Kirstie Alley Keep the 'Cheers' Bar Open?"

13. Freeman, "'Cheers' Finale at 25."

14. J. D. Reed, "The Tears behind the Cheers," *People*, October 29, 1990. https://people.com/archive/cover-story-the-tears-behind-the-cheers-vol-34-no-17/.

15. Ken Levine, "My Favorite Kirstie Alley Scene," . . . *by Ken Levine, The World as Seen by a TV Comedy Writer* (blog), July 8, 2011. http://kenlevine. blogspot.com/2011/07/my-favorite-kirstie-alley-scene.html.

16. "Home Is the Sailor," *Cheers*.

17. "The One Where Sam Shows Up," *Frasier*, S2E16. Directed by James Burrows; written by Ken Levine and David Isaacs. NBC, February 1995.

18. "The Improbable Dream, Part 1," *Cheers*, S8E1. Directed by James Burrows; written by Cheri Eichen and Bill Steinkellner. NBC, September 1989.

19. Ibid.

20. "Finally! Part 2," *Cheers*, S8E16. Directed by James Burrows; written by Ken Levine and David Isaacs. NBC, February 1990.

21. Susan King, "Decades Later and We Still Remember Their Names: The Cast of 'Cheers' Reflects on the Beloved Series," *Los Angeles Times*, May 16, 1993. https://www.latimes.com/entertainment/tv/la-et-st-cheers-end-19930516-snap-story.html.

22. Ibid.

23. "Love Me, Love My Car," *Cheers*, S11E10. Directed by James Burrows; written by David Lloyd. NBC, December 1992.

24. Mike Duffy and Susan Stewart, "Last Call for a Distinguished Cast at 'Cheers,'" *The Day* (New London, CT), May 16, 1993. https://news.google.com/

newspapers?nid=1915&dat=19930516&id=ZDJHAAAAIBAJ&sjid=
XPgMAAAAIBAJ&pg=1166,3318588&hl=en.

25. "Rebecca Gaines, Rebecca Loses, Part 2" *Cheers*, S11E24. Directed by James Burrows; written by David Lloyd. NBC, May 1993.

26. "A Kiss Is Still a Kiss," *Cheers*, S6E10. Directed by James Burrows; written by David Lloyd. NBC, December 1987.

27. "Yacht of Fools," *Cheers*, S6E16. Directed by Thomas Lofaro; written by Phoef Sutton. NBC, February 1988.

28. "Let Sleeping Drakes Lie," *Cheers*, S6E18. Directed by James Burrows; written by David Lloyd. NBC, February 1988.

29. "Backseat Becky, Up Front," *Cheers*, S6E25. Directed by James Burrows; written by Cheri Eichen and Bill Steinkellner. NBC, May 1988.

30. Harmetz, "Television: Can Kirstie Alley Keep the 'Cheers' Bar Open?"

31. Ibid.

32. Josh Wolk, "'Cheers' Said Goodbye 25 Years Ago: Raise a Toast with These 9 Essential Episodes," *New York Times*, May 18, 2018. https://www.nytimes.com/2018/05/18/watching/cheers-best-episodes.html.

33. "Norman's Conquest," *Cheers*, S2E20. Directed by James Burrows; written by Lissa Levin. NBC, February 1984.

34. "My Fair Clavin," *Cheers*, S6E11. Directed by James Burrows; written by Phoef Sutton. NBC, December 1987.

35. "Abnormal Psychology," *Cheers*, S5E4. Directed by James Burrows; written by Janet Leahy. NBC, October 1986.

36. "The Gift of the Woodi," *Cheers*, S7E19. Directed by James Burrows; written by Phoef Sutton. NBC, April 1989.

37. Ibid.

38. Rob Owen, "Sexual Harassment Has a Long History as a Comedic Punchline on TV," *Pittsburgh Post-Gazette*, November 30, 2017. https://www.post-gazette.com/ae/tv-radio/2017/11/30/Sexual-harassment-has-a-long-history-as-a-comedic-punchline-on-TV/stories/201711300085.

39. Ibid.

40. Ibid.

41. James Hannah, "TV Sitcoms Are Rife with Sexual Harassment, Study Says," *The Telegraph* (Nashua, NH), December 27, 1994. https://news.google.com/newspapers?nid=2209&dat=19941227&id=eItKAAAAIBAJ&sjid=LpQMAAAAIBAJ&pg=6550,6711961&hl=en.

42. Ibid.

43. "I'll Be Seeing You, Part 2," *Cheers*, S2E22. Directed by James Burrows; written by Glen and Les Charles. NBC, May 1984.

44. "The Visiting Lecher," *Cheers*, S7E22. Directed by James Burrows; written by David Lloyd. NBC, May 1989.

45. "Woody or Won't He," *Cheers*, S8E17. Directed by Andy Ackerman; written by Brian Pollack and Mert Rich. NBC, February 1990.

46. Alyssa Milano, Twitter, October 15, 2017. https://twitter.com/Alyssa_Milano/status/919659438700670976/?lang=en.

47. Ryan McGee, Meredith Blake, Todd VanDerWerff, Noel Murray, Phil Dyess-Nugent, Erik Adams, Donna Bowman, and Keith Phipps, "*Cheers*: 'Friends, Romans, Accountants'/'Truce or Consequences,'" A.V. Club, December 8, 2011. https://tv.avclub.com/cheers-friends-romans-accountants-truce-or-conseq-1798170817.

7. SAM AND DIANE

1. David Isaacs, "Sitcom Master Class: Creating Comedy through Character," in *Inside the Room: Writing Television with the Pros at UCLA Extension Writers' Program*, ed. Linda Venis (New York: Gotham Books, 2013), 182.

2. Brian Raftery, "The Best TV Show That's Ever Been," *GQ*, September 27, 2012. http://www.gq.com/story/cheers-oral-history-extended.

3. Leah Rozen, "Ted Danson Leers Again on *Cheers*," *People*, May 11, 1987. https://people.com/archive/cover-story-ted-danson-leers-again-on-cheers-vol-27-no-19/.

4. Raftery, "The Best TV Show That's Ever Been."

5. Ibid.

6. Ibid.

7. Ibid.

8. Jim Bawden, "Critic Nibbles on Tidbits with TV Stars," *Toronto Star*, June 24, 1986.

9. Rozen, "Ted Danson Leers Again on *Cheers*."

10. Susan King, "Decades Later and We Still Remember Their Names: The Cast of 'Cheers' Reflects on the Beloved Series," *Los Angeles Times*, May 16, 1993. https://www.latimes.com/entertainment/tv/la-et-st-cheers-end-19930516-snap-story.html.

11. Quoted in Warren Littlefield, *Top of the Rock: Inside the Rise and Fall of Must See TV* (New York: Doubleday, 2012), 41.

12. Raftery, "The Best TV Show That's Ever Been."

13. Martin Gitlin, *The Greatest Sitcoms of All Time* (Lanham, MD: Scarecrow Press, 2014), 45.

14. "Sumner's Return," *Cheers*, S2E5. Directed by James Burrows; written by Michael J. Weithorn. NBC, November 1983.

15. "I'll Be Seeing You, Part 2," *Cheers*, S2E22. Directed by James Burrows; written by Glen and Les Charles. NBC, May 1984.

16. "Sam's Women," *Cheers*, S1E2. Directed by James Burrows; written by Earl Pomerantz. NBC, October 1982.

17. Peter Kerr, "NBC Comedy 'Cheers' Turns into a Success," *New York Times*, November 29, 1983. https://www.nytimes.com/1983/11/29/arts/nbc-comedy-cheers-turns-into-a-success.html.

18. Vince Waldron, *Classic Sitcoms: A Celebration of the Best in Prime-Time Comedy* (New York: Mcmillan, 1987), 471.

19. Ken Bloom and Frank Vlastnik, *Sitcoms: The 101 Greatest Comedies of All Time* (New York: Black Dog and Leventhal Publishers, 2007), 60.

20. Kevin Fitzpatrick, "The Most Absolutely Awful TV Couples," UGO.com, February 14, 2012. http://www.ugo.com/tv/worst-tv-couples.html.

21. Taffy Brodesser-Akner, "Ross and Rachel vs. Sam and Diane: Who Is the Better Couple?" *Vulture*, October 3, 2016. https://www.vulture.com/2016/10/tv-couples-ross-rachel-sam-diane.html.

22. "Chambers vs. Malone," *Cheers*, S5E13. Directed by James Burrows; written by David Angell. NBC, January 1987.

23. Brodesser-Akner, "Ross and Rachel vs. Sam and Diane."

24. "Sam's Women," *Cheers*.

25. "Home Is the Sailor," *Cheers*, S6E1. Directed by James Burrows; written by Glen and Les Charles. NBC, September 1987.

26. Ken Levine, "Friday Questions," . . . *by Ken Levine, The World as Seen by a TV Comedy Writer* (blog), April 22, 2016. http://kenlevine.blogspot.com/2016/04/friday-questions_22.html.

27. "Adventures in Paradise: Part 2," *Frasier*, S2E9. Directed by James Burrows; written by Ken Levine and David Isaacs. NBC, November 1994.

28. "The Show Where Diane Comes Back," *Frasier*, S3E14. Directed by James Burrows; written by Christopher Lloyd. NBC, February 1996.

29. "Don Juan in Hell," *Frasier*, S9E1–2. Directed by Kelsey Grammer; written by Sam Johnson, Chris Marcil, and Lori Kirkland. NBC, September 2001.

30. "Loathe and Marriage," *Cheers*, S11E15. Directed by James Burrows; written by Ken Levine and David Isaacs. NBC, February 1993.

31. "Rebecca Gaines, Rebecca Loses," *Cheers*, S11E23–24. Directed by James Burrows; written by David Lloyd. NBC, May 1993.

32. "Do Not Forsake Me, O' My Postman," *Cheers*, S11E5. Directed by James Burrows; written by Ken Levine and David Isaacs. NBC, October 1992.

33. Bar Wars VII: The Naked Prey," *Cheers*, S11E19. Directed by James Burrows; written by Ken Levine and David Isaacs. NBC, March 1993.

34. "A Diminished Rebecca with a Suspended Cliff," *Cheers*, S10E17. Directed by James Burrows; written by Dan O'Shannon and Tom Anderson. NBC, February 1992.

35. "'Cheers' to Burrows' Favorite Episodes," *USA Today*, November 24, 2015.

36. Josh Bell, "10 Great Sitcom Romances," About.com, February 16, 2009. https://web.archive.org/web/20090216190223/http://tvcomedies.about.com/od/listsrecommendations/tp/sitcomromances.htm.

CONCLUSION

1. "My Life in Four Cameras," *Scrubs*, S4E17. Directed by Adam Bernstein; written by Debra Fordham. NBC, February 2005.

2. "Simon and Marcy," *Adventure Time*, S5E14. Directed by Adam Muto; written by Cike Sanchez and Rebecca Sugar. Cartoon Network, March 2013.

3. *Guardians of the Galaxy, Vol. 2*. Directed by James Gunn; written by James Gunn. Marvel Studios, 2017.

4. "Somewhere Else," *The Good Place*, S2E13. Directed by Michael Schur; written by Michael Schur. NBC, February 2018.

5. "How Long Does It Take to Watch Every Episode of *Cheers*?" Binge-clock.com, October 30, 2018. https://www.bingeclock.com/s/cheers/t/380561/2741813156.

6. Ken Bloom and Frank Vlastnik, *Sitcoms: The 101 Greatest Comedies of All Time* (New York: Black Dog and Leventhal Publishers), 62.

BIBLIOGRAPHY

Associated Press. "Splitting Up Takes Nights for Sam, Diane of 'Cheers.'" *Toledo Blade*, May 3, 1984. https://news.google.com/newspapers?id=4VZQAAAAIBAJ&sjid=LA4EAAAAIBAJ&pg=6868%2C2662620.

A.V. Club. *Inventory: 16 Films Featuring Manic Pixie Dream Girls, 10 Great Songs Nearly Ruined by Saxophone, and 100 More Obsessively Specific Pop-Culture Lists*. New York: Scribner, 2009.

A.V. Club Staff. "*Cheers*: 'Give Me a Ring Sometime/Sam's Women.'" A.V. Club, November 11, 2011. https://tv.avclub.com/cheers-give-me-a-ring-sometime-sam-s-women-1798170424.

"Bar Tour." *Cheers Season 3*. DVD Special Features, Disc 4. Paramount, 2004.

Bawden, Jim. "Critic Nibbles on Tidbits with TV Stars." *Toronto Star*, June 24, 1986.

Bell, Josh. "10 Great Sitcom Romances." About.com, February 16, 2009. https://web.archive.org/web/20090216190223/http://tvcomedies.about.com/od/listsrecommendations/tp/sitcomromances.htm.

Bianculli, David. *The Platinum Age of Television: From* I Love Lucy *to* The Walking Dead, *How TV Became Terrific*. New York: First Anchor Books, 2017.

"Bio Channel: Kelsey Grammer (Full Documentary)." YouTube, February 28, 2018. https://www.youtube.com/watch?v=hepVnn_fm6g.

Bjorklund, Dennis A. *Toasting Cheers: An Episode Guide to the 1982–1993 Comedy Series with Cast Biographies and Character Profiles*. Jefferson, NC: McFarland Press, 1997.

Bloom, Ken, and Frank Vlastnik. *Sitcoms: The 101 Greatest Comedies of All Time*. New York: Black Dog and Leventhal Publishers, 2007.

Brant, Marley. *Happier Days: Paramount Television's Classic Sitcoms 1974–1984*. New York: Billboard Books, 2006.

Brodesser-Akner, Taffy. "Ross and Rachel vs. Sam and Diane: Who Is the Better Couple?" *Vulture*, October 3, 2016. https://www.vulture.com/2016/10/tv-couples-ross-rachel-sam-diane.html.

Buck, Jerry. "Actress Bebe Neuwirth Brings Flexibility to Her Rigid Role on NBC's 'Cheers.'" *Tulsa World*, May 24, 1992. https://www.tulsaworld.com/archives/actress-bebe-neuwirth-brings-flexibility-to-her-rigid-role-on/article_68b484f7-1f16-5bf3-8012-3bc22c3de825.html.

———. "Colasanto Strayed from Directing to Take Role as 'Cheers' Bartender." *Schenectady Gazette*, August 4, 1984. https://news.google.com/newspapers?id=SRMhAAAAIBAJ&sjid=YHMFAAAAIBAJ&dq=cheers%20coach%20worldly%20wise&pg=2377%2C1168140.

Buell, Spencer. "Michael Che Made Another Boston Joke, This Time at the Emmys." *Boston Magazine*, September 18, 2018. https://www.bostonmagazine.com/news/2018/09/18/michael-che-boston-emmys/.

Butler, Jeremy G. *Television: Critical Methods and Applications*, 4th ed. London: Routledge, 2011.

Buzzanell, Patrice M., and Suzy D'Enbeau. "Aging Masculinity in Popular Culture: The Case of *Mad Men*'s Roger Sterling." In *Aging Heroes: Growing Old in Popular Culture*, edited by Norma Jones and Bob Batchelor, 131–42. Lanham, MD: Rowman & Littlefield, 2015.

Carter, Bill. "The Tonic That Keeps 'Cheers' Bubbling Along." *New York Times*, April 29, 1990. https://www.nytimes.com/1990/04/29/arts/television-the-tonic-that-keeps-cheers-bubbling-along.html?pagewanted=all.

Castleman, Harry, and Walter J. Podrazik. *Watching TV: Six Decades of American Television*, 2nd ed. Syracuse, NY: Syracuse University Press, 2010.

"'Cheers' to Burrows' Favorite Episodes." *USA Today*, November 24, 2015.

Coles, Stephen. "*Cheers* Logo and Opening Titles." Fonts in Use, October 29, 2013. https://fontsinuse.com/uses/5067/cheers-logo-and-opening-titles.

Cronin, Brian. "Did the United States Government Create a Special Never-Broadcast Episode of Cheers?" LegendsRevealed.com, October 18, 2017. http://legendsrevealed.com/entertainment/2016/10/18/did-the-united-states-government-create-a-special-never-broadcast-episode-of-cheers/.

———. "TV Legends Revealed: Why You Don't Mess with Carla on *Cheers*." *Comic Book Resources*, January 10, 2013. http://spinoff.comicbookresources.com/2013/01/10/tv-legends-revealed-why-you-dont-mess-with-carla-on-cheers/.

Darowski, Joseph J., and Kate Darowski. Frasier: *A Cultural History*. Lanham, MD: Rowman & Littlefield, 2017.

Delaney, Tim, and Tim Madigan. *The Sociology of Sports: An Introduction*. Jefferson, NC: McFarland Press, 2009.

Duffy, Mike, and Susan Stewart. "Last Call for a Distinguished Cast at 'Cheers.'" *The Day* (New London, CT), May 16, 1993. https://news.google.com/newspapers?nid=1915&dat=19930516&id=ZDJHAAAAIBAJ&sjid=XPgMAAAAIBAJ&pg=1166,3318588&hl=en.

Dullea, Georgia. "'Cheers' Has Brewed Trouble for Patrons of the Real Boston Watering Hole." *Chicago Tribune*, October 6, 1985. https://www.chicagotribune.com/news/ct-xpm-1985-10-06-8503080137-story.html.

Eskridge, Sara K. "'There Goes Old Gomer': Rural Comedy, Public Persona, and the Wavering Line between Fiction and Reality." *Southern Cultures*, December 2014.

EW Staff. "The Year That Was." *Entertainment Weekly*, December 24, 1993. http://www.ew.com/article/1993/12/24/year-was.

Fitzpatrick, Kevin. "The Most Absolutely Awful TV Couples." UGO.com, February 14, 2012. http://www.ugo.com/tv/worst-tv-couples.html.

Flynn, Daniel J. "Cheers to the Bull & Finch." *American Spectator*, March 24, 2014. https://spectator.org/57725_cheers-bull-finch/.

Freeman, Marc. "'Cheers' Finale at 25: Untold Stories from inside the Writers Room." *Hollywood Reporter*, May 20, 2018. https://www.hollywoodreporter.com/amp/live-feed/cheers-at-25-untold-stories-inside-writers-room-1113428.

Froelich, Janis D. "George Wendt: Norm Reflects on His TV Series, Life and Drinking." *Deseret News*, October 16, 1990. https://www.deseretnews.com/article/127517/GEORGE-WENDT--NORM-REFLECTS-ON-HIS-TV-SERIES-LIFE-AND-DRINKING.html.

Gitlin, Martin. *The Greatest Sitcoms of All Time*. Lanham, MD: Scarecrow Press, 2014.

"Glen and Les Charles on Casting 'Cheers'—EMMYTVLEGENDS.org." YouTube, December 12, 2012. https://www.youtube.com/watch?v=TbaaM_l0baw.

"Glen and Les Charles on Creating the Characters on 'Cheers'—EMMYTVLEGENDS.org." YouTube, December 12, 2012. https://www.youtube.com/watch?v=g7oe7wI_kas.

"Glen and Les Charles on the 'Cheers' Theme Song—EMMYTVLEGNEDS.org." YouTube, December 12, 2012. https://www.youtube.com/watch?v=zi3EsEvuJuE.

"Glen Charles: Writer/Producer." *The Television Academy Foundation: The Interviews*. December 8, 2003. https://interviews.televisionacademy.com/interviews/glen-charles.

Greenwald, Andy. "Men in Black: The Show?" *Grantland*, January 23, 2013. http://grantland. com/features/tv-mailbag-time/.

Hannah, James. "TV Sitcoms Are Rife with Sexual Harassment, Study Says." *The Telegraph* (Nashua, NH), December 27, 1994. https://news.google.com/newspapers?nid=2209&dat= 19941227&id=eItKAAAAIBAJ&sjid=LpQMAAAAIBAJ&pg=6550,6711961&hl=en.

Harmetz, Aljean. "Television: Can Kirstie Alley Keep the 'Cheers' Bar Open?" *New York Times*, September 20, 1987. https://www.nytimes.com/1987/09/20/arts/television-can-kirstie-alley-keep-the-cheers-bar-open.html.

Hentoff, Nat. "'Cheers': No Blacks at the Bar." *Washington Post*, August 24, 1984. https:// www.washingtonpost.com/archive/politics/1984/08/24/cheers-no-blacks-at-the-bar/ b4490fe5-d9e0-487d-8fae-bb075a525a4c/?utm_term=.01eef5121437.

"How Long Does It Take to Watch Every Episode of *Cheers*?" Bingeclock.com, October 30, 2018. https://www.bingeclock.com/s/cheers/t/380561/2741813156.

Hundley, Heather. "Sex, Society, and Double Standards in *Cheers*." In *Transmitting the Past: Historical and Cultural Perspectives on Broadcasting*, edited by J. Emmett Winn and Susan L. Brinson, 205–22. Tuscaloosa: University of Alabama Press, 2005.

Isaacs, David. "Sitcom Master Class: Creating Comedy through Character." In *Inside the Room: Writing Television with the Pros at UCLA Extension Writers' Program*, edited by Linda Venis, 174–91. New York: Gotham Books, 2013.

Jackson, Marc Evan. "Ch. 26: Michael Schur, Creator." *The Good Place: The Podcast*. Podcast audio, September 21, 2018. https://www.nbc.com/the-good-place/exclusives/tgp-podcast.

"James Burrows." Directors Guild of America, December 23, 2014. https://www.dga.org/ News/Guild-News/2015/Jan2015/Awards-Jim-Burrows-LATV.aspx.

Jones, Chris. "'Cheers' to Sam and Diane, a Pair Whose Names You Know." *Chicago Tribune*, September 23, 2016. https://www.chicagotribune.com/entertainment/theater/reviews/ct-cheers-live-review-ent-0923-20160922-column.html.

Kaufman, Joanne. "A Great Mixer, Kirstie Alley Is the Toast of Cheers—Where Nobody Gives a Dram about Her Predecessor." *People*, November 30, 1987. https://people.com/archive/a-great-mixer-kirstie-alley-is-the-toast-of-cheers-where-nobody-gives-a-dram-about-her-predecessor-vol-28-no-22/.

Keets, Heather. "Remembering Nicholas Colasanto as Coach on 'Cheers.'" *Entertainment Weekly*, February 11, 1994. https://ew.com/article/1994/02/11/remembering-nicholas-colasanto-coach-cheers/.

Kerr, Peter. "NBC Comedy 'Cheers' Turns into a Success." *New York Times*, November 29, 1983. https://www.nytimes.com/1983/11/29/arts/nbc-comedy-cheers-turns-into-a-success. html.

King, Susan. "The Creative Brew: Glen and Les Charles, James Burrows." *Los Angeles Times*, May 16, 1993. https://articles.latimes.com/1993-05-16/news/tv-35836_1_glen-charles.

———. "Decades Later and We Still Remember Their Names: The Cast of 'Cheers' Reflects on the Beloved Series." *Los Angeles Times*, May 16, 1993. https://www.latimes.com/ entertainment/tv/la-et-st-cheers-end-19930516-snap-story.html.

Klein, Paul L. "Why You Watch What You Watch When You Watch." *TV Guide*, July 24, 1971.

Kurp, Josh. "The Greatest TV Writers Room Ever." *Vulture*, June 2011. http://www.vulture. com/2011/06/the-greatest-tv-writers-rooms-ever.html.

"Les Charles: Writer/Producer." *The Television Academy Foundation: The Interviews*. December 8, 2003. https://interviews.televisionacademy.com/interviews/glen-charles.

Levine, Ken. "The *Cheers* Conspiracy." *. . . by Ken Levine, The World as Seen by a TV Comedy Writer* (blog), March 27, 2018. http://kenlevine.blogspot.com/2018/03/the-cheers-conspiracy.html.

———. "The *Cheers* Episode We Wrote That Is Now Very Timely." *. . . by Ken Levine, The World as Seen by a TV Comedy Writer* (blog), May 5, 2013. http://kenlevine.blogspot.com/ 2013/05/the-cheers-episode-we-wrote-that-is-now.html.

———. "The *Cheers* Set." *. . . by Ken Levine, The World as Seen by a TV Comedy Writer* (blog), February 12, 2017. http://kenlevine.blogspot.com/2017/02/the-cheers-set.html.

———. "Friday Questions." . . . *by Ken Levine, The World as Seen by a TV Comedy Writer* (blog), April 22, 2016. http://kenlevine.blogspot.com/2016/04/friday-questions_22.html.

———. "How Did We Handle Drinking on *Cheers*." . . . *by Ken Levine, The World as Seen by a TV Comedy Writer* (blog), December 23, 2010. http://kenlevine.blogspot.com/2010/12/how-did-we-handle-drinking-on-cheers.html.

———. "How to Be a Good Showrunner." . . . *by Ken Levine, The World as Seen by a TV Comedy Writer* (blog), November 10, 2012. https://kenlevine.blogspot.com/2012/11/how-to-be-good-showrunner.html.

———. "How to Hide the Miracle of Life." . . . *by Ken Levine, The World as Seen by a TV Comedy Writer* (blog), April 3, 2007. http://kenlevine.blogspot.com/2007/04/how-to-hide-miracle-of-life.html.

———. "The Kiss of Death for Eddie LeBec." . . . *by Ken Levine, The World as Seen by a TV Comedy Writer* (blog), July 21, 2006. http://kenlevine.blogspot.com/2006/07/kiss-of-death-for-eddie-lebec.html.

———. "The 'Lost' *Cheers* Scene." . . . *by Ken Levine, The World as Seen by a TV Comedy Writer* (blog), February 5, 2017. http://kenlevine.blogspot.com/2017/02/the-lost-cheers-scene.html.

———. "May Day (Malone)." . . . *by Ken Levine, The World as Seen by a TV Comedy Writer* (blog), May 1, 2016. http://kenlevine.blogspot.com/2016/05/may-day-malone.html.

———. "My Favorite Kirstie Alley Scene," . . . by Ken Levine, The World as Seen by a TV Comedy Writer (blog), July 8, 2011. http://kenlevine.blogspot.com/2011/07/my-favorite-kirstie-alley-scene.html.

———. "The Story behind the *Cheers* Bar War Episodes." . . . *by Ken Levine, The World as Seen by a TV Comedy Writer* (blog), July 18, 2010. http://kenlevine.blogspot.com/2010/07/story-behind-cheers-bar-war-episodes.html.

———. "The Story behind the *Cheers* Theme." . . . *by Ken Levine, The World as Seen by a TV Comedy Writer* (blog), September 21, 2014. http://kenlevine.blogspot.com/2014/09/the-story-behind-cheers-theme.html.

Lewis, Jon E., and Penny Stempel. *Cult TV: The Comedies.* London: Pavilion Books, 1998.

Lewisohn, Mark. *Radio Times Guide to TV Comedy.* London: BBC Worldwide, 2012.

Littlefield, Warren, with T. R. Pearson. *Top of the Rock: Inside the Rise and Fall of Must See TV.* New York: Doubleday, 2012.

McCarthy, Dan. "The *Cheers* Conspiracy." *Boston Magazine*, March 20, 2018.

McGee, Ryan, Meredith Blake, Todd VanDerWerff, Noel Murray, Phil Dyess-Nugent, Erik Adams, and Donna Bowman. "*Cheers*: 'Pick a Con, Any Con'/'Someone Single, Someone Blue.'" A.V. Club, January 26, 2012. https://tv.avclub.com/cheers-pick-a-con-any-con-someone-single-someone-1798171308.

———. "*Cheers*: 'I'll Be Seeing You.'" A.V. Club, April 26, 2012. https://tv.avclub.com/cheers-i-ll-be-seeing-you-1798172563.

McGee, Ryan, Meredith Blake, Todd VanDerWerff, Noel Murray, Phil Dyess-Nugent, Erik Adams, Donna Bowman, and Keith Phipps. "*Cheers*: 'Coach Returns to Action'/'Endless Slumper.'" A.V. Club, December 15, 2011. https://tv.avclub.com/cheers-coach-returns-to-action-endless-slumper-1798170877.

———. "*Cheers*: 'Friends, Romans, Accountants'/'Truce or Consequences.'" A.V. Club, December 8, 2011. https://tv.avclub.com/cheers-friends-romans-accountants-truce-or-conseq-1798170817.

McLevy, Alex. "Gary's Olde Town Tavern Gave *Cheers* a Nemesis—and a Perfect Foil." A.V. Club, April 5, 2016. https://tv.avclub.com/gary-s-olde-town-tavern-gave-cheers-a-nemesis-and-a-per-1798245924.

Mitz, Rick. *The Great TV Sitcom Book*, expanded ed. New York: Perigree Books, 1983.

Mulkerrins, Jane. "In the Mood for Danson." *The Telegraph* (London), February 25, 2013. https://www.telegraph.co.uk/culture/tvandradio/9883086/In-the-mood-for-Danson.html.

Murthi, Vikram. "When *Cheers* Became *Cheers*: An Appreciation of 'Endless Slumper.'" *Vulture*, December 6, 2017. https://www.vulture.com/2017/12/cheers-an-appreciation-of-the-endless-slumper-episode.html.

Nemetz, Dave. "Food Fight! The Messy True Story behind the Classic 'Cheers' Episode, 'Thanksgiving Orphans.'" Yahoo.com, November 24, 2015. https://www.yahoo.com/entertainment/news/cheers-thanksgiving-orphans-episode-true-story-054056375.html.

———. "How 'Cheers' Replaced Coach: James Burrows Looks Back, 30 Years Later." Yahoo.com, February 12, 2015. https://www.yahoo.com/entertainment/blogs/tv-news/cheers-james-burrows-coach-woody-010936771.html.

———. "How Gary Portnoy Made 'Cheers' the Place Where Everybody Knows Your Name." Yahoo.com, April 3, 2013. https://www.yahoo.com/entertainment/news/how-gary-portnoy-made--cheers--the-place--where-everybody-knows-your-name---230349578.html.

"Nick Colasanto: His Final Season." *Cheers Season 3*. DVD Special Features, Disc 4. Paramount, 2004.

O'Connor, John J. "Critic's Notebook: 'Cheers' Is Dead, but There's Always the Wake . . ." *New York Times*, May 21, 1993.

Olenski, Steve. "Is Norm the New Norm? The 'Cheers' Effect on Marketing." *Forbes*, August 16, 2018. https://www.forbes.com/sites/steveolenski/2018/08/16/is-norm-the-new-norm-the-cheers-effect-on-marketing/#9ac5fef682e8.

Owen, Rob. "Sexual Harassment Has a Long History as a Comedic Punchline on TV." *Pittsburgh Post-Gazette*, November 30, 2017. https://www.post-gazette.com/ae/tv-radio/2017/11/30/sexual-harassment-has-a-long-history-as-a-comedic-punchline-on-tv/stories/201711300085.

Raftery, Brian. "The Best TV Show That's Ever Been." *GQ*, September 27, 2012. http://www.gq.com/story/cheers-oral-history-extended.

Reed, J. D. "The Tears behind the Cheers." *People*, October 29, 1990. https://people.com/archive/cover-story-the-tears-behind-the-cheers-vol-34-no-17/.

Reisman, Arnie. "Where Everybody Borrows Your Name." *Vineyard Gazette*, March 25, 2016.

Reuters. "Leno Calls Telecast on 'Cheers' 'a Mistake': Drunken Cast Members Ruined 'Tonight' Broadcast from Boston Bar, He Says." *Los Angeles Times*, May 28, 1993.

"Reviews of New Television Shows." *Variety*, October 6, 1982.

Rothenberg, Fred. "Ask Why NBC . . . " *Lewiston Journal*, September 24, 1983. https://news.google.com/newspapers?id=3Q8gAAAAIBAJ&sjid=imUFAAAAIBAJ&dq=cheers%20television%20%7C%20tv&pg=1347%2C3808893.

Rozen, Leah. "Ted Danson Leers Again on *Cheers*." *People*, May 11, 1987. https://people.com/archive/cover-story-ted-danson-leers-again-on-cheers-vol-27-no-19/.

Sepinwall, Alan, and Matt Zoller Seitz. *TV (The Book): Two Experts Pick the Greatest American Shows of All Time*. New York: Grand Central Publishing, 2016.

"Setting the Bar: A Conversation with Ted Danson." *Cheers Season 1*. DVD Special Features, Disc 4. Paramount, 2003.

Shales, Tom. "Coach Really 'Got 'Em,' and He Will Be Missed." *Chicago Tribune*, February 19, 1985. http://www.chicagotribune.com/news/ct-xpm-1985-02-19-8501100295-story.html.

Stahl, Jessica. "Is 'Cheers' Still Funny?" *Washington Post*, March 7, 2014. https://www.washingtonpost.com/news/arts-and-entertainment/wp/2014/03/07/is-cheers-still-funny/?noredirect=on&utm_term=.fd4e070ee0de.

StarTrek.com Staff. "Mark Allen Shepherd Was Born to be Morn—Part 1." Star Trek Discovery, April 11, 2011. http://www.startrek.com/article/mark-allen-shepherd-was-born-to-be-morn-part-1.

"The Story behind the Cheers Theme." Garyportnoy.com, n.d. https://www.garyportnoy.com/cheers-story/.

"Strictly Top Shelf: The Guys behind the Bar." *Cheers Season 2*. DVD Special Features, Disc 4. Paramount, 2004.

Susman, Gary. "10 Greatest TV Pilot Episodes." *Time*, September 8, 2013. http://entertainment.time.com/2013/09/09/10-greatest-tv-pilot-episodes/slide/ready-for-takeoff/.

"Ted Danson, on Life (and 'Death') after 'Cheers.'" *Fresh Air*. NPR, September 16, 2009. https://www.npr.org/templates/transcript/transcript.php?storyId=112884242.

Waldron, Vincent. *Classic Sitcoms: A Celebration of the Best in Prime-Time Comedy*. New York: Mcmillan, 1987.

Weiner, Carrie. "11 Years Ago 'Cheers' Bid Farewell to Shelley Long." *Entertainment Weekly*, May 1, 1998. https://ew.com/article/1998/05/01/11-years-ago-cheers-bid-farewell-shelley-long/.

Welk, Brian. "'Cheers' Finale at 25: 12 Best Moments from 'One for the Road.'" *The Wrap*, May 20, 2018. https://www.thewrap.com/cheers-finale-25th-anniversary-best-moments-from-one-for-the-road/.

White, Brett. "'Cheers' Has the Greatest (and Messiest) Thanksgiving Episode of All Time." *Decider*, November 23, 2017. https://decider.com/2017/11/23/cheers-thanksgiving-episode/.

Winston, Jay. "The Designated Driver Campaign: Why It Worked." *Huffington Post*, March 18, 2010; updated May 25, 2011. https://www.huffingtonpost.com/jay-winston/designated-driver-campaig_b_405249.html.

Wolk, Josh. "'Cheers' Said Goodbye 25 Years Ago: Raise a Toast with These 9 Essential Episodes." *New York Times*, May 18, 2018. https://www.nytimes.com/2018/05/18/watching/cheers-best-episodes.html.

———. "*Parks and Recreation* Showrunner Michael Schur Gives a Masterclass on *Cheers*." *Vulture*, September 1, 2011. http://www.vulture.com/2011/09/cheers_parks_and_recreation_mi.html.

Zakarin, Jordan. "'Cheers' Turns 30, and Cliff Clavin Delivers His Memories." *Hollywood Reporter*, October 1, 2012. https://www.hollywoodreporter.com/news/cheers-30th-anniversary-john-ratzenberger-ted-danson-375263.

Zurawik, David. "Last Call for Cheers: The Boston Bar Is Just a Sitcom Set, but for Viewers It Has Become a Real Place, Where Friends Hang Out." *Baltimore Sun*, May 16, 1993. https://www.baltimoresun.com/news/bs-xpm-1993-05-16-1993136158-story.html.

INDEX

ABOUT THE AUTHORS

Joseph J. Darowski holds a PhD from Michigan State University and teaches English at Brigham Young University. He has published previous research on popular culture topics ranging from Superman to *The Office*. He previously authored *X-Men and the Mutant Metaphor: Race and Gender in the Comics* and coauthored Frasier*: A Cultural History* with Kate Darowski.

Kate Darowski holds a master's degree from Parsons School of Design, where she studied the history of decorative arts and design with an emphasis on twentieth-century modern design and pop culture in design. She attended Brigham Young University–Hawaii, where she majored in cultural studies. She coauthored the book Frasier*: A Cultural History* with Joseph J. Darowski.